Modeling in Wax
for
Jewelry and Sculpture

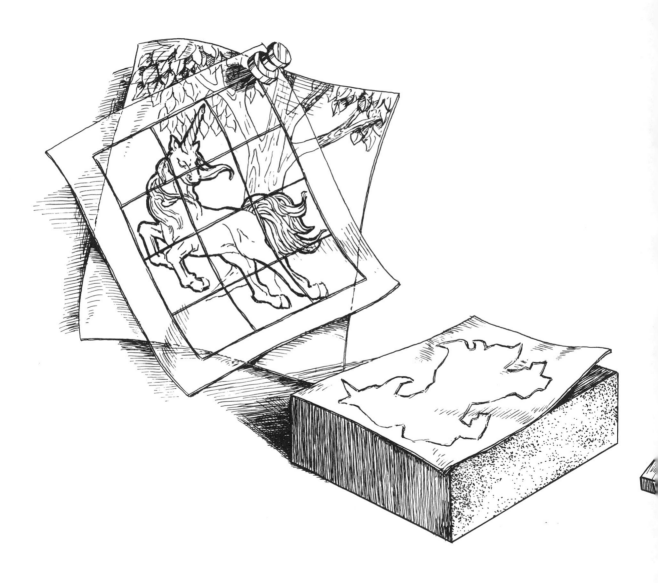

Modeling in Wax
for
Jewelry and Sculpture

Lawrence Kallenberg

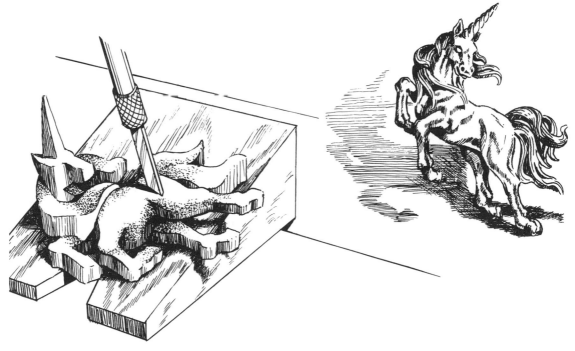

Chilton Book Company   Radnor, Pennsylvania

For Annie

All illustrations by the author

Copyright © 1981 by Lawrence Kallenberg
All Rights Reserved
Published in Radnor, Pennsylvania 19089, by Chilton Book Company

Library of Congress Catalog Card No. 80-70384
ISBN 0-8019-6896-8

Designed by William E. Lickfield
Manufactured in the United States of America

12 13   6 5

Contents

Chapter 5
Wax Carving—Part Two: Green Wax

Chapter 6
Wax Build-up

Chapter 7
Sheet Wax and Wax Rods

Chapter 8
Accidental Effects

Chapter 9
Specialized Wax Techniques

Preface

THIS BOOK was written because, to my knowledge, no one had ever devoted a complete text to the subject. There has been a chapter here and perhaps a chapter there, or else a book on one particular aspect of the craft, but no comprehensive work had ever been produced. This seemed a pity, since the medium has always been an accepted one for both fine and ornamental art. An ancient technique, modeling wax for lost wax casting has now been updated by modern approaches and equipment, making its range of possibilities truly remarkable. This book has attempted to explore some of these possibilities in the hope that the professional will expand his knowledge of the field and that, perhaps even more important, the novice will be inspired to try this highly rewarding craft.

I would like to express my appreciation to the many students who, over the years, have suggested that I write such a book; to John and Arlene Sharpe, former jewelry school owners, who encouraged me in the early stages of the project; to Richard DiBello, who helped me experiment with the properties of different waxes; to Victor Goldberg, whose extensive knowledge of the craft he shared freely with me; to Arthur Kutcher, for all the trade secrets he gave me; to Jack Weinraub, master mold-cutter; to Adolfo Mattiello, inventor of the Matt gun; to Peter Bovin, whose revised text I studied carefully; to Toby Davis, Maurice Katz, and Mr. and Mrs. Bill Seregi, who allowed me to rummage through their vaults for illustrative material. Especially, I would like to thank Ann Seregi for her intelligence, encouragement, help, and patience.

LAWRENCE KALLENBERG

New York City, January 1981

viii

Modeling in Wax
for
Jewelry and Sculpture

Chapter I

The Process of Lost-Wax Casting

THE wax model is the heart of the jewelry industry. A model-maker takes a design, either his own or someone else's, elegantly outlined on a piece of paper, and gives it form. He is the bridge between the pure artistry of the designer and the pure craft of the metalworker; he must have more common sense than either, for it is his task to interpret the meaning of a few pencil lines or brush strokes into a fully formed sculptural piece which may be cast by one person, cleaned by a second person, soldered by a third, and polished by yet another. The model-maker must understand each of these jobs in order for the designer's thought to be realized. The way he shapes the wax is the way hundreds, or even thousands, of pieces of jewelry cast into precious metal, perhaps set with precious stones, will be formed and sold.

For the artist, utilizing cast metal to produce a unique sculpture or a limited series of numbered figurines, the wax is not only the heart of the process but the thought and fulfillment as well. It is a sculpture, complete as far as the artist can take it. It is only left to the technicians to transform the fragile substance of the original into the permanence of metal: brass, bronze, pewter, silver, or gold.

The professional jewelry model-maker, the artist, the craftsperson creating a small line of silver pieces, and the hobbyist are all forced to rely upon the professional for casting their waxes into metal and preparing them for future reproduction. It is important, if not essential, before ever touching the wax itself, to understand the mysterious process called "lost-wax casting," a process by which wax is turned to gold. This discussion will not be an overly technical one. There is no real point to memorizing the melting point of bronze when you will never need the information. But it is necessary for a wax model-maker to be familiar

1

with a process that is inextricably bound with the production of his own work, without which his own work would remain forever incomplete.

CARVED WAX TO CAST METAL

Lost-wax casting is a very old concept. It was used by the Mayan Indians centuries ago to produce the highly intricate gold objects we so admire in museum collections. The same process, with many technical improvements, is used today to produce almost every piece of jewelry manufactured on a large scale in the United States. Because of its simplicity, it is the perfect way of reproducing, from a single original model, the artist's handiwork exactly the way the artist created it. Each reproduction is cast from a mold of the original.

The artist or model-maker carves a wax model, which is set into a metal container; plaster is poured in until it completely covers the wax model. When the plaster has set, the container is placed in a special oven until the wax flows out through a channel in the plaster. All that is left of the model is a cavity bearing an exact imprint of the original. Into this cavity, molten metal is shot, usually by centrifugal force; when the metal sets, the plaster is washed away and the model—now transformed into the permanence of metal—remains. It is then filed and polished until it is even more perfect than the wax had been, and from this metal model, a rubber mold is made. The metal original is set aside; molten wax is injected into the cavity of the rubber mold and the entire process is repeated, only now an unlimited number of wax reproductions can be cast in metal.

Only two qualities inherent in the wax are important for us to understand at this point. The wax—which is formulated specifically for either carving or casting—is able to hold the most intricate details and the most elaborate twists and turns that you can devise. It also melts at a fairly low temperature and leaves no residue. It is around these two properties that the entire process of lost wax casting, as we have just described it, is structured.

SPRUING

When a wax model is given in to be prepared for casting, the first step which it undergoes is a procedure called spruing. Of all the aspects of the actual casting process, spruing is the most important for the model-maker to understand well.

Spruing is a process whereby wax rods—sprues—ranging in diameter from less than ⅛ inch up to more than ¼ inch, depending upon the size of the piece, are permanently attached to your wax model. When the wax is "lost," the sprues will then become conduits for the molten metal on its way to taking on the form of the model. These wax sprues jutting out of the model on all sides will converge to form a single thick rod of

2

wax, so that the completely sprued model will look not unlike a lopsided bouquet of long-stemmed flowers (Fig. 1.1a).

In general, it is best—unless you really trust the casting house—for the model-maker to sprue up his own work, provided he understands the principles of the operation. Often, if the caster does the work, the sprue will be stuck either in the most outlandish place or into the most inaccessible cavity, or else a blob of sprue wax will obscure the most precise detail work, requiring hours of hand-engraving on the metal to rectify. The conscientious caster, however, will make sure that the sprues, above all else, are placed correctly to insure proper flow of the molten metal; that is his primary concern—as it should be ours. If the sprues are not placed correctly, there is a very good chance that, in casting, our model will be ruined.

The direction in which the sprue is placed will ultimately be the direction in which the molten metal will flow through the conduits to fill up the cavity of the burned-out plaster. Clearly a sprue set at a right angle to the model will result in uneven flow, causing tiny gas bubbles to form, which, upon bursting, leave pockmarks in the metal: a condition called porosity. Sprues should insure that metal will flow into all parts of the model. Naturally, a thicker section will require either a thicker sprue or more sprues. Sections in the model which are very thin, or isolated from the bulk of the piece, or turned backward toward the source of the flow, should have their own individual sprues. There are three essential things to remember when setting sprues. The first is that the molten metal, shot out by centrifugal force, will tend to travel in a straight line away from the reservoir; it will not flow readily around a 90-degree turn and it will not flow readily backwards toward its source. The second is that the metal is cooling even as it is running into the cavity; and the third is that the force of the metal flow diminishes the farther it travels from the source.

Wax Flow

The first point and its ramifications are clear. Do not sprue the work so that it looks like a mushroom, with the stem supporting a perfectly level plateau; the metal cannot spread itself out thinly and evenly over a basically flat surface set at 90 degrees to the direction of the flow. Instead, angle the model so that its general orientation is in the direction of the intended flow, attaching sprues toward one side of the model rather than in dead center. According to this principle, anytime a section is at a right angle from the direction of the flow, in order to insure that it will cast properly, an extra sprue, a curved one if possible, should be added to the end of it (Fig. 1.1b). This will provide two channels through which the molten metal may enter the cavity and assume the form of your model.

3

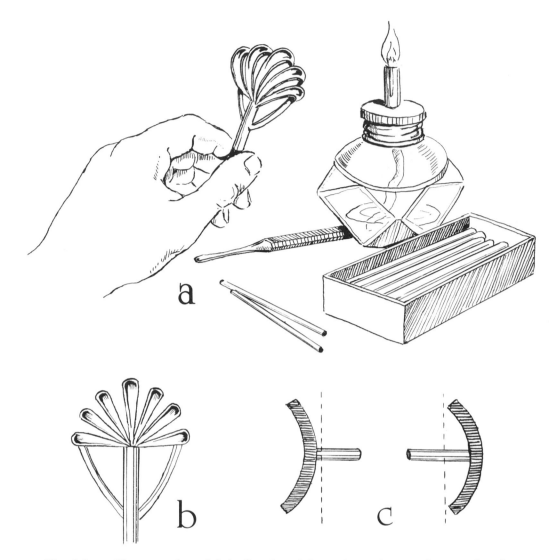

Fig. 1.1 a. The sprued model. b. Spruing right-angle sections. c. Sprues placed on convexities are more easily removed.

As for the second and third points, although they seem perfectly obvious, they are the prime factors to consider when setting sprues. Indeed, the two factors actually combine to form one problem, which, simply stated, is that the sections of the piece farthest away from the source are less apt to receive a sufficient flow of metal. If the piece is improperly sprued, these outlying sections will end up unduly thin or pitted or, worst of all, nonexistent. Therefore, in order for an adequate amount of sufficiently molten metal to reach these sections, the sprues must compensate for the cooling and lack of force. This may be accomplished by making certain that the thickest section of your piece is closest to the reservoir. This placement insures adequate flow to the section

4

which will demand the greatest amount of metal, and also provides a second small reservoir to feed the more distant sections.

Metal hardens from the outside inward. The thinner the section of the model, the narrower will be the space between the walls of the plaster mold after the wax has been "lost." The metal would cool too quickly at this bottleneck to move into the neighboring sections easily. A thicker section, having more space between the walls, would remain fluid longer and be less likely to clog the flow. If there are two thick sections separated by a thin section, multiple sprues are required. If the piece is fairly large, compensate by placing additional sprues about two-thirds of the way up, in order to aid the force of the metal just as it is about to wane.

Practical Considerations

Spruing is complicated by the fact that the ideal sprue placement, in terms of controlling and directing the flow of the metal, might fall in a section that has intricately carved detail work. Such placement could obliterate an hour's work—and cause five hours' extra work with an engraving tool later. Therefore, more often than not, a compromise must be made; place the sprue in the most logical position—under the individual circumstances. Be selective. Remember, it is the model-maker who cleans up the metal casting of the original wax. Only he really knows whether a sprue set in the middle of a series of narrow parallel grooves is preferable to three sprues set deep inside the cavity of the back. These choices must be made anew each time. However, there are a few standard procedures which will render the unpleasant job of sawing and grinding the sprues less painful.

If there is a choice between setting the sprue in either a concavity or a convexity, choose the convexity. The metal will flow into it more readily and, later, the sprue may be sawed off nearer the base, making the grinding and polishing jobs much more easily accomplished (Fig. 1.1c). Given a choice between setting the sprue on either an edge or on a flat surface, the edge is preferred. Not only is it easier to remove the sprue precisely, but it is much safer. It is easy to judge, by the profile, just how much metal to leave and how much to take away. On the flat surface, which is often less than 1 millimeter away from the other side, there is always the danger of grinding away too much and leaving the spot significantly thinner than the rest—a situation which will come back to haunt you later when you try to pull a wax from the rubber mold and discover piercework where none had existed before.

It is also better at first to over-sprue than to under-sprue. Cleanup time will be greater, of course, but repair time will also be far less. No amount of polishing can eradicate porosity; it is not a surface condition but goes all the way through the metal. If ultimately it comes down to a choice between a difficult cleanup and insuring proper flow on the original wax model—even, sorrowfully, a choice between obscuring a lovely bit of detail work and insuring proper flow—always consider the flow of the metal first.

If you are timid about spruing up a piece of work that might have taken you forty or fifty hours to produce, speak with the caster. Most casters, except perhaps for the very large production houses or the occasional crank, will welcome questions. These people generally are grateful for the opportunity of working on something which is challenging or something in which the artist takes pride—instead of their usual runs of countless dome rings that all look the same. Just tell the caster what spots he should avoid when setting the sprues and he is almost certain to comply. If you have no caster in your vicinity and must send your work out of town, wrap the piece very carefully and include a diagram of those sections to be kept clear of sprues. The great majority of casters will respect the model-maker's wishes; they do not take for granted the artist's opinion and they like to keep him satisfied. On original waxes, as opposed to the second waxes pulled from rubber molds, they shower a great deal of attention. A wax pulled from a mold, if lost in the casting, can always be replaced; an original wax model, if lost, is lost forever—and so, generally, is the customer.

After the wax has been sprued properly, it must then be prepared for the process called investment: an operation wherein a specially formulated plaster is poured around the model to create a mold.

INVESTMENT

First the sprued model is set into a rubber disc, called a sprue base, which has an inner rim that contains a wad of soft pliable wax, usually scrap (Fig. 1.2a). It is into this wad of wax that the ends of the sprues are placed and affixed with heat. The wad, having later been burnt out along with the rest of the network of wax, will form the main reservoir for the molten metal. According to the size and complexity of the model, the size of this reservoir varies. The greater the reservoir, the longer the metal will remain molten. This reservoir, when it has set, is given a specific name; it is called a button. When the caster melts down his metal, in order to ascertain how many pennyweights to put in his crucible, he must account not only for the projected weight of the model but for the sprues and the button as well.

The wax model, supported by its system of sprues rising from the wax button and set in its rubber sprue base, is almost ready for investing. It is only for the caster to set a metal flask into place in the sprue base and begin.

Flasks are stainless steel cylinders, not unlike sawed-off pieces of plumbing pipe, ranging in diameter from less than 2 inches to more than 4 inches and in height to more than 9 inches. Larger flasks can be made if the need arises. The size of the flask, naturally, is predicated upon the size and number of the pieces to be invested. There must be ample room

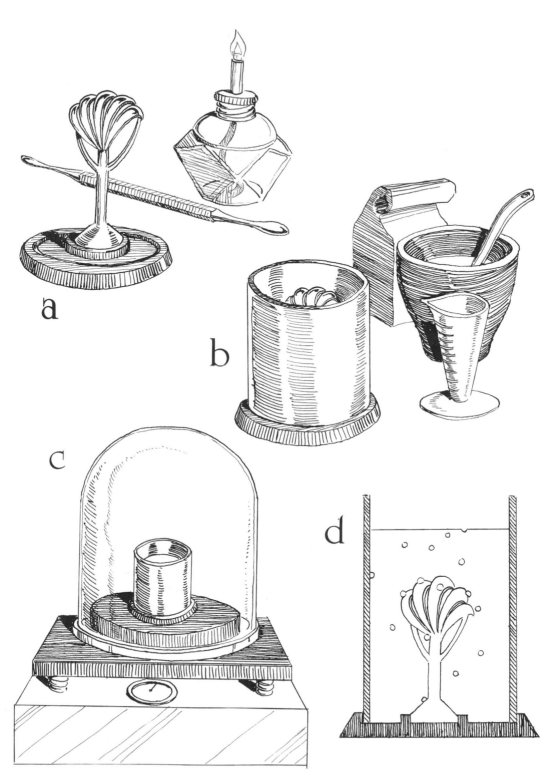

Fig. 1.2 a. Model set in sprue base. b. Model with flask in position, ready for investing.
c. Debubblizer. d. Cross section of investment flask.

between the model and the walls of the flask on all sides, as well as to the rim. For original models, the caster will often use a small flask, over which he can maintain greater control, and invest only one piece. For his production pieces, he will choose a larger flask to reduce the number of operations. After he has selected the appropriate flask, the caster fits it into the channel in the rubber sprue base designed to accommodate it, thus creating a leakproof vessel into which he will pour the liquid investment (Fig. 1.2b).

In its powdered form, investment looks like ordinary plaster; it is mixed with water like plaster, and it sets like plaster. In fact it *is* a type of plaster, which does not burn or crack when subjected to the enormous temperatures of molten metal. Not only does it not crack under very high temperatures; it actually expands slightly as it sets, pushing its way into every niche and line of the model to make an exact impression of the original carving. It is also fairly easily dissolved in water after the casting process is complete. Without these properties, each metal piece would emerge from casting so rough that proper cleanup would take hours.

Debubblizing

The investment is mixed with water to form a slurry which is poured into the flask, completely submerging the wax model inside. The whole unit—wax model, sprues, sprue base, flask, and slurry—is immediately placed in a vacuum machine, called in the trade a debubblizer, which sucks the entrapped air bubbles up to the surface of the investment (Fig. 1.2c). Were this process eliminated, air bubbles might cling to the model. Once the investment had set, these bubbles would form cavities that would receive the molten metal during casting (Fig. 1.2d). The model then would be augmented by an arbitrary surface texture of small balls, called nodules, which would have to be ground off at the cost to the jeweler of much time and energy.

The vacuum process also insures that the slurry finds its way into all crevices of your model, coming into contact with the wax at all points along its surface. To aid the process, the debubblizing machine is mounted on a spring base which vibrates while the slurry is setting. The average setting time is about an hour. After the slurry has set into a solid block snugly fitting around the wax model, the rubber sprue base is removed from the stainless steel flask. The model is ready to vanish forever, leaving only its negative impression in the investment.

BURN-OUT

The process whereby the wax is evacuated from the plaster is called burn-out. It is a very simple process. The flask, with the investment and the wax inside it, is placed on a grill in a special oven (Fig. 1.3a) with the wax button downward. The temperature in the oven is raised gradually until the wax inside the investment begins to flow. It flows out of the

8

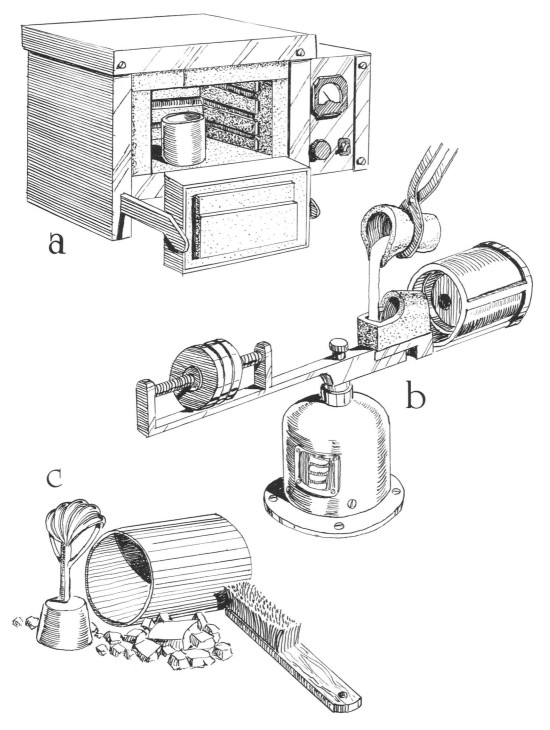

Fig. 1.3   a. Burn-out oven. b. Centrifugal casting machine. c. The cast model.

button first, since the wax used to create the button melts at the lowest temperature. Then the wax sprues, which have a melting point somewhat higher than the button, begin to flow, first down into the cavity left when the button had melted and then out of the flask altogether. The last to melt is the wax model itself; it will begin to flow at a temperature roughly 50 degrees higher than the sprues which had supported it. It will flow down the channels left when the sprues had melted out, into the space left by the button, and then out.

However, residue of the wax still clings to the walls of the cavity, even though the solid center has melted away. The temperature in the oven, therefore, must continue to be raised well beyond the maximum melting point of the wax, up to the enormously high temperature of 1400°F. At this temperature, the carbon residue—which is all that remains of the wax—will turn to gas and escape through the microscopic pores in the investment. The oven is then turned off and the temperature is allowed to return gradually to a point somewhere between 1100° and 700°F—depending upon the thickness of the model and the choice of metal in which it is ultimately to be cast. The flask, with the wax completely burnt out of the cavities in the investment, is now ready to accept molten metal. This burn-out process, of all the stages involved in casting a metal object from a wax original, is the most simple; yet it is the key to the entire process to which it gives its name: lost-wax casting.

METAL CASTING

It is now left to the caster to shoot molten metal into the spaces in the investment once occupied by the wax. There are two ways of doing this: centrifugal casting or vacuum casting. In both cases a physical pressure is exerted upon the metal, forcing it to flow into the opening of the flask, through the network of sprues, and into the cavity of the model, filling it completely. If you can visualize the circuitous route that the metal has to travel, even doing loop-the-loops while filling in the laciest of filigree patterns, you may be able to imagine the kind of force required to cast your piece.

Centrifugal Casting

For many years, centrifugal force—the force that propels objects away from the center of rotation—has been utilized in the casting of jewelry. The process and the equipment used are both very simple. The basic centrifugal casting machine is spring-driven. A pair of metal arms are attached to a heavy spring set in the base; at the end of one arm is a clamp to hold the flask and a fitting for the crucible which will contain the molten metal; at the end of the other arm is a counterweight (Fig. 1.3b). To work the machine, the caster simply winds the arm backwards a few turns and releases it; the pull of the spring as it returns to its normal position supplies enough centrifugal force to fill up the largest flask. Most professionals have highly sophisticated centrifugal casting machines, driven by electrical motors which can control the velocity of the rotation according to the size of the flask, the relative complexity of the model, and the kind of metal to be used.

In any case, basic procedure is the same. The still-hot flask is removed from the burn-out oven with a pair of tongs and locked firmly in the clamping mechanism provided for it at the end of one of the arms of the casting machine. The side of the flask with the opening is placed facing inward toward the hub. A specially formed silicon carbide crucible with an opening on top and a nozzle-like hole on one side is fixed into the button opening. The arm of the machine is turned several times and locked; all that remains to do is to pour the molten metal into the crucible, and spin.

Melting of Metal

Metal is generally melted in its own crucible. The solid metal is weighed out, put in the crucible, and set in the furnace. It is an easy job to compute the amount needed for each piece. Weigh the wax model and the sprue network, then multiply the weight by the specific gravity of the metal to be cast. For example, multiply the weight of the wax by 11 if the model will be cast in sterling silver, by 13½ if 14-karat yellow-gold, by 16 if 18-karat gold. If you need a more precise measurement, get the weight of the wax in grains, multiply by the exact specific gravity of the metal, instead of an approximation (for example, the specific gravity of sterling silver is actually 10.40, not 11), and then divide by 24 to arrive at the projected weight in pennyweights (dwt), the standard measurement of weight in the jewelry industry. Consult the Appendix for a complete list of weights and measures.

The caster, having ascertained the weight of the metal, adds one-quarter more for the button and begins to raise the temperature in the melting furnace. Silver and 14-karat yellow-gold begin to flow at around 1650°F; 18-karat gold flows at about 100° higher, while platinum flows at such a high temperature—3224°F—that special methods have to be employed to cast it. For most metals, though, the procedure is the same.

Once the temperature has risen to the flowpoint of the metal, the crucible containing the molten metal is removed from the furnace with tongs; the metal is poured from the melting crucible into the casting crucible; the arm on the casting machine is released and the metal is shot into the still-hot flask by centrifugal force. In less than a few seconds, the molten metal has passed through the opening, traveled through the network of sprues and—if everything has gone according to plan—has completely filled in the mold of the original wax model.

The injected metal hardens gradually, from the walls inward. Naturally, setting time depends upon the actual thickness of the cavity to

11

be filled. As it is cooling, the metal contracts slightly. The lower the specific gravity of the metal, the greater will be the contraction upon setting. So, although the molten metal will have completely filled in the hollow mold in the investment, touching all points along the inner surfaces, the final solidified metal casting will allow a fraction of a millimeter of space to separate it from the investment wall. In short, the final casting will be slightly smaller by volume than your original model had been—by about 0.5 to 1 percent. This shrinkage is negligible, and you should not even consider it when making your model, even if you are making a ring of a particular size. It is only if you contemplate reproducing your model in quantity that the shrinkage factor becomes something that the model-maker must seriously consider.

The cast piece must now be freed from the flask: another simple operation. After the flask has cooled slightly, the caster will immerse it in cool water until the investment becomes spongy and falls away from the metal. Then, with either an air hose or a stiff brush, he will remove the last particles of investment still clinging to the model. For the first time, the cast model may actually be seen and examined (Fig. 1.3c). The sprues are then clipped off, about ⅛ inch (3 mm) away from the model (the sprue network and the button are, of course, remelted and recast later in someone else's flask), and the caster's job is done—for now.

Vacuum Casting

Centrifugal casting, although it is the most widely used form of casting, is not, however, the only one. Vacuum casting has recently been used more and more extensively, especially for larger flasks that would be cumbersome to handle on the centrifuge. This process utilizes an air pump to create a vacuum. The flask is placed, button-side up, on a flat plate, directly over a suction hole. Unlike the method we discussed for centrifugal casting, the molten metal is poured directly into the flask. Thus far, the procedure exactly follows the most ancient method of casting, where the molten metal was poured into a mold and allowed to find its own level, utilizing only the laws of gravity. Here, when the machine is turned on, a vacuum is created under the flask, causing the molten metal to be sucked downward through the sprue network and into the cavity of the model. The force generated is not as powerful as centrifugal force; therefore, it takes the metal longer to travel to the extremities of the mold and, by the time it gets there, it has already cooled somewhat. Centrifugal casting, which sends hotter, more fluid metal into the cavities of the mold is able to pick up much finer detail in the casting. In either case though, all operations leading up to the actual casting of the metal are standard. And, in both cases, the end result is the transformation of your wax model into the permanence of precious metal.

POLISHING

The final cast piece, however, is not yet a thing of beauty. It is dull. It has imperfections, clipped-off sprues protruding on all sides, perhaps some nodules, perhaps fire-scale or porous places. It does not even look like precious metal. Silver looks like chalk; gold looks like clay. It is hardly something that anyone would buy. Therefore, before anything else is done to it, the model must be cleaned so that all imperfections have been removed, and polished until it gleams.

Silver is considerably easier to polish than 14-karat yellow-gold because it is softer. Small imperfections may be burnished over without the necessity of grinding. Contours may be bent slightly, sections domed up or flattened. All model-makers who plan to use their work for mass production always cast their original into silver—regardless of into what metal the final reproductions are going to be cast. (The only compensation made, according to the metal intended for casting the finished piece, is to regulate the model's thickness; gold, being a much denser substance than silver, can sustain a far thinner wall. Therefore, the model-maker, knowing his piece will eventually be cast into gold, can safely—with an eye toward economics—make his original much lighter than if silver were going to be the metal used.)

This, however, is not the place for the polishing process to be outlined. Since every model-maker should know how to polish his own models in the metal—whether he intends to mass-produce or do one-of-a-kind pieces, I have set aside chapter 10 specifically for a discussion of finishing techniques. For now, it is only important to know that the cast piece must be polished, that it does not come out of the investment full-blown. In the polishing process, the total volume of the piece, which is already almost one percent smaller than your original wax, is reduced a second time. This, of course, is only the logical outcome of a process which utilizes a number of abrasives to remove whatever imperfections might mar your piece. The amount of this second reduction depends primarily upon the type and number of the imperfections. For example, removal of nodules does not in any way intrude upon the exterior contours of your piece. Scratches, on the other hand, or pitting—any type of imperfection which is incised *into* the surface—require the surface to be reduced to the lowest depth of the imperfection (Fig. 1.4). Naturally, the deeper the scratch, the more material will have to be removed to compensate for it, and therefore the greater will be the overall reduction

Fig. 1.4   Reduction of model due to surface imperfections.

of the model. That is exactly why a good model-maker will not give out the wax for casting until every last imperfection has been removed. It is only the rankest of amateurs who will say: "I'll take care of it later." This sort of model-maker will discover that his piece has been reduced by as much as 5 percent in the polishing, which is actually 6 percent smaller by volume than the original wax model. Conversely, a good model-maker can expect no more than a 2 percent reduction of the piece through polishing, 3 percent overall.

These very slight reductions in the size of your piece begin to add up after a while. However, it is only for the mass-produced market that a model-maker really has to confront the problem of shrinkage. This is because the greatest single reduction in the size of the already shrunken piece occurs in making a mold from the metal model, a rubber mold.

RUBBER MOLDS

For the purpose of reproducing a number of pieces from a single original model, rubber is the ideal material. The specially formulated rubber used in mold-making is able to hold an impression of even the most delicate detail work. It is also pliable, so that wax reproductions may easily be pulled from it. It is able to withstand the heat of the molten wax; and it is long-lasting, so that many reproductions are possible from a single rubber mold.

The rubber comes in either strips, sheets, or rolls, and is individually cut to the correct size. It also comes in a variety of grades and in a sizeable range of qualities. It is upon the grade and quality of the rubber that the shrinkage factor depends; the denser the rubber, the less it will contract after vulcanizing. But here too, discretion and economics must play a part. A grade-A quality rubber, which might be ideal for a highly detailed and precise model, would be a waste of money on a rough-hewn silver bead, whereas a spongier rubber would never do justice to the finer model.

So first the piece must be appraised by the mold-maker, not only for the quality of the rubber it demands, but for the approach he will eventually take to cut it from the vulcanized mold. After this has been done, the chosen rubber is cut to fit into an aluminum or zinc-magnesium frame, packed down in layers until somewhat more than half the frame is completely filled with the rubber (Fig. 1.5a).

The model, to which a sprue that looks like a golf tee has been soldered, is placed in the frame on top of the rubber, with the end of the sprue touching the inner wall of the frame (Fig. 1.5b). More sheets of rubber are then packed down tightly on top of the model, sandwiching it entirely, until an equal number of rubber sheets have been placed on top and bottom of the model. The rubber, which rises one or two layers higher than the level of the frame, is ready to be vulcanized.

14

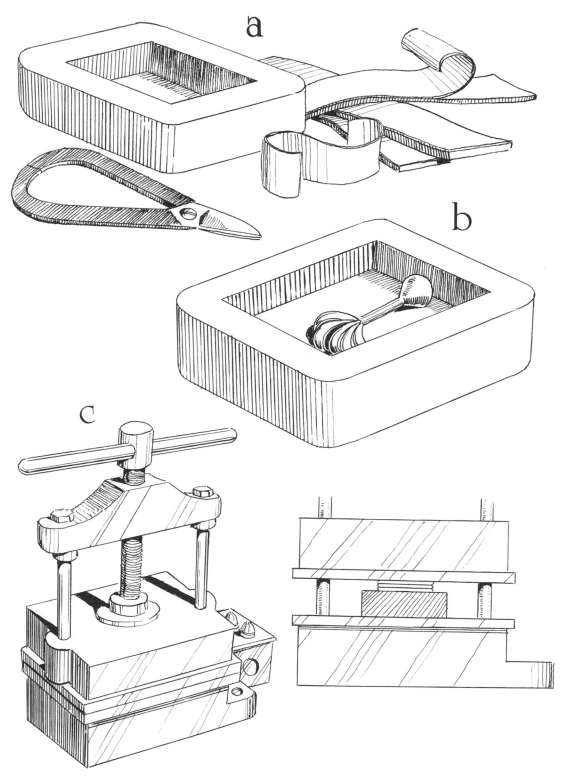

Fig. 1.5   a. Frame for making rubber mold. b. Metal model placed in frame. c. Vulcanizer.

Vulcanizing

A vulcanizer is an electrically controlled device which resembles a cross between an etching press and something from the Spanish Inquisition (Fig. 1.5c). The aluminum frame containing the rubber-packed model is placed between two aluminum plates (rubber, like wax, does not stick to aluminum), so that the top plate just barely comes into contact with the topmost layer of rubber. The machine is turned on and the plates begin to heat up, melting the rubber at around 300°F. As the rubber begins to flow, a crank is turned to bring the two plates closer together, causing the now-viscous rubber to become compressed completely around the model and to flow into all empty spaces and air pockets within the frame. This operation is repeated until the two aluminum plates come into complete contact with the aluminum frame and the rubber is compressed as much as possible between the plates. The mold is now done. After it has cooled, the now solid block of rubber containing the silver model within it—like an avocado formed around its pit—is popped out of its frame and given to the person who slices open the rubber, freeing the model and creating a mold from which thousands of pieces of jewelry may be cast.

Mold Cutting

Rubber-mold cutting, like every other operation we have discussed, is quite simple. The rubber-mold cutter, after having appraised his piece, hooks the vulcanized block of rubber to the side of his bench—usually with an ordinary beer-can opener or bent nail—and makes a few tentative cuts around the edges with a surgically sharp knife (Fig. 1.6a). He must free the model in such a way that the rubber falls into two halves that can be fitted together again easily and exactly. So he begins by either cutting a male-female locking mechanism into the four corners of his mold or by slicing a saw-toothed pattern completely around the edge (Fig. 1.6b).

Once this has been accomplished, he can turn his attention to the real work at hand: cutting the model out of the rubber. The model is completely embedded inside the mold; there is no way of being absolutely certain just exactly where it is. The best that the mold-cutter can do is rely on memory and bend the mold open as far as it can go, stretching the rubber so that eventually the contours of the model start to show. Once the form of the model becomes discernible through the rubber, the mold-cutter may pick and choose, within reason, the placement of the final cuts.

However, unlike casting and vulcanizing, where a successful product is more or less guaranteed if you are careful, a good rubber mold depends upon the individual skill and experience of the mold-cutter. Anyone can

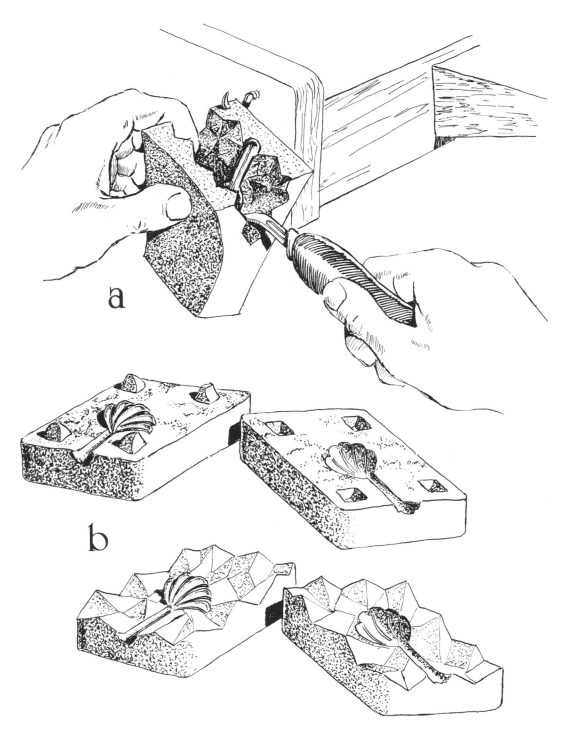

Fig. 1.6   a. Cutting a rubber mold. b. Comparison of different cutting techniques.

17

slash the rubber mold into two pieces and free the model; only a real professional can do the job so that no difficulties arise later, either in casting or in finishing.

There are many things which a rubber-mold cutter must keep in mind, the first of which is the ultimate object—the pulling of a perfect wax from the rubber. If the wax, which is still highly flexible when it is taken out of the mold, can only be removed by twisting and turning, a distortion is bound to occur, a distortion which will be permanently documented in each reproduction. Therefore, ease of removal is a prime factor in determining how the mold-cutter will approach the task. A basically flat piece entails no problems; the mold-cutter simply slits along the edges so that the mold divides equally and the wax is just lifted out (Fig. 1.7a). A ring, on the other hand, especially one which boasts a highly domed hollow crown, demands much more sophisticated techniques so that the pulling of the wax may be effected without distortion. In fact, the more complex the piece, the more the ingenuity of the rubber-mold cutter will be tested.

However, there are some things which even the best rubber-mold cutter in the world cannot accomplish. It is the job of the designer/model-maker to understand what is possible and what is not possible in cutting a mold. A hollow filigree bead, for example, is absolutely impossible to produce in one piece from a rubber mold; there is no way to free the rubber inside the ball, assuming that the melting rubber can even work its way inside the openings of the silver model. In order to produce a hollow bead, the model-maker must present it to the caster in two halves. The mold-cutter can then position his cut around the rim of each hollow hemisphere, and removal from the mold is an easy matter (Fig. 1.7b). After polishing, the two halves are soldered together and the bead is done. This same principle applies to any hollow, fully formed three-dimensional object. It must be cast in two halves; the two halves reproduced in the rubber mold and, then, soldered together.

Similarly, objects having very severe undercuts cannot be pulled from a rubber mold without some distortion. Anything that comes to a bottleneck should be avoided. For example, a large hollow bead rising from a flat surface can be reproduced in the rubber—there will be a large enough opening for the rubber to flow inside the cavity and take on the impression of its exact contour—but that which is hollow in the model becomes solid in the mold and, after the wax has been formed, there will be no way possible to squeeze that solid rubber ball through the tiny opening in order to release the wax without distorting it (Fig. 1.7c). One way of avoiding this is to make sure that wherever you have a deep core, the base of that core should not exceed the width of the opening—even though the outside contours might create the illusion of uniform thickness within (Fig. 1.7d). In fact, very deep cores should be avoided altogether, if possible, since the rubber will contract unevenly

18

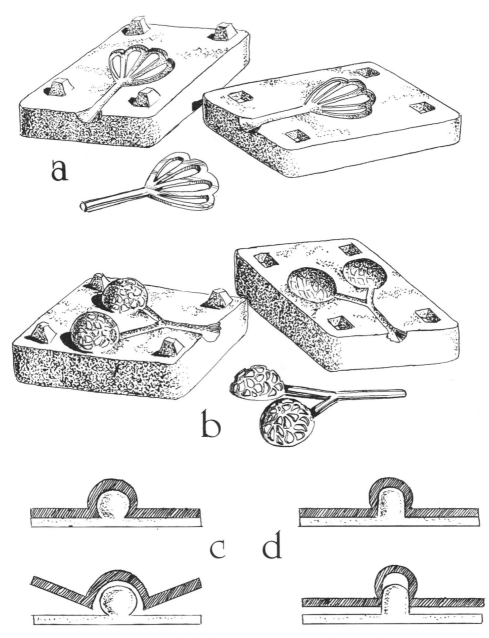

Fig. 1.7 a. A simply cut mold. b. Cutting hemispheres from mold. c. An improperly sized core. d. A properly sized core.

around long extended hollows, causing the wax to become excessively thin in spots. A simple understanding, on the part of the model-maker, of the basic principles of rubber-mold making will ultimately produce a cleaner, better piece, as well as goodwill between the model-maker and the mold-cutter: no mean accomplishment; he is a worthwhile ally.

The mold-cutter's job, however, is not finished after deciding how to split the mold to insure minimum distortion in the wax. He must seriously consider where the split should fall along the surface of the model. This is the hallmark of the fine rubber-mold cutter, because wherever this parting line, as it is called, runs, there will be a slightly raised line caused by the overflow of wax seeping through the unavoidable space between the halves. Quite often, the mold-cutter will have to make a trade-off between distorting the wax and laying his parting line across the most intricately carved section of the piece. A poorly placed parting line can cause the jeweler hours of unnecessary cleanup; it could even amount to reengraving entire sections of the piece each time one is cast. I once did a model of an Art Nouveau piece, a lady with long, flowing hair. Numerous hours were spent on incising lines into the hair to accentuate the pattern of the tresses. Numerous hours more were spent accentuating those lines in the cast metal model so that they would be as sharp and as clean as possible, since detail does have a tendency to become less distinct in the rubber mold. When I got my first reproduction back, not only did the parting line run across the nose and cheek of the lady's face, it ran at a right angle to the direction of the hair. Each strand had to be filed and separated individually. Needless to say, I quickly had another rubber mold made—by another rubber-mold cutter.

In general, the mold-cutter, with an eye toward ease in cleanup, tries to run his parting line along the edge of a piece. This is the easiest sort of seam to remove: the jeweler simply files down the edge of the casting and all evidence of the parting line vanishes. Failing this, the mold-cutter will put his parting line across the broadest plain surface he can find, preferably one that is domed up, so that the jeweler will have no difficulty in filing or grinding the seam. If this method is inappropriate as well, the mold-cutter hides the parting line in the most obscured section of the piece, usually in the back, or where settings or another casting are intended to fit.

Once the parting line has been decided upon, the cut is made and the silver model is removed from the rubber. Then the mold-cutter has to manicure his product. Release lines—lines which are cut into the inner surface of the rubber to facilitate removal of the wax from the mold—are made. Incised imperfections which might have escaped the model-maker's attention and which now show in the rubber as raised ridges or nipples are burned away with a hot tool. If necessary, additional sprue channels are cut directly into the rubber to augment the flow of wax through the main sprue. Most important, though, sections which appear too thin are burned out slightly to allow more room for the wax to enter.

Shrinkage

Unexpected thin spots are the great bane of the model-maker who is about to put his piece into production. And, in most cases, these thin

20

areas should not really be totally "unexpected"; they are caused by inadequate compensation in the original wax model for the shrinkage which will occur afterward. The finished cast silver original is at least 3 percent smaller by volume than the original wax had been. Now, to that sum, must be added the shrinkage factor of the rubber.

A rubber mold, unlike the original mold in the investment, is not inert after it has set. As long as the silver model is still wedged firmly inside it, it will conform exactly to the dimensions of the model. However, once the model has been released, the rubber will expand to fill some of the space that had been taken up by the metal, much as a rubber ball held tightly in the hand will expand when the pressure is released. The result is that the mold impression is appreciably smaller than the model from which it was made. Depending upon the rubber, this shrinkage may be as little as 3 or 4 percent, for Castaldo rubber, to as much as 8 percent for the less expensive brands. So, the model-maker is dealing with a very major shrinkage factor which can range from 6 percent overall, at the very least, to as much as 12 percent and more. And there are yet three more operations to be done, each one of which will further reduce the size of the finished piece.

PULLING A WAX

The first of these operations is the injection of molten wax into the rubber mold. This is done either with a hydraulically powered wax injector that strongly resembles some sort of primitive samovar (Fig. 1.8a) or else through centrifugal force, exactly as the metal casting was done; only instead of molten metal being injected into an investment mold, molten wax is injected into a rubber one. The centrifugal method, although it is able to capture more detail and be better controlled, is seldom used in the large casting houses; it is too slow. The quicker samovar model is now the standard for almost all wax injection.

Special casting wax, different from the wax used to carve the original—more quickly melted, more quickly cooled, more brittle when set, more fluid in its molten state—is placed in the wax injector and allowed to melt into a more or less viscous liquid. The rubber mold is fitted together and placed in an aluminum clamp to insure complete contact (Fig. 1.8b). The opening in the mold, which looks like a counter-sunk hole, is placed against the nozzle of the injector (Fig. 1.8c). Depending upon the mechanism of the individual machine employed, a spigot is opened, a handle is pumped, or the mold is simply pressed up hard against the nozzle and a thin stream of wax shoots out of the injector, up the sprue channel, and into every crevice of the cavity in the rubber mold.

The wax is allowed a few moments to set; then the mold is taken out of the clamp and separated. The wax, which is still flexible at this point, is carefully pulled from the mold. The process has come full-circle,

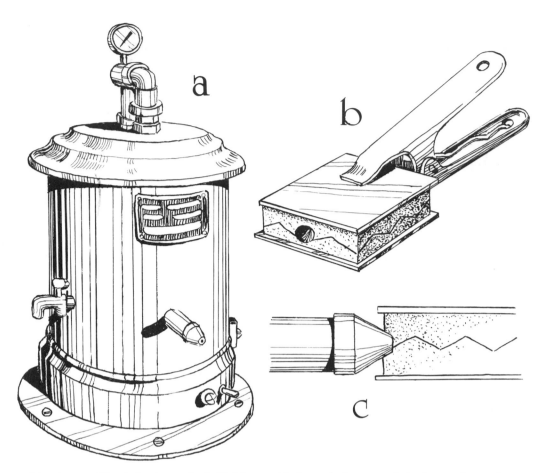

Fig. 1.8 a. Wax injecting unit. b. Rubber mold clamp in frame. c. Injection unit nozzle.

back to a wax model to be cast. Only this wax model, obviously, is considerably smaller than the original. Not only has it been reduced once when the original model was cast into metal, reduced a second time in the polishing, a third time in the rubber mold, now it is reduced yet again—another 1 percent—as the fluid wax injected into the mold contracts upon setting. This wax will then be cast into metal and the metal will again contract 0.5 to 1 percent. Then the cast piece will be cleaned and polished, further reducing the size of the piece by another 1 to 2 percent: an overall reduction from the original wax model to the finished piece of jewelry of 10 to 15 percent by volume, depending upon the quality of the work and the type of materials used. This shrinkage factor is only an approximation; there is no way to gauge it accurately. A model-maker must simply remain aware of this shrinkage at all times and enlarge the original piece accordingly.

The lost-wax casting process—even with all its numerous procedures—is a very simple one to understand. Nor is the model-maker really called upon to understand it in depth, as the caster must. However, a really serious model-maker must appreciate the fact that the wax model is not an end but rather only the first step in the creation of an object of lasting value and beauty.

Chapter 2

Equipment

AT least four-fifths of all the jobs a professional model-maker is called upon to perform require the ability to render a gracefully carved form from a solid block of wax. Whatever additional techniques might be acquired to make the job easier or quicker or more precise, these only serve to supplement the essential act. Without a sound knowledge of sculpting, the novice cannot really hope to produce the many beautiful objects made possible through the lost-wax method of casting.

Instead of marble and wood, a model-maker uses different grades of specially prepared waxes. Instead of a mallet and chisel, he uses an assortment of small tools either bought or hand-made. A model-maker's tools are his fortune. And, since wax offers no resistence to the metal tool, no friction to dull the cutting surface, one investment can, literally, last a lifetime.

Naturally, the choice of tools is dictated by the intended type of work. However, no matter how simple or ambitious your aspirations, certain equipment must be purchased before you can begin. This equipment can be divided into three catagories: work area, lighting, and carving tools. The relative sophistication of this equipment must be hashed out only between you and your pocketbook.

WORK AREA

The wax model-maker is very fortunate when it comes to selecting his work space, especially when compared to the jeweler or metalsmith who needs, ideally, one complete room in which to work, a room with a door so that cyanide pellets will not be mistaken for candy and metal filings will not find their way into the bathtub. A wax model-maker, on the other hand, uses completely innocuous materials and, even at the

24

end of a long day's work, has only to collect a few tablespoons of fine wax powder from the floor. The only factors to be considered when selecting a work area are the fragility of the wax and the precision required to work it: no thoroughfares, no spots above boilers where vibrations may be felt, no places where sudden loud noises might distract you. Just about any relatively sequestered corner near an electrical outlet is fine.

Workbench

Once you have chosen your nook, you need to find a solid working surface and a comfortable chair. The ideal surface is a jeweler's bench (Fig. 2.1a). A jeweler's bench is specifically designed to meet all the demands of the model-maker/jeweler. It is heavy and sturdy, in order to absorb vibrations and not shake, regardless of the most zealous application of file to wax. It is equipped with a drop drawer, specifically intended to eliminate the necessity of sponging down the floor after a vigorous session, and a tool drawer for storage. Most important, it has spaces designed to accomodate a bench pin and an armrest, both of which are necessary for maintaining maximum control over the work. In fact, the model-maker does *all* his work on the bench pin, which projects out far enough from the front of the bench to allow him freedom to hold his work securely while carving it.

Bench pins are available in several sizes and should "feel good" in the hand. A good way of determining the best size is simply to reach around the middle of the bench pin, touching the thumb to the middle finger. If your fingers do not reach, try a smaller size. Whether you buy a jeweler's bench or not, a bench pin is a necessity.

An armrest is optional; however, unless you can find a place to brace your elbow, arm-weariness may very quickly interfere with your control. A word of caution here to lefties. If you are about to spend the $125 to $200 for a jeweler's bench, make sure that it has *two* narrow slots for armrests, one on each side of the bench pin. Too often, there is but a single right-handed slot. Keep in mind, too, that your author is right-handed (witness all the drawings of left hands throughout the text) and that instructions will be geared to righties. Simply read "left" for "right" and there should be no problems.

The jeweler's bench, although ideal, is quite expensive and not readily available in areas outside large cities—although they can be ordered through catalogs and shipped. For considerably less than half the price, however, any fairly adept carpenter can put together an acceptable work table. It must be sturdy, and the working surface must be able to withstand the wear and tear of sharp metal tools being dropped on it continually. A very good bench may quickly be constructed from a frame of 2-by-4s attached at the corners, by means of eight heavy-duty right-angle brackets, to four legs—similarly fashioned of pine 2-by-4s, and reinforced by crossbeams on three sides (Fig. 2.1b). Across the top of this structure,

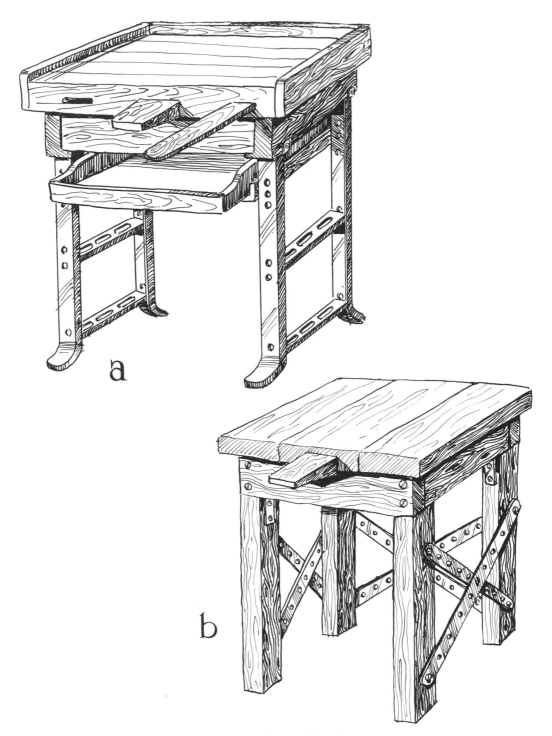

Fig. 2.1   a. Jeweler's bench. b. Homemade workbench.
26

hardwood planks are laid. Birch and maple are excellent woods to use; oak because of its open grain is less acceptable. A 1½-inch butcher block or cutting board also makes a fine surface. Simply drill holes into your hardwood board, and screw or dowel it into the base.

However, one necessary refinement must be considered before the working surface is secured to the frame. If you do not have a routing tool to drill out the slot for the bench pin, you must allow at least a 1½-inch overhang of the hardwood board at the front of the bench. This will allow you to clamp your bench pin onto the bench, either by attaching it onto the lip of the bench with C-clamps, or by drilling a hole through both bench and bench pin and slipping a wingbolt through. Or, for somewhat more money than you would ordinarily pay for a standard bench pin, buy a bench pin with a special metal holder (Fig. 2.2).

This bench pin with its metal holder is a very useful addition to any toolbox. With it, you can, if necessary, convert any solid table into a workbench, as long as the table has a 1½-inch lip. In fact, with a little ingenuity, you may erect a proper workbench from any number of pedestrian objects. For the last dozen or so years, I have turned out my models on a used typewriter table, using, as a bench pin, a shoemaker's last, size six, which fits into my hand delightfully.

Chair

Prolonged sitting can be a very tedious business and, if your chair is uncomfortable, quite a disagreeable one. The relative comfort of the seat, however, is something which may be ameliorated by means of foam cushions; nor is the softness of the seat even the prime factor to be considered when selecting a chair. The height of the chair in relationship to the height of the bench is much more important, and this can only be ascertained, after some experimentation, by each individual. Your legs should go under the bench at a right angle to your body, and the bench pin should be pointed directly at your breastbone. If it is higher than the breastbone, armweariness will result; lower, and you will get a stiff neck from bending too far down over your work.

LIGHTING

Once the bench and chair have been decided upon and set in place, the next step is to select a light source. I cannot stress strongly enough the importance of proper lighting. The professional model-maker stares intently at his work for at least eight hours every working day. Lighting which is either inadequate or glaring can produce violent headaches; it can also do permanent damage to the eyes. If you are concerned about economizing, economize on the bench—or even on the tools; do not economize at the expense of your eyes.

Do not work with only the illumination of the ceiling globe; a light source far above you will cast the shadow of your head directly onto

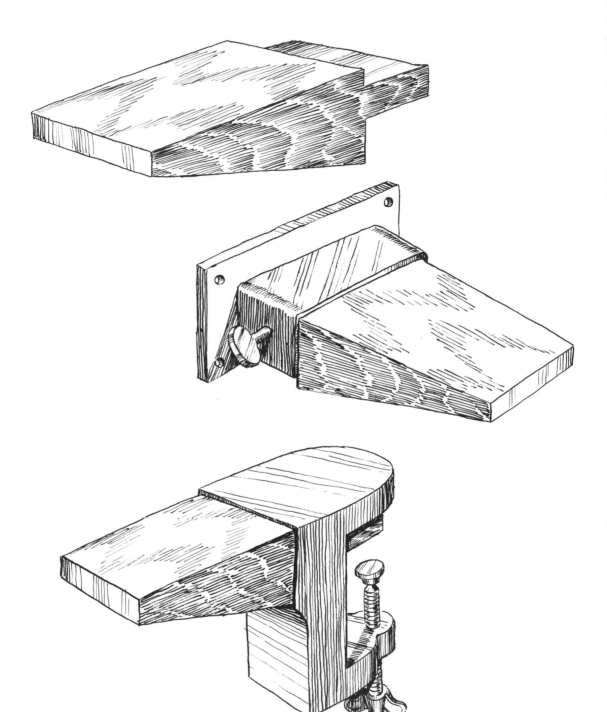

Fig. 2.2   Bench pins.

28

your work. Do not use a high-intensity lamp; you will continue to see its glare long after you have closed your eyes. Indeed, in my opinion, incandescent bulbs of any kind produce shadows that are too well-defined and highlights that bounce too much for any really prolonged work of a precise nature to be accomplished. The ideal light source, of course, is natural light and, failing that, fluorescent light.

Fluorescent light is soft; there are no harsh shadows with which to contend and no glittering highlights; and yet, the illumination is quite sufficient for even the closest work. Fluorescent lamps boast one or two or even three 15-watt bulbs. The most well-known brand, the Dazor lamp, comes with three different type bases as well (Fig. 2.3). The lamp, like everything else on the workbench, must be steady. A wobbly light can be disconcerting, to say the least. The Dazor lamp—and many of the Dazor-style lamps—comes in a model which has a weighted base, which is particularly useful if you intend to use your lamp elsewhere in the house. The more usual model, however, comes equipped with either a clamp-on base or a base which may be permanently attached to your workbench with wingbolts or screws. Dazor lamps come with either two or three bulbs, ranging in price from $45 to $75.

The ideal arrangement is to set up two two-bulb lamps on either side of the bench and have them cross-firing at the work. In this way, even the very soft shadows produced by the fluorescent bulbs are eradicated, and the sharpness of the detail work can be more accurately gauged. Alternating light sources, left and right, also give a more realistic perspective. Do not take your light source for granted. Even if you are fortunate enough to escape a headache, there is virtually no way that truly fine wax models can be executed in a shadow cast by your head.

CARVING TOOLS

Each wax model-maker has his own techniques—favorite ways of working. And each wax model-maker relies on certain tools rather than on others to get the job done. Some prefer knives, others files, still others prefer to work primarily with the flexible shaft machine.

The choice of tools depends, in large measure, upon the kind of work you wish to produce, because the finished piece you desire dictates the type of wax you will use—and all waxes cannot be worked with the same tools. For example, a highly intricate carving requires wax so hard and brittle that most knives will cause your work to chip or split when you least expect it. Do not rush out to buy your tools until you have fairly well decided upon the kind of pieces you wish to produce.

Knives

The knife is the most easily obtainable tool and, perhaps in the long run, even the most useful. There are many knives on the market, but very few of them are really suited to the highly precise work of the model-

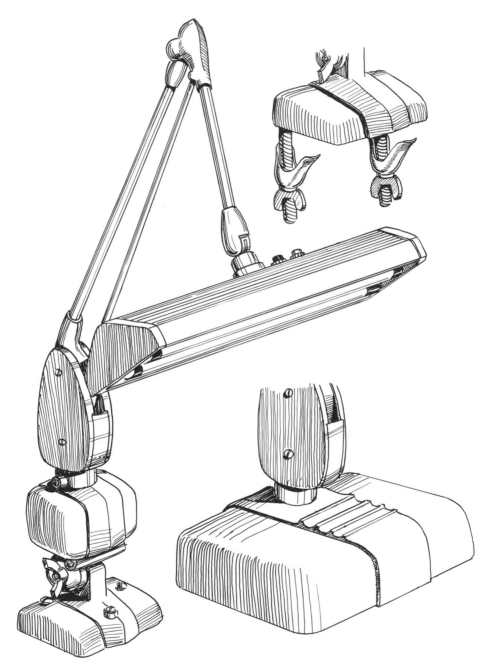

Fig. 2.3 Dazor-type lamp.

30

maker. Carving wax is not the same as whittling wood. The ideal knife for the purpose of carving wax is the standard X-Acto knife with a 5/16-inch diameter aluminum handle. It is light; it is strong; and its blades, which come in a variety of shapes, are replaceable (Fig. 2.4a). The blade which I find most useful is the standard blade that comes with it: the number-11 blade. The knife is available everywhere: in art supply stores, in hobby shops, even in stationery stores, and the cost is under $2—with a box of replacement blades (several years' supply) costing less than $1.

For many jobs, however, the angle of the number-11 blade is too severe: a smaller X-Acto stencil knife equipped with aluminum handle and replaceable number-4 blades has a 45-degree cutting edge (Fig. 2.4b) which is quite useful in scraping and smoothing operations. X-Acto also puts out an assortment of frisket knives used by advertising lay-out artists. These knives are tiny and, therefore, easily adapted to carving fine details into the wax; however, some of them are quite expensive. If a proper handle can be improvised, the replacement blade alone is a sufficient purchase.

An excellent handle, not just for knives but for scribing points and various cutting burrs, is a mechanical drafting pencil. Eagle makes one for its thicker leads. Simply insert the tiny knife from the front, and you have a perfectly balanced precision tool (Fig. 2.4c).

These three are the only knives I use; the pleasure of throwing away a dull blade is worth the very modest extravagance; however, there are model-makers who buy very good knives and retain them for years. The advantage of this lies in the sharpening of the blade to whatever cutting edge is deemed correct for the job. A few swipes across an Arkansas sharpening stone and the blade, because of the superior quality of the steel, takes on an edge which can be made finer than any machine-honed edge. Also, because the blade is permanently mounted in the handle, the slight wobble inherent in a knife which accepts replaceable or inter-changeable blades is never a factor.

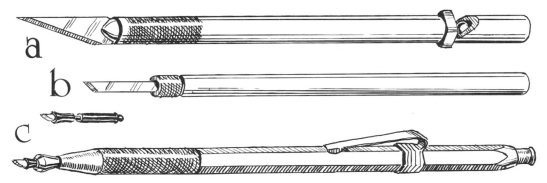

Fig. 2.4   a. X-Acto knife with #11 blade. b. X-Acto #4 stencil knife. c. Swivel blade in mechanical drafting pencil.

These knives require care. If you are planning to buy a set of good carving tools, you must be prepared to sharpen them when they grow dull. Despite the mystique which has grown up around sharpening knives, it is actually a very simple operation. You need a good sharpening stone, a few drops of oil, and a steady hand. The most important of these is the stone. You are dealing with miniature tools; a tiny nick caused by an inferior stone might be insignificant on a six-inch hunting knife but on so tiny an edge it can be a catastrophe. The best stone to use is the Arkansas stone which may be bought in any fine hardware store or jewelry or art supply house. The standard size stone is a nice luxury, but just as useful for our miniature tools are thin slips of Arkansas stone, if mounted in a little wooden box or even in plaster to keep them rigid as you use them. Other stones such as the Arkeram stone, a stone created of the Arkansas stone powder which has been fused by heat, and the India oilstone are also acceptable.

Simply add a few drops of oil to the surface of the stone, to facilitate even cutting without drag, and begin. Hold the knife securely so that the entire bevel of the cutting edge is uniformly touching the stone (Fig. 2.5a). Maintaining even pressure, describe either a circle on the stone or else move the knife back and forth in a straight line. Beginners find the second method more easily accomplished but, since a back and forth motion demands stops and starts and constant readjustment of pressure, the result is apt to be irregular. I would suggest that, while practicing on a less-than-absolutely-precious tool, you try to perfect the circular stroke, which allows a continuous and even pressure to be maintained. Taking care not to alter the angle at which you are sharpening your blade, make approximately a dozen circles with the knife; then, turning the knife over and striking the same angle of the bevel as before, sharpen the second side for a dozen swipes.

Checking is done by looking at the edge of your blade; if you can see it, chances are it needs more sharpening. Double-check it by pushing the sharpened edge slowly across the surface of your fingernail. It should raise up a tiny shaving, similar to the shavings created when wood is planed (Fig. 2.5b). If it slides at all, go back to the Arkansas stone. Study under a high magnification will show that use of the stone will produce a tiny burr on your cutting edge, which will cause the blade to drag and inadvertantly leave tiny scratches in your work. This burr can easily be removed by flopping the blade back and forth on a small piece of leather stretched taut, or else by polishing the blade on a piece of jeweler's emery polishing paper, grade 3/0 or 4/0. Even working the blade backward on the side of your hardwood bench pin will do the job (Fig. 2.5c). Anyone who is capable of carving wax is capable of sharpening a knife. Just work carefully and a keen edge will be the result.

Finding knives should be no problem. Any well-stocked art supply store offers an assortment of small knives, originally designed for cutting

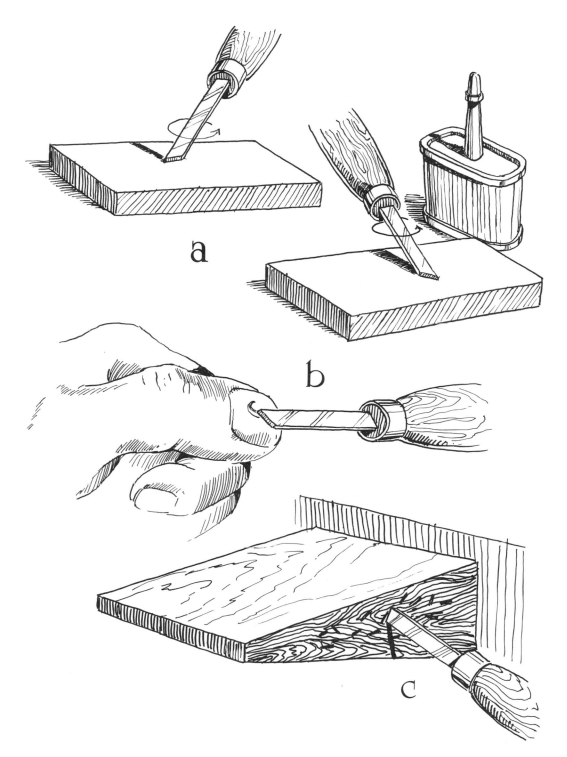

Fig. 2.5   a. Using a sharpening stone. b. Testing on fingernail. c. Removing the burr.

stencils, which are perfectly suitable for working fine details into the wax. A good hardware store is also an excellent source for cutting instruments. Depending upon the extent of the stock, they often carry sets of miniature chisels, gouges, and wood-carving tools. Do not, however, buy any tools with engraver's round-palm handles: these are specifically designed to push against dense material, allowing the heel of the hand to supply maximum pressure. Since wax is so easily cut, such a handle is unnecessary and very cumbersome when trying to work on a small scale. Stay with the elongated handles—the thinner the handle, the better.

Craft and hobby shops, jewelry supply houses, and well-stocked lumberyards all carry tools, not specifically designed for wax carving of course, but very easily adapted to the task: frisket knives, swivel knives, etching tools, wood and linoleum block printing tools, engravers' blades, miniature tools designed to carve intricate balsa models, wood-turning tools—the possibilities are endless. And consider scientific supply houses with their wealth of dissecting instruments, or surgical supply houses, or what is perhaps the single finest source of exotically shaped cutting implements: dental supply houses.

A brief survey of a dental supply catalog will unearth a wealth of knives, picks, and spatulas in almost every conceivable shape (Fig. 2.6). They are ideal for carving wax—and much less expensive than instruments of comparable quality purchased from a jewelry supply house. These instruments are not sharp enough for carving, but with the Arkansas stone, a razor-sharp edge may readily be obtained. Once the correct cutting edge has been honed, use on the wax will never dull it. It is only in the unavoidable contact of metal tool to metal tool within the toolbox that the edge loses its keenness. However, a small leather carrying pouch with individual pockets for each knife will prolong the life of the tools indefinitely.

Files

The files that the model-maker employs should, with few exceptions, be purchased only from a jewelry supply house. They are not cheap, and most of even these fine files have not been designed specifically for working wax; they are primarily metal-working tools. The one exception is the standard 8-inch wax file (Fig. 2.7a), a half-round tool with one side having a coarse cut and the other side having a medium cut. This file is designed to work into cavities, such as the inside of ring shanks, or else to rough out large flat planes or sweeping curves without wax becoming clogged in the grid. The only substitute for this very useful tool would be to buy two half-round files of different cuts from a hardware store and, even then, there would be a chance that the wax might clog up so that you would do more cleaning than filing.

34

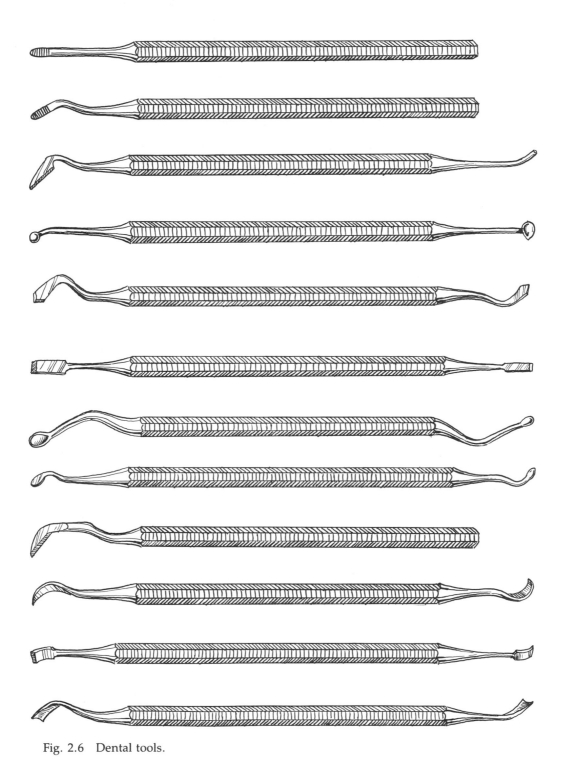

Fig. 2.6   Dental tools.

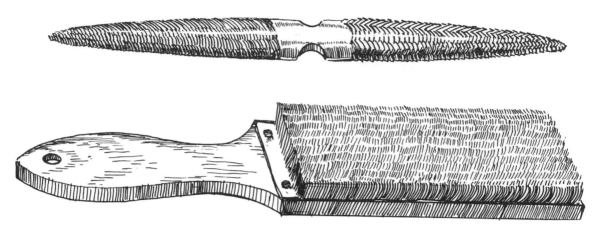

Fig. 2.7   Wax file and file cleaner.

Files may be cleaned fairly easily by scraping them with a specially designed file cleaner that contains hundreds of short wires, all curved in one direction, set into a flat wooden paddle (Fig. 2.7b). However, when one is concentrating on shaping a piece of wax, constant recourse to the cleaner can be a great annoyance. Avoid it, if you can, by purchasing the one file intended for wax-work.

Of the other files available, only the miniature ones—the riffle, the escapement, and the needle files—are of interest to us. Each of these files comes in an assortment of cuts, lengths, and shapes. These files are intended for metal-work, specifically for watch-repair and delicate fittings; therefore they must be adapted. Most are available in six or even eight "cuts," ranging from very coarse (cut-00) to very fine (cut-8). Neither end of the spectrum is particularly useful to a model-maker. The coarse cut leaves deep scratches and the fine cut will clog up after one or two swipes. If one is to err, however, err on the side of the coarser cut because even the median cut—cut-4—is too fine for any work but final finishing touches. Only consider a cut-4 if there is no way to reach the spot with a knife or a polishing agent; for example, inside tiny holes where a round or half-round needle file might be the only means of finishing the inner surface. As a regular practice, select the cut-2 or, less often, the cut-3. These grids are coarse enough to take down the material quickly without undue clogging, and yet they are fine enough to leave the surface fairly smooth.

The two most popular types of miniature files are the needle file and the escapement file. There is, in reality, little difference between them. The escapement files come with square handles which make them slightly more steady in the hand than the needle files, which regularly come with knurled round handles (Fig. 2.8a). The proportion of cutting surface to handle, also, is different. In the escapement file, the blade is the same length as the handle or less, to facilitate working in out-of-the-way places. In the needle file, the blade is usually longer than the handle, so that there is more cutting surface per file. The needle files also come in an assortment of lengths, ranging from 4 inches to 7¾ inches. The escapement files are generally available in only one length—5½ inches.

In making a choice between the two types of files, you must determine how large and intricate you intend your work to be. The bigger (and for our purposes, three inches is huge) and the simpler the work, the more you would tend toward the needle files. The smaller and more intricate the work, the greater the use you would make of the escapement files. An assortment of each is ideal—if you can afford it. One thing I would *not* suggest is that you buy a ready-packaged set of assorted files, despite the useful little carrying case. In such a set, you can get no variety in cut or length or type, and more often than not you will end up with a file or two that might have been perfect for opening tiny gears inside a watch, but which will remain forever unused by you. Weigh each purchase with extreme care in order to ascertain its ultimate usefulness.

Although the relative coarseness of the cut and the length of the cutting surface are important, the essential feature of each file is its shape. No one file can suffice for all jobs; therefore, at least a dozen different shapes are available. The job of selecting the most useful ones, however, is not as difficult as it might first appear. Many files are simply refinements of a single basic shape. For example, files with esoteric names such as cant, escape-wheel, and balance-wheel are all minor variations on the basic barette file, perhaps the most useful single file you can buy.

The barette file (Fig. 2.8b) is a flattened triangular file with a single cutting surface. It is one of the few files that do not utilize all surfaces, but this makes it a very useful tool. You can file in the tiniest of areas without worrying about inadvertantly nicking other areas. It can be controlled, its use focused, more than any other file. In its longer lengths and coarser cuts, it is the ideal choice for rough-shaping exterior contours as well as interior details.

A barette file, however, is inappropriate inside concavities or rounded openings. For this function, the choice is the half-round file (Fig. 2.8c), which cuts on both its rounded and flat surfaces. It may be used in rough-shaping as well as in detail work and, although it cannot be focused as readily as the barette file, it is a much more versatile tool. Indeed, if you were to buy only one file, the half-round would be the one to choose.

Between the barette file and the half-round file, most of the jobs that the model-maker is liable to encounter can be well taken care of. However, there are other files which are particularly useful for specialized

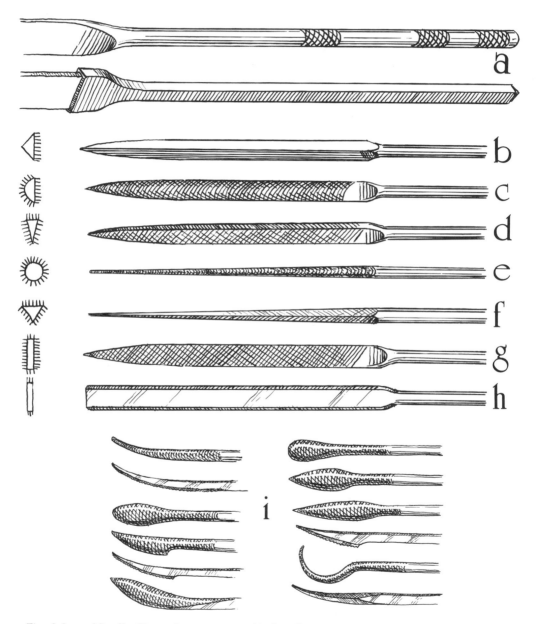

Fig. 2.8   a. Needle file and escapement file handles. b. Barette file. c. Half-round file. d. Knife file. e. Round file. f. Tri-corner file. g. Warding file. h. Joint-finishing file. i. Riffle files.

types of work. Foremost among these is, I think, the knife file (Fig. 2.8d), which is the file that I most frequently employ. The file is shaped like a steep-sided triangle coming to a sharp edge. However, the edge does very little of the work; most of the cutting is done with the sides. The action of this file is primarily a slitting and opening one. It is used to define interior details and is, therefore, most useful if small.

Another tool used almost entirely for interior details is the round file (Fig. 2.8e), whose basic function is to enlarge and even-out circular holes. Although not particularly useful for carving miniature sculptures, this tool is the mainstay of production model-makers who work with prong and bezel settings. Similarly useful for this sort of highly precise geometrical work is the tri-corner or three-square file (Fig. 2.8f), which is also particularly useful for incising lines into the surface of your piece.

The last two files are also primarily used by the production model-maker: the warding file and the joint-finishing file (Fig. 2.8g and 2.8h). The warding file, the pillar file, and the equalling file all have similar profiles in cross section and all serve a fairly similar function: taking down perfectly flat or squared-off sections of wax. The warding file is tapered toward the point of the blade to permit a greater variety in the width of the cut (an advantage when working as small as a model-maker must), while the equalling and pillar file both have a uniform blade. The pillar file is also different from the other two, in that it has no cutting surface on the edges. The companion file to the pillar is the joint-finishing file, which cuts only on its edges, its wide sides being blank. This file's only purpose is slitting but, the production model-maker involved in making uniform galleries and open-work finds it a blessing.

These are all the files you will probably ever need, even if you come to rely primarily on the use of files, rather than on knives or the flexible shaft machine. But it is more than simply a matter of temperament which will dictate the type of tool that a model-maker prefers; it is really the type of work he is commissioned to do. A highly convoluted miniature sculpture is more easily done with knives or the flexible shaft machine. When a piece requires precise fitting of several castings together, or when a design is basically geometrical in nature—as in most modern jewelry—the natural choice would be the file. One push of a barette file is able to produce a more strictly flat surface than a dozen hours of work with a knife.

However, there are files available which have been specifically designed for working forms freer than the purely geometric shapes produced so readily by standard escapement or needle files. These are the riffle files (Fig. 2.8i) which come in any number of varieties, each one designed to reach a different out-of-the-way place. In my opinion, riffle files are entirely too expensive for the average model-maker. Exotically shaped tools never really fit exactly where they are needed; a rolled-up piece of emery paper often does the job better.

A basic file set should include:

7 ¾"   barette needle file, cut-2
7 ¾"   half-round needle file, cut-2
6 ¼"   three-square needle file, cut-2
5 ½"   barette escapement file, cut-3
5 ½"   half-round escapement file, cut-3
5 ½"   knife escapement file, cut-3
5 ½"   round escapement file, cut-4

Naturally, this set can be expanded to include other shapes, cuts, and lengths. It may even be reduced by eliminating the two longest needle files. When buying files, buy the best ones that you can afford, usually either Swiss or French made, because the file will last forever if you use it only on the wax. The average cost of a good file is between $4 and $5. Do not use your files to clean your cast metal pieces; it will dull your cutting surface so that you will have to exert more pressure in order to take down the material, thereby diminishing the control you have over the implement. Do not use your file for anything other than filing: no using it as a scribe to mark lines on the wax; no using it as a spatula to add wax to the piece; no using it as a lever to pry apart pieces temporarily tacked together. The file does not have any spring to it. If it is made to bend, even a little, the point will snap off.

Take care of your files in the toolbox. More damage will be done by the abrasion of one tool knocking up against another than can ever be done while working on the wax. Either buy or make a little leather or plastic pouch with pockets, or else simply roll your files up in a cloth to separate them from each other and from your other tools. Do not place your files precariously at the edge of the bench; one fall is usually enough to snap off the point. These are fine tools, expensive tools; if properly cared for, they should last a lifetime.

Saws

Two saws are usually enough for any model-maker: one for cutting off slabs of wax from the solid block, and the other for the more intricate sawing of the pattern from the slab. For the rough work, an inexpensive hacksaw purchased from a hardware store is a perfect instrument. Get one with fairly large, wide-spaced teeth, or the wax will clog up the blade. Do not buy a standard rip or cross-cut saw; the sawcut will be very rough and irregular. A little bit of glycerine on the hacksaw blade will make the job easier.

More thought, however, is required in the selection of the finer saw frame and the interchangeable blades you will use in it. Saw frames for intricate fret sawing are best purchased through a jewelry supply house. There are several types, some with a rigid frame, some with a frame whose opening may be adjusted by loosening a wing bolt; some are made of round steel rod; some are made of oval rod (Fig. 2.9). None of these differences is particularly important.

Of great importance, however, is the depth of the frame. Saw frames come in varying depths, ranging from 2¼ inches all the way to the 8-inch saw frames intended for cutting out patterns from very large pieces of metal. What you receive in versatility from a large frame, you lose in control. When the frame is 8 inches from the cutting blade, the slightest waver in control is accentuated at the point of contact, causing irregularities in the sawcut. Nor does the average model-maker, working on such a miniature scale, even require a deep frame. For me, the shallower the frame, the better. Model-makers seldom attempt pieces larger than a few inches in any direction; therefore, a 2¼-inch frame is ideal. It offers maximum control, which, after all, is the model-maker's prime concern.

There is one more attribute which a saw frame must have; the locking device which holds the saw blade should be forged of high-quality steel and, if possible, be replaceable. Unlike the metal jeweler, who uses only flat saw blades, the wax model-maker also utilizes spiral blades which

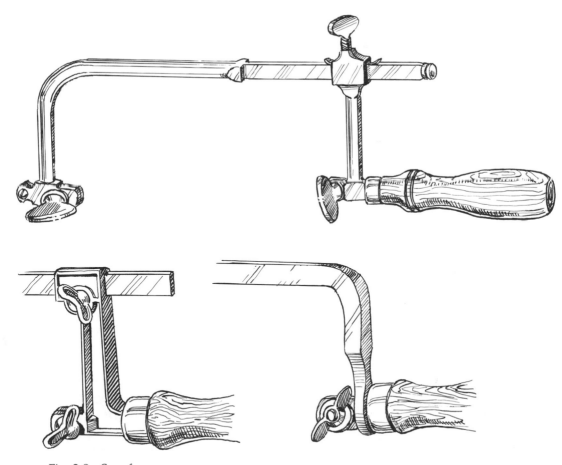

Fig. 2.9 Saw frames.

have a tendency to erode a channel into the steel plate of the locking device, causing the thinner flat blade to slip in its mooring.

The wax model-maker has recourse to three types of saw blades, each having a distinctly different function. The mainstay of the model-maker is the spiral blade. Because wax offers little resistance when compared to metal, a blade which cuts in all directions, as the spiral blade does, is a great convenience. It eliminates the necessity of removing the blade and starting a new cut from the opposite direction. This is fine for rougher sawing, outside contours, and larger shapes; however, as is the case with many things, there are drawbacks. Since the blade does not naturally create its own track, the cut is very difficult to control with precision. Using a fine, number-2 blade will help, but the imprecision can never be eliminated altogether. For more exacting jobs, such as pierce-sawing intricate patterns into the wax, a standard flat jeweler's blade is preferred.

Flat blades come in two styles: piercing saws and so-called flat saws. In fact, both are flat, but the piercing blades have rounded backs to facilitate shifts in cutting direction, and are the better of the two styles. The range of sizes is greater too, even though you only really need two different blade sizes: a rough number-4 or number-5 and a finer 4/0 or 5/0 blade (refer to the Appendix for the complete table of saw blade sizes). Each of these blades serves a specific function. The rougher blade is used in place of the spiral blade when precise cutting is imperative. It is not as versatile as the spiral blade; its path is only forward. It is also slower, and breaks easily. And, in spite of all precautions, the wax clogs in the teeth and has to be cleaned out regularly with the file cleaner. Therefore, it is best to make the substitution of the piercing saw blade for the spiral blade only when extreme accuracy in the cut is demanded. Small patterns of cut-outs, perfectly straight lines, and exacting gallery work would all require a piercing blade. A good way to determine which blade to utilize in a particular situation is to ascertain in advance if you can indulge in the luxury of plying the file freely. If you do have ample room, use the spiral blade; if the space is tight and filing away mistakes seems inordinately difficult, choose the piercing blade.

The other flat blade, the thin 4/0 or 5/0, cannot be used in place of a spiral blade. It has really only one highly specialized use—but that use is so important that the addition of a dozen blades is necessary to almost every model-maker's toolbox. This blade is used for slitting. Very often, to facilitate casting or cleaning or hollowing out a piece, it is necessary to remove an entire section and replace it later. When the need for this procedure arises, the very sawcut becomes a factor in planning the reconstruction of the entire piece. In the act of cutting, material is powdered away. The thickness of the saw blade determines just how much material is lost. And even though it is difficult to cut through a piece of wax with a very fine blade, it is even more difficult to build up a thin layer, perfectly

42

formed, in order to reform the original contours of the space that had been sawed away.

Spatulas

A model-maker, even one who intends only to carve, must be prepared for all contingencies. Unfortunately, one of the major contingencies that everyone, sooner or later, must confront is breakage. Wax is very fragile, especially when worked to thicknesses of less than 1 millimeter. Fissures appear. Things snap. You saw off too much. Unsatisfactory sections have to be replaced. In order to correct mistakes, as well as for more constructive reasons which will be discussed fully in a later chapter, it is often necessary to melt new wax onto the original carved piece. Wonderfully, the new wax, once hardened, shows no trace of the mistake. This miracle may be effected with two simple tools: a spatula to hold and apply the wax, and an alcohol lamp to melt it.

Even though a spatula is nothing more than a steel rod with both ends flattened and shaped, there is such a myriad of shapes, sizes, and thicknesses that selection might be difficult. But here, as in most things, the simpler, the better and I have found that the most useful shape is the basic spoon, which can be purchased from jewelry or dental supply houses.

Spatulas are explained and illustrated in detail in Chapter 6 on wax build-up.

Alcohol Lamps

Alcohol lamps, or spirit lamps, are very simple vessels which can be readily made or cheaply purchased. They are, basically, covered glass jars with a wick threaded through a hollow tube wich is designed to keep the flame away from the reservoir (Fig. 2.10). To convert a small glass jar with a metal screw-on top, simply drill a ⅜-inch hole through the top and wedge 1½ inches of hollow metal tubing—available in most hardware or plumbing supply stores—into the hole. Secure the tubing, either by slotting one end and opening the slots inside the lide or by applying a little solder around the joint. Then just thread your wick, also available in hardware stores, up into the tube until ¼ inch appears through the top.

If you would rather, a good alcohol lamp can be bought for under $5 from a scientific or a jewelry supply house, or from a hardware store. These commercial lamps are made of very thick glass and come in an assortment of shapes, some pretty, and some not. Many of the more sophisticated models come with a thumb screw in the lid which, ideally, is supposed to raise or lower the wick. In my experience, this mechanism never works properly, and is a vast nuisance. Buy a cheaper model that does not feature it.

It is important to note that—despite the obviousness of the statement—an alcohol lamp should be filled only with alcohol. Other fluids,

43

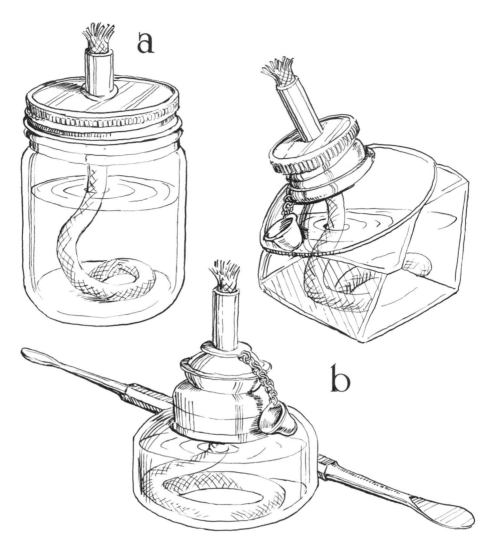

Fig. 2.10 a. Homemade alcohol lamp. b. Commercial alcohol lamps.

such as kerosene and gasoline, do not produce a clean-burning flame; soot tends to build up quickly on the spatula and eventually black spots which could ruin the piece become embedded in the wax. Other flammable fluids, such as lacquer thinner and acetone, are so downright dangerous that the glass jar could conceivably explode. Nor will all types of alcohol do the job. Rubbing alcohol, for example, cannot really sustain a decent flame. Use only denatured alcohol (sometimes labeled denatured solvent) bought from a hardware store.

Gauges

For the jeweler or serious craftsman who must be concerned with exact measurements, either to compute the final weight of the cast piece

44

or to create mountings for existing castings or for stones, measuring gauges are essential. At the first and final stages of working a piece, I always have at least one nearby.

Gauges, in model-making, are used for three purposes; flat measurements, outside measurements on three-dimensional forms, and inside measurements on three-dimensional forms. For flat measurements, a standard ruler is fine. Get a plastic one, if you can, because plastic will not scratch wax, while a metal ruler will. Get one that is calibrated in millimeters, which is the standard unit of measurement for the jewelry industry. On more sophisticated gauges, the millimeter regularly appears either along with a vernier inch scale or as a substitute for it.

For outside measurements (and certain inside ones as well), the natural choice is calipers (Fig. 2.11a). Calipers are all basically the same: a rule with a set of adjustable jaws that slide back and forth on a track. Available from jewelry supply houses, drafting supply houses, or good hardware stores, they come either in metal or plastic and, depending upon how much you wish to pay, have an assortment of features. Some have locking screws which keep the measurement constant; some have dials which show the measurement easily; some even have their own carrying cases. The only features, however, which are really important are the inclusion of a set of inside measuring jaws and an easy-to-read millimeter scale. As for the material, plastic is again as good or better than metal—and about one-fifth the price. Remember, though, calipers are only as good as the exactness of the jaws; they must close flush at all points. Plastic calipers are very fragile; excess heat can warp them. Never drop them into your toolbox. One inexact measurement could result in a catastrophe.

The only gauge which *must* be metal is the degree/ligne gauge (Fig. 2.11b), also called a spring gauge because the jaws spring shut when tension is released on the other end. For the model-maker, especially with the price of gold climbing every day, this instrument is indispensable. It is used to measure the thickness of the wall of a piece of jewelry in order to determine how much wax must be hollowed out from the core; the thinner the wall, naturally, the less expensive the finished piece. The curved jaws of the gauge are especially designed to fit into out-of-the-way places, such as inside a large dome ring. On such pieces, a wall of 1 millimeter (approximately ¹⁄₂₅ inch) is considered excessively thick, with 0.75 millimeter being the accepted standard. There is almost no way to determine thickness accurately without a degree gauge.

Unfortunately, the tool has been specifically designed for use on metal and, in order to use it on wax, it must be modified. Even then exercise great care when using it. The jaws, although curved to reach into out-of-the-way places, have squared-off corners which hamper complete use of the gauge in deep tight spots. They come together at two small squared-off points, too wide to gauge correctly the thickness of

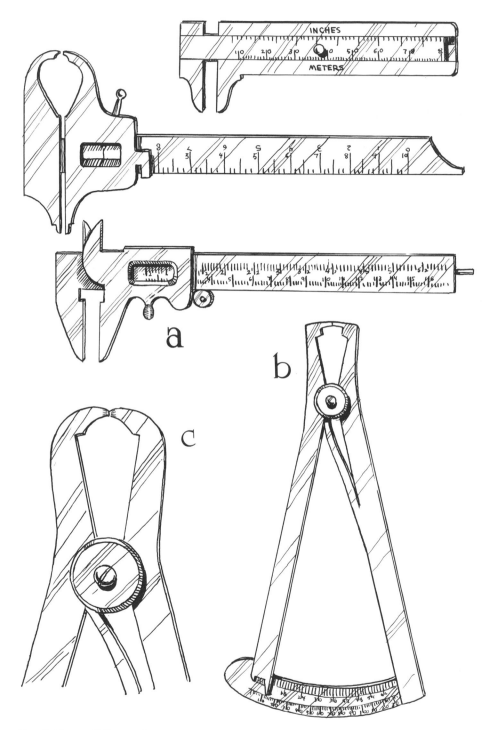

Fig. 2.11 a. Calipers. b. Degree/ligne gauge. c. Modification of jaws.

46

very small, intricately detailed pieces. The corners also tend to scratch wax, aided by the natural snapping action of the spring steel jaws. Do about five minutes' work on a grinding machine or about thirty minutes' work with an old file. The outer corners must be rounded off (Fig. 2.11c); the point of contact must be reduced to as small a surface area as possible; the contour of the jaws, sharply die-stamped, should be rounded off all the way to the meeting point of the jaws.

FLEXIBLE SHAFT UNIT

A complete flexible shaft unit—motor, handpiece, hanging rod, and burrs—costs over $150. Do not rush out to make such an investment unless you are absolutely serious about becoming a wax model-maker. Work first with the files and the knives, and be sure that you enjoy the work, and that you truly require the use of the flexible shaft machine. If you intend to utilize free-form techniques where molten wax is gradually built up to create organic or nugget-like effects, the drill would be an unnecessary luxury. However, if you wish to become adept at producing the fine gold jewelry you see in stores, you cannot truly approach the task, professionally, without the flexible shaft unit. The savings in time alone—not even considering the increase in precision—will pay for the machine in less than a month.

The flexible shaft unit consists of a motor and a pole on which to hang it, a foot rheostat which regulates the number of revolutions per minute the motor will produce, a handpiece which allows you to work virtually without hindrance, and a number of interchangeable burrs in different shapes and sizes.

The best motor, and the motor most popular among professional jewelers, is the Foredom model CC (Fig. 2.12a). I have had mine for eighteen years. It is sturdy, almost maintanance-free, and dependable. It is not a high-speed motor but, for wax, the lower the speed, the better. If you are tempted to work at too high a speed, the heat of friction will melt the work right out of your hand. The only other motor I would recommend would be the Foredom model F, which is a less expensive light-duty model, well suited to working such a resistance-free material as wax. However, if you intend to refine or polish your pieces after they have been cast into metal—particularly into 14-karat gold—the model F will balk at the strain and break down quickly.

Both of these motors, as well as motors put out by other companies, are marketed either as complete units with the handpiece included or else as individual units onto which your own handpiece may be attached. There is some savings on the complete set, but the handpiece which is included is the standard number-30 handpiece, which is a heavy-duty, all-purpose metal-working tool (Fig. 2.12b). It is a very thick, heavy handpiece which works like any standard electric drill with a chuck that can accommodate the finest twist drill as well as any shank size up to $\frac{5}{32}$

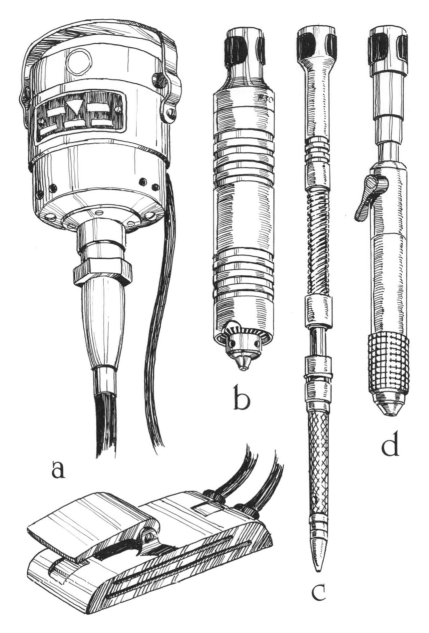

Fig. 2.12   a. Motor and rheostat foot pedal. b. Number-30 handpiece. c. Collet-style handpiece. d. Faro handpiece.

inch. However, the very factor which makes this tool so durable—its heft—could make it less than ideal for the wax model-maker who requires the utmost in pin-point precision and whose work is often so tiny and intricate that nothing but the slimmest tool is able to reach in to do the job.

It has been my experience that the number-30 handpiece is simply too big for the average-size hand. Among my students, almost no woman

48

has been able to handle it easily on delicate work and most men, too, find it difficult to control. I suggest that, when you go to the jewelry supply store—about the only place where these particular tools can be purchased—you play with the handpieces for a while before making your choice. If you must order by mail, obtain the length and diameter of the different pieces, and shape a broom handle or dowel to those dimensions. The handpiece alone costs around $40, and some consideration should go into its purchase.

Except for the number-30, almost all handpieces utilize either a standard $\frac{3}{32}$-inch collet or a selection of interchangeable collets ranging from $\frac{1}{32}$ inch to $\frac{1}{8}$ inch (Fig. 2.12c). A collet is basically a tube of spring steel which has been slotted partway down. When the tube is in place in the hollow handpiece, a mechanism pushes the slit sides together, firmly grasping your drill or burr. When the mechanism is released, the tube springs back to its original opening size and the drill drops out. Such a mechanism takes up less room than the chuck and key mechanism of the number-30 handpiece. In fact, some collet-style handpieces actually taper down to a $\frac{3}{16}$-inch point.

However, before rushing out to buy any handpiece, a word of caution; what feels good cold in your hand might have certain unpleasant surprises in store when you actually begin to use it. These very narrow, pencil-thin handpieces pay the price for their delicacy; because the mechanism is so near the outer wall, they become terribly hot. Also, because these handpieces do get so hot, they require a good deal of lubrication to keep from burning up. The oil has a tendency to seep out through the clamping mechanism and get on your hands—and eventually into your work. Nor are they particularly long-lived. Those that clamp the collet shut by means of snapping open in the middle of the shaft, after a while often snap open permanently. Those that shut the collet by pushing a sleeve down toward the point loosen up unexpectedly. Those that have an exposed spring mechanism can pinch your hand while depositing their load of hot oil into the wound.

There is, thankfully, one collet-style handpiece which eliminates many of the negative features inherent in the model while retaining the slimness and ease of handling—the Faro handpiece (Fig. 2.12d), which closes its collet by means of a lever set into the shaft. It is thin, although not quite as thin as the other models described, but it does not get hot in the hand. There is no need to fumble with a chuck key; a turn of the lever releases the burr. And it is durable. The only drawback is that it takes only standard $\frac{3}{32}$-inch shafts, making it unusable for almost all twist drills, except those set into standard shafts. But for your purpose—light, exacting work—it is as close to an ideal handpiece as you can hope to find.

While the flexible shaft unit is best for all the types of work required of a model-maker, it is not the only solution to jobs where a rotary action is necessary. Special flexible shafts which can be tightened into standard electric drills are available at good hardware stores for considerably less than the price of the more sophisticated unit. Dremel puts out a small compact unit with the motor inside the handpiece. Both of these devices, while not ideal for carving, are quite useful for the one job that is virtually impossible for anything other than rotary cutting: hollowing out concavities to lighten the weight for casting.

Burrs

Whichever unit you ultimately select, you must then choose your burrs, the small grinding tools which bear more than a passing resemblance to the steel tips the dentist snaps onto his drill. These burrs come in a wide selection of shapes and sizes (Fig. 2.13), some of which are almost essential to model-making.

Burrs really serve the function of files, but instead of working with a backward and forward motion, they work with a circular one. The same rules which governed the selection of files applies to burrs; in general, a coarse cut is better than a fine cut. In fact, the rule applies much more to burrs than to files, because the burr moves many times faster, increasing the possibility of melting the wax. Most burr shapes come in two different cuts: single-cut and crosscut. The crosscut may be worked only at extremely low speeds and then only for final surface smoothing; the mainstay of the wax model-maker is the single-cut burr. Once again, with the exception of the very coarse three-bladed wax burr usable for only the very roughest shaping, no burr has been specifically designed for wax. However, I have found that, in most cases, the coarse single-cut burrs are admirably suited for working on wax. The fine single-cut burrs, like the crosscut ones, are only for finishing work. As for the quality of the steel—tungsten, vanadium, carbide—it makes no difference as long as you use them solely on wax.

Burrs come in different shapes for different jobs but, by far, the most useful is the standard round. With it, you can cut a straight line, drill through the wax for pierce-sawing, and clean out a hollow to whatever thickness you desire. The spectrum of sizes for round single-cut burrs runs from 9/0, which is 0.1 millimeter in diameter and used for the most intricate details, all the way up to the huge 11.1 millimeter number-34, which is used for quick routing of especially large sections. The job is always quicker and better if you choose the largest possible burr that will fit. The hollow will be smooth, exactly conforming to the contour of the burr, instead of the pitted or lined effect you will create from worrying the surface with a burr that seems safer but is, actually, far too small.

The other mainstay is the cylinder which, though not as versatile as the round, more satisfactorily replaces the function of a file; the larger ones will rough-shape material into planes—like a file, but in a tenth of the time—and the smaller ones will produce sharp corners and very precise contours.

50

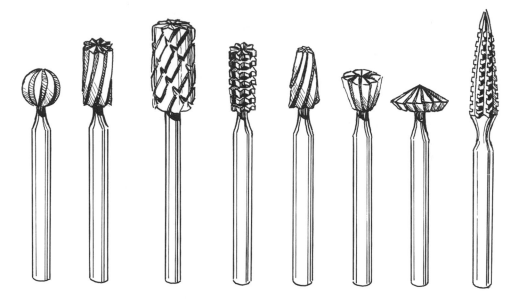

Fig. 2.13 Burrs for the flexible shaft unit.

To the basic cylindrical burr (also called the cylinder square), three or four variations may be added: the cone square, which cuts in finer details; the krause burr, which cuts in still finer details as well as opens up holes to produce highly elaborate fretwork; the inverted cone, which cleans up the walls of squared channels and produces sharp V-shaped cuts in the wax; and the hart burr which incises lines into the surface of the work.

Each burr serves the function of a particular file. The all-purpose round burr is as versatile as the half-round file. The cylinder square very nearly serves the function of the barette file. The cone square is used in place of the knife file, the krause burr in place of the round file, and the inverted cone in place of the tri square. As for other shapes—I personally have very infrequently found a use for them.

One suggestion: get a small piece of wood, about 1½ inches thick, and drill holes into it. Stand your burrs up in it; this will keep you from wasting time fumbling around for the right size and shape, and it will also keep your burrs from being damaged in the toolbox. Sometimes, the supply house will have the compartmentalized plastic containers in which the burrs had been originally packaged; these are also good.

A very basic selection of burrs would include:

> round, single-cut: sizes 6/0, 2/0, 0, 2, 6, 9, 14, 20, 30
> cylinder square, single-cut: 1, 4, 10
> cylinder, high-speed: 19, 28
> cylinder square, crosscut: 2
> cone square, single-cut: 3/0, 0, 2

cone square, crosscut: 2
inverted cone, single-cut: 1, 4, 9
hart: 10
krause: 2
twist drills (attached to $\frac{3}{32}$-inch shank): 3/0, 2, 5

All the tools which I have recommended here, I have in my own toolbox. Preference among tools varies from individual to individual. As a professional model-maker, I must consider time as a factor; therefore I, personally, rely most heavily on the flexible shaft unit, doing all my rough-shaping and most of my intricate details with it. I usually finish my wax model with files, if it is geometric or has pierce-work, or knives, if it has delicate carved details. But again, each model-maker is different, his problems are different, his goals are different and it is up to each model-maker to select the method of approach which, ultimately, is right for him.

Chapter 3

Wax Models from Molds

YOU have already seen, in Chapter 1, that the use of molds is an integral part of lost-wax casting, that a mold of the carved wax model is made in investment, and that a mold of the finished casting is made in rubber so that many pieces can be reproduced. The mold has been the essential feature of this type of casting since ancient times. However, molds need not always be made from a wax original. Carving directly in the wax is a relatively new phenomenon. Until quite recently, no wax had been formulated capable of sustaining the quality of detail that is required of a finished piece of jewelry. Practically all models were made originally in metal and reproduced directly in rubber. The only function which was served by wax was to be melted into the rubber mold, to solidify, and to be lost in the actual casting.

Before taking up the wax block and carving it, it may be helpful to learn a little more about wax and its function in the casting process. This chapter will go back to a traditional method of making a mold for lost-wax casting, using neither wax nor metal for the original model, but rather modeling clay: a familiar material that is simple to work. With it, you will easily be able to understand the technical aspects of the process, as well as some of the sculptural ones.

BAS-RELIEF BELT BUCKLE

Begin with a photograph or a drawing of practically anything which is a self-contained unit: an animal, a plant, any sort of ornament which suggests a high relief—because you are going to make a bas-relief, an ornament which suggests three-dimensionality but which actually is carved only on the front side and is perfectly flat in back. Amost all jewelry, incidentally, is fashioned on the principle of the bas-relief.

A good source for photographs is, of course, magazines—especially nature magazines, but there are also books on the market which reproduce various types of ornaments: ornaments derived from natural forms, ornaments from a particular historical period, ornaments used for particular purposes. I would suggest, even here at the very outset, that you begin to collect a library of such books, gathering, in addition, photographs of anything which could reasonably be fashioned into jewelry, and organize them into some sort of file. Or, if you have the ability to draw, by all means save those sketches or studies which might readily be transformed into jewelry designs, or into designs for any other type of ornamentation as well.

Once the photograph or drawing has then been selected, it must be modified to fit within the limits of aesthetics and practicality. If, for example, you have chosen a plant with many isolated stems and tendrils—knowing the impossibility of carving such thin strands in clay—you must alter the arrangement of the stems so that they overlap, forming a more solid unit in silhouette. Similarly, you must be able to render the details of the original into a size which is applicable for our purpose. Do not be satisfied to use the photograph exactly as you have found it.

The method for reducing or enlarging is a very simple and mechanical one. Using a piece of tracing paper, simply make a grid over your original drawing, dividing the surface up into squares (Fig. 3.1a). Then ascertain the size of your projected finished piece (no bigger than 3 inches; the average caster does not have the facilities to accommodate anything larger) and make a grid which is proportional to the original one, only smaller or larger as the situation demands. Then, simply fill in the squares one at a time, as if each one were a tiny picture to be reproduced on a smaller scale (Fig. 3.1). The reduced drawing will almost magically complete itself.

If you would like to know both dimensions of a finished piece, you can use a standard algebraic formula to determine them. Assume that the original drawing is 3 inches by 5 inches, and that you want the finished piece to be 2 inches long.

You set up the formula as follows:

$$\frac{3 \text{ in.}}{5 \text{ in.}} = \frac{x}{2 \text{ in.}}$$

Cross-multiply to eliminate the fractions:

$$3 \text{ in.} \times 2 \text{ in.} = 5 \text{ in.} \times x, \text{ or } 6 \text{ in.} = 5x$$

Divide both sides by 5 to find x:

$$1\frac{1}{5} \text{ in.} = x$$

So the finished piece will be $1\frac{1}{5}$ inches by 2 inches.

Once the rendering has been accomplished, you may begin the actual work of transforming this two-dimensional creation into something

Fig. 3.1   Reducing and simplifying a bas-relief rendering.

which catches highlights and casts shadows, something you can feel as well as see: a tiny sculpture. Indeed, it is the prime function of the model-maker to interpret that extra dimension from nothing more than the suggestions offered by a drawing. It is the model-maker—not the artist who created the design—who must give complete form to an idea, shaping and modulating that form so that it becomes a thing of beauty.

The first project, a man's western-style belt buckle, will give you a short excursion into the third dimension, concentrating, for now, on bas-relief, and leaving full sculpture for later.

Tools and Materials

Block of Plasticine, non-hardening clay, number 4
X-Acto knife, number-11
Wooden modeling tools (or a ¼-inch wooden dowel)
Plate glass, 5 inches by 5 inches
Small can of investment or casting plaster
Rubber mixing bowl
Inexpensive watercolor brush
Empty cottage cheese or whipped butter container
Small aluminum pot
Inexpensive serving ladle
Small container of glycerine
One-pound block of Ferris green carving wax
   or
Box of pink sheet wax, gauge 16 or 18
   or
Block of Ferris red Mold-A-Wax
Few rods of ⅛-inch sprue wax
Alcohol lamp and spatula
Few sheets of sandpaper, numbers 2, 0, 4/0
Small piece of felt cloth

The glass, under which you will place your drawing, should be plate glass for safety measures. Any glazier will be glad to cut down a piece of glass for you and grind the sides to insure that no sharp edges remain. As a further precautionary measure, it might be a good idea to bind the edges of the glass with cloth tape, either white adhesive tape or one of the plastic-coated kinds. The use of the plate glass serves several functions—not just for this project, but for many others which will be discussed later; it should be a staple of every model-maker. It will provide a transparent shield through which to view the drawing, actually to work directly on the drawing, without dirtying it. It will also serve as a stick-resistant surface that doubles as a base for carving and casting activities.

Clay is a substance familiar to practically everyone; it is a fixture in almost all kindergarten classes. However, the clay which is designed for children's playtime, although basically the same stuff, is much too soft and malleable to be of much use in carving and holding small details. The clay that you will use should be purchased from an art supply store, where it is available in a range of grades, from the familiar soft clay up to a very hard material which takes detail well. Roma Plastilina, for example, comes in five hardnesses, each having the basic non-hardening qualities of modeling clay; they all may be softened and worked in the hands but the harder grades, the 4 and the 5, lend themselves well to work with a knife as well as to manual shaping. In fact, the texture of these harder grades of Plastilina is not unlike the texture of some types of wax. You should select the very hardest grade of clay available and be prepared to work it with a knife, as well as with your hands and wooden tools.

The wooden tools that are generally used on clay are readily available, rather inexpensive and fun to play with. However, a single wooden ¼-inch dowel, cut into 6-inch sections and carved with a knife, will produce enough tools to mold a David in modeling clay (Fig. 3.2). It would be good practice also, if—even at this early stage in your approach to model-making—you were to accustom yourself to making at least some of the tools you will require. When a really specialized type of cut is necessary,

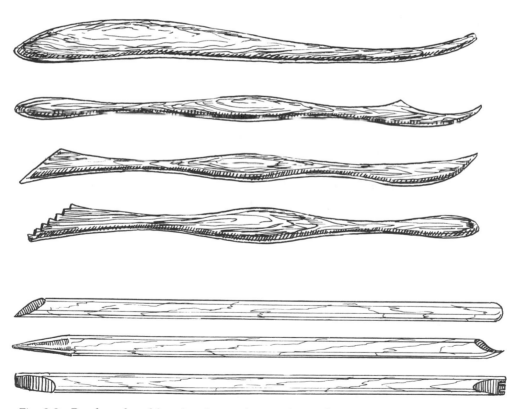

Fig. 3.2 Purchased and handmade wooden carving tools.

57

no tool on the market is ever able to accomplish the job correctly. Therefore, the model-maker has no recourse but to fashion his own implement to the particular specifications of the task at hand.

Clay Model

Your approach to creating a clay model should be a very systematic one, with each step figured out well in advance. There is nothing as frustrating as being forced to discard a piece after hours of labor simply because of incomplete preparations. Therefore, work slowly.

The first step is to cut a thin slab of clay, about ⅛ inch (3 mm) thick, and apply it directly onto the glass plate, cutting it with a wooden tool so that it roughly follows the outline of the design underneath (Fig. 3.3a). This slab is to be the basic shape upon which all of the additional ornamentation is to be bonded. The slab should not be perfectly level, but should have a slight belly in the center which slopes gently out to the edges (Fig. 3.3b), conforming to the slightly bent contour of the standard western-style belt buckle. The back will be given a matching curve later in the process.

Once the clay slab, modulated to form the shape of a buckle, is in place on the glass plate, simply sharpen the outline by refining it with your X-Acto knife. This not only will make the contour exact but will provide a defined thickness—approximately ¹⁄₁₆ inch (1.5 mm) at its finest—around the edges of the piece (Fig. 3.3c). The piece should then be smoothed with a wooden tool to remove any kinds of imperfection. Even though you are only working in clay at this stage, get into the habit of being as precise as possible; it will stand you in good stead later.

The functional part of the belt buckle is almost completed at this point, and the ornamentation is next. In jewelry, the model-maker must always consider the function of the piece first. If a ring cannot be worn, no matter how beautiful it might be, it is worthless as a piece of jewelry. Therefore, the model-maker works on the ring shank before even beginning to carve in details on the crown. All pieces of jewelry must pass two tests: "Can it be worn," and "Can it be worn comfortably." It is only after the piece has passed these two tests that the question of aesthetics is considered.

The basic approach to sculpture is to consider a piece in terms of planes or levels. In a bas-relief you must assign heights to all the salient features of the design, noting which features should be at approximately the same level, which higher, which lower. My buckle shows a standard floral design. Before I ever touch a tool to the clay, I try to assign distinct planes to the major elements of my design. The flowers, I feel, should attract the most attention; therefore, they will be the highest. The leaves should be gracefully undulating; therefore, the next level will be the thickest—to allow ample room to make the leaves twist and turn. The

58

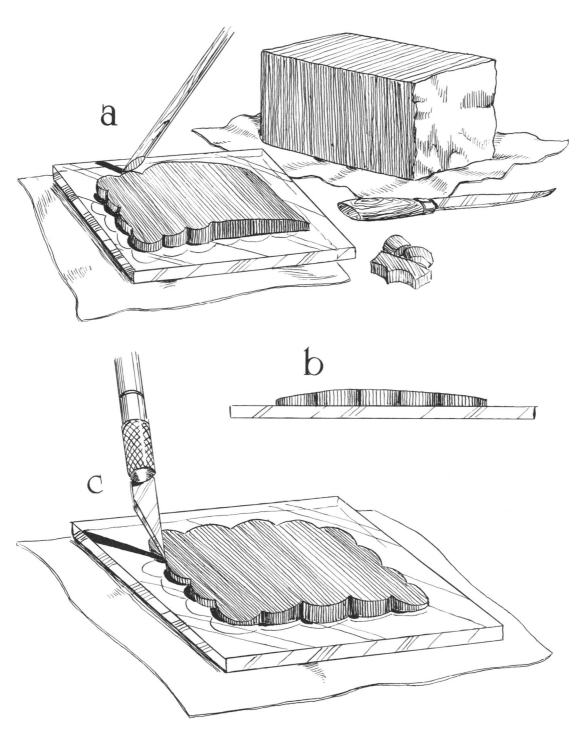

Fig. 3.3 a. Shaping the base layer of clay. b. Side view of base layer. c. Refining the outline.

lowest level, barely rising above the basic plane of the buckle, will contain the stems.

Usually, the model-maker is helped by the designer in assigning levels to the sections of the piece. The designer very seldom submits just a simple outline drawing; he will either shade it, leaving the lower levels in varying degrees of shadow, the darkest representing the most deep, or else he will render his idea from a slight angle to give at least some sort of hint as to the profile of the piece. But ultimately, it is the model-maker who determines the proportions.

For the floral design, the buckle is divided into three distinct planes, the bottom one being the buckle form itself. From the block of clay, cut off two more slabs, one ⅛-inch (3 mm) thick, the other ¼-inch (6.5 mm) thick. The latter will be the lower of the two layers (Fig. 3.4a). Using the same procedure as before, slip the original drawing underneath a clear section of the glass plate, to use as a stencil. Instead of cutting the clay to the form of the entire buckle, cut out only those sections which belong in the middle level of the profile (Fig. 3.4b). Apply this layer to the base in the proper position, creating, as you do so, two distinct planes. Repeat the procedure, using the ⅛-inch (3 mm) slab (Fig. 3.4c).

Do not go immediately to putting veins on the leaves or petals on the flowers. Within each basic plane, there are other planes which must be determined first, and these are not necessarily parallel to the three major ones. While not really a difficult job, determining the angles of these secondary planes often requires a good deal of consideration. Do not be timid however; the clay—like the wax in which you will be working later—can always be replaced if you cut off too much.

You must reduce the subtleties of the design down to the most basic movements, thinking in terms of black and white. In fact, it is often useful to make another tracing of the original, a tracing which—instead of lines—presents the piece in terms of masses, each mass representing one distinct plane. Or, failing that, try to visualize the underlying direction of each section of the piece. If you leave every flower to face directly toward you, the piece will be static, like a plywood garden ornament. It is the job of the model-maker to imbue a piece with life and movement; he must make it dynamic.

Cut the plane representing each flower at a different angle, facing each in a slightly different direction. Take your lamp and aim it at the piece from a very low angle to display the light and dark areas most severely; look at the piece critically in this way, turning it every which way, until the angle and the direction of each plane have been determined and the overall effect is a pleasing one. Every cut you make should be a straight one; it is much easier to see a pattern of lights and darks when the planes meet at sharp boundaries (Fig. 3.5a). At this point, the gracefully undulating curves which generally are the hallmark of a good model would only be a hindrance. This is the part of the job—the arrangement

60

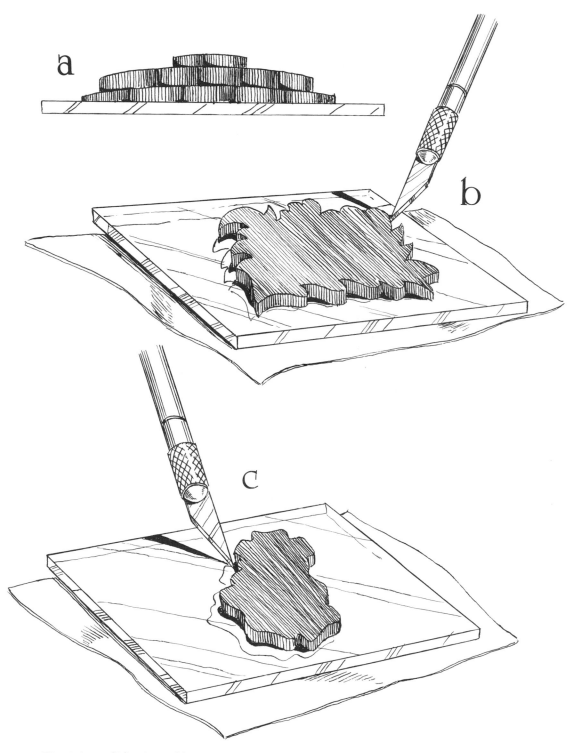

Fig. 3.4   a. Side view of layers. b. Shaping the middle layer. c. Shaping the top layer.

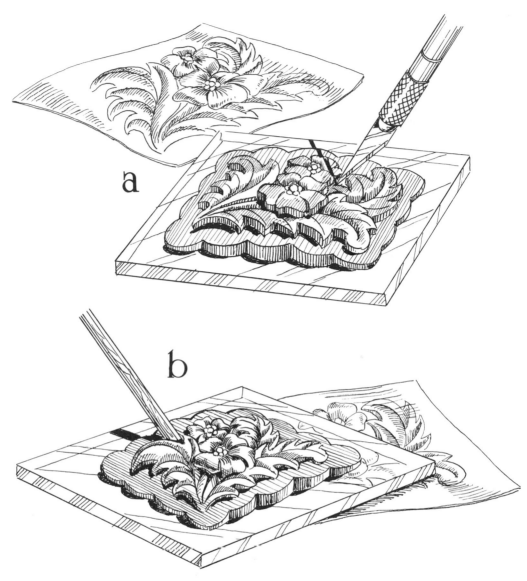

Fig. 3.5 a. Defining the secondary planes. b. Finishing the details.

of the different planes, the variation in the size of the planes, in their directions, in their relationships one to the next—that I find the most enjoyable. It is also the most challenging and the most important. Almost anybody can acquire enough technique to scratch in fine details; it takes a special kind of ability to arrange forms so that they come alive.

Once this arrangement of planes has been accomplished, you are free to play with your assortment of wooden tools, shaping the severe forms into well-modulated curves, refining outlines, and getting all the individual units of the piece to move together in harmony (Fig. 3.5b). If you have made your underlying structure dramatic enough, this mod-

62

ulation should enhance the beauty of the piece, restoring the subtlety of form suggested by the original design. Feel free to smooth the clay, alter the detail—even if it differs from the design—texture it, even pierce it if that will make it more beautiful, remembering however, that it is primarily a utilitarian piece you are making: a belt-buckle.

The clay model now only requires a few final touches. Incised lines will sometimes raise a burr in the clay; these must be cut away carefully with the X-Acto knife. The surface should be smoothed to remove any imperfections; a bit of glycerine—not too much—on the clay will facilitate this operation nicely. Do not stint on the finishing operations. You are going to make a mold from this model, and every imperfection which is allowed to slip by at this point will come back to haunt you later.

Investing

The clay model, thus completed, is ready for the next step: investing. Remove the bottom from a waxed cottage cheese container, making a sort of cylinder open on both sides: in short, a flask. This paper flask is then set down on the plate glass so that there is at least a ½-inch border on all sides of the clay model. It is fixed in place with a strip of plastic-coated tape that runs completely around the base of the container, creating a fairly water-tight vessel (Fig. 3.6a). Smear glycerine on the exposed glass inside the flask to insure a nonstick surface.

Investment, as discussed in Chapter 1, is a very specialized type of plaster and even though you are not concerned here with the property which allows it to endure extremely high temperatures, it is helpful that it expands slightly when setting. Investment is fairly expensive, however, and sometimes unavailable in small cans, regularly being marketed in hundred-pound drums. A fine grade of casting plaster may then be substituted. *Do not* buy your plaster from a hardware store; get it at an art supply store. The plaster which is used to fill up the cracks in walls is simply not fine enough to hold all the detail of your model. You will soon discover, especially if you plan to do model-making as a profession, that a small savings on the materials you use may truly cost you hours of additional work correcting flaws which should never have occurred.

Of course, you have to be selective. The most expensive thing need not necessarily be the best. Often you will find that, by improvising, you can very nicely substitute a more inexpensive item. Such is the case with your rubber mixing bowl, which may be purchased from either the art supply store or the jewelry supply house. The reason you must use a rubber bowl to mix plaster has to do with the high cost of plumbing. An unused portion of wet investment or plaster cannot be disposed of down the sink; it will clog up the pipes. The plaster can only be thrown out after it has set—into the garbage bag; however, if it sets in an ordinary pot, there is no way to remove it except with a hammer and chisel. Mix it in a rubber bowl and, once it sets, all you need do is squeeze the sides

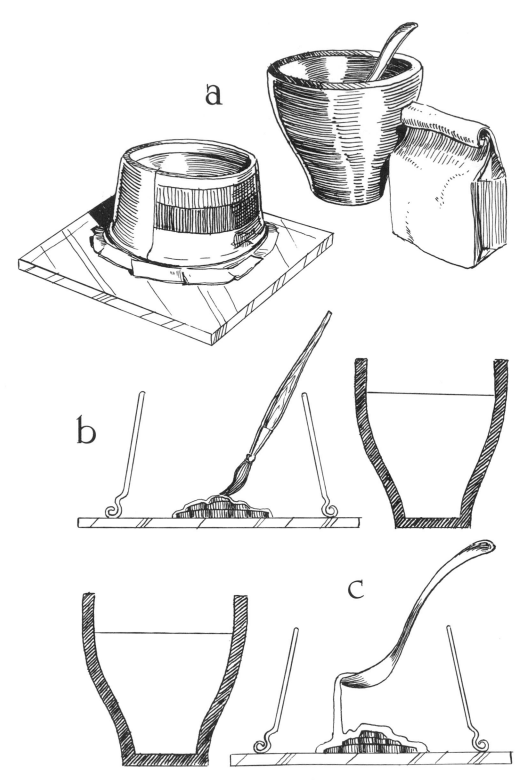

Fig. 3.6   a. Paper flask set in place around clay model. b. Painting the investment onto the model. c. Spooning the investment into the flask.

of the bowl together and the solid plaster falls out readily. But, since the only property of the rubber essential to its use as a mixing bowl is its flexibility, any substantial rubber (or even plastic) container will do. I have found that not one but two ideal mixing bowls can be fashioned from one inexpensive rubber ball with a 4- or 5-inch diameter. Just slice it in half along the seam, and you are ready to begin mixing your investment.

The mixing ratio is roughly four or five parts of water to one part of investment or plaster. First add the water to the bowl. You can control the setting time of the plaster by controlling the temperature of the water: the warmer the water, the more quickly the plaster will set. For now, cool water is best; you want to allow the plaster sufficient opportunity to run into every niche and depression in the clay model. The setting time may be even further controlled by the number of times you stir the mixture, and here again, it is best to stir it very little. The plaster should be quite fluid, without air bubbles, which are a natural result of vigorous stirring. The proper method for mixing plaster is to add the powder, a little at a time, to the water, breaking apart any undissolved clods with your fingers, until all of the powdered plaster has been used up and you have a fairly viscous liquid, about the consistency of light sweet cream.

Working quickly, because the material sets fairly rapidly, especially in warm weather, take your watercolor brush and dab the liquid plaster into the deepest recesses of the model, taking care not to disturb any of the detail-work. Then, brushing lightly, deposit a thin coat of plaster over the entire clay model as if you were simply painting it, making certain that the plaster adheres to all areas of the clay (Fig. 3.6b). If any area repels the plaster, keep working over that area until the plaster does take. Once this priming coat has been put on—and while it is still fairly wet—dip a plastic spoon into the now-thickening bowl of plaster and begin to spoon the mixture directly on top of the painted model (Fig. 3.6c). There should be some running down the sides of the model onto the glass plate, but gradually a fairly thick layer of plaster—about ½ an inch—will be built up all around the model, completely obscuring its form. Once this has happened, pour the remaining plaster into the flask, but aim the flow directly onto the glass plate all around the model until the level of the plaster at the borders of the flask rises up to the level of the plaster covering the model (Fig. 3.7a). Once the level in the flask is uniform throughout, just pour the remainder of the plaster in until it reaches the lip of the flask and let it set.

Do not rush the setting time. Quite often a model-maker who has been the very paragon of patience throughout the entire carving procedure will rush his way through a totally mechanical operation and find that his entire piece has been ruined. Go out and take a walk. You should not even touch any part of the paraphernalia—not the flask, nor the plaster, nor the glass plate upon which it all rests—until you are certain

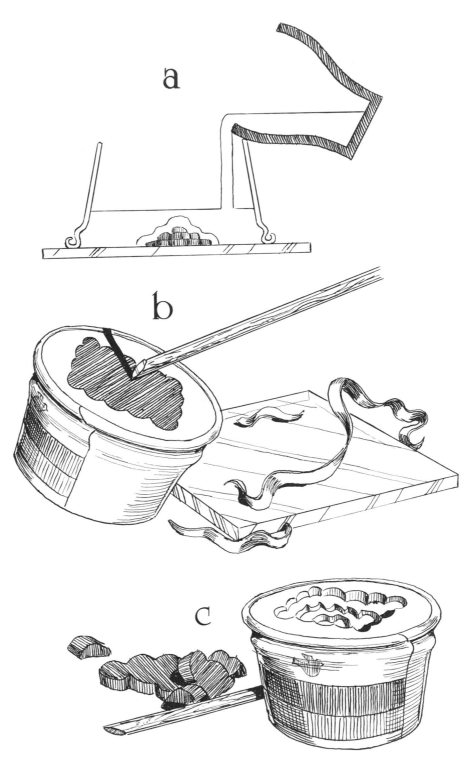

Fig. 3.7   a. Pouring the remaining investment into flask. b. Removing the clay.
c. Completed plaster mold.

that the mold has set completely. One way to double-check is to scratch the plaster lightly with a pin; if the material falls away into a powder leaving a sharp line in the plaster, chances are your mold is ready.

Remove the tape which attaches the flask to the plate and begin, by sliding and twisting the flask across the glass surface—not by immediately pulling the flask away from its base—to free the flask. The clay is adhering to both the plaster mold and to the glass plate on which it has been shaped. If you simply pull the flask away, there is the chance that the clay will pull away from the mold rather than from the plate, taking with it some of the more delicate sections of the plaster.

Once the flask has been freed, invert it so that the smooth level underside of the clay model is exposed, and working carefully with a flat wooden tool, begin to remove the clay (Fig. 3.7b). Since the plaster is relatively soft, try to avoid touching it at all with the tool; scratches or nicks might result which would then be permanently reproduced in the wax. Work outward from the densest section of the clay, prying it up or picking it out a little at a time until all the clay has been removed and there is a cavity bearing the impression of the clay model (Fig. 3.7c). If any residue of the clay remains in the mold, a cotton swab dipped in oil will help remove it; just use a dry swab after the wet one to absorb some of the oil which might remain and perhaps blur the finer details.

Wax Model

The mold is complete, a hollow set down into a perfectly level plaster surface. Now you will make a wax model from the mold.

This will be your first exposure to wax and, depending upon the design of the piece, there are three different types of wax—and three distinct wax techniques—which may be used to obtain a proper model for casting.

The most traditional method is wax pouring, with the wax that most professional model-makers employ as their mainstay: Ferris green wax. Ferris is a brand name. There are other companies, particularly Kerr, which put out a wide variety of waxes but, in my opinion, the finest carving wax on the market is Ferris. It comes in three varieties, each having distinct properties: green, purple, and blue. In later chapters, I shall discuss these waxes much more fully. For now it is only important to know that green wax melts at about 230°F; and when it melts, it runs like water; when it sets, it becomes hard enough to file or carve with a knife.

Ferris green wax comes in one or five-pound blocks. In either case, saw off the appropriate amount of wax before you begin to melt it. There is no rule that states that you cannot melt down the whole block and simply reuse the unused portion after it has hardened; however, after melting, the wax—which is wonderfully hard in its block form—becomes significantly softer. It is better to approximate the amount required to fill the cavity and then double that amount to allow for the wax which will stick to the pan.

For melting, the smallest aluminum saucepan or pot is best; smallest because your models will always be miniature, and aluminum because wax will not stick to an aluminum surface. Melt the wax over the lowest possible heat; you do not want to burn the wax, and you do not want to boil it. Burning will alter the consistency, and boiling will introduce bubbles that can make the final model look like a piece of Swiss cheese. The best procedure to prevent these catastrophies is to watch the melt constantly. The wax that is in direct contact with the aluminum will melt first, leaving a solid chunk floating on the surface of the melt. Depending upon how large the amount of wax you are using, the molten wax could conceivably boil before the solid piece has melted completely. Turn off the heat altogether and allow the solid piece to melt just from the heat of the already liquid wax. To be doubly certain, check the temperature regularly with a candy thermometer; it should not exceed the flowpoint.

When the wax has completely melted, it is ready to go into the glycerine-coated plaster mold, which should be warmed in the oven to prevent bubbles from forming in the molten wax due to sudden changes in temperature at the points of contact with the plaster. Do not pour the molten wax directly from the pan into the mold; this will cause a turbulence within the wax that can also create bubbles. Instead, take a large aluminum spoon and ladle the wax slowly from a very shallow height into the mold (Fig. 3.8a). The wax must be extremely fluid to run into all the crevices of the mold, so first the wax is ladled into those sections which are deepest or which have the greatest amount of detail work. Then, once the deepest depressions have been filled, the wax is deposited onto the still bare areas until, gradually, the entire cavity is filled right up to the level of the rim.

Then take another walk. Do not disturb the wax until you are absolutely certain that it has hardened completely through. Too often, the thin hard skin which forms on top is mistaken for complete solidity and the wax is tampered with before it has really set. Do not be impatient—*ever*—when working with wax models. When the wax has indeed set, you may remove it from the mold.

Depending, again, upon the relative complexity of the model, removal of the wax may be accomplished in several ways. If the model is smooth and without any real undercutting, a few raps with any hard object on the back of the plaster mold should suffice to dislodge it fairly cleanly. If the piece, however, is fairly complex, simply immerse the whole flask in a pot of warm water—and take another walk. By the time you return, enough of the plaster will have absorbed the water to facilitate removal of the wax. Just break it away between your fingers. Any bits that cling, you may remove carefully with a pointed stick. The powdery

68

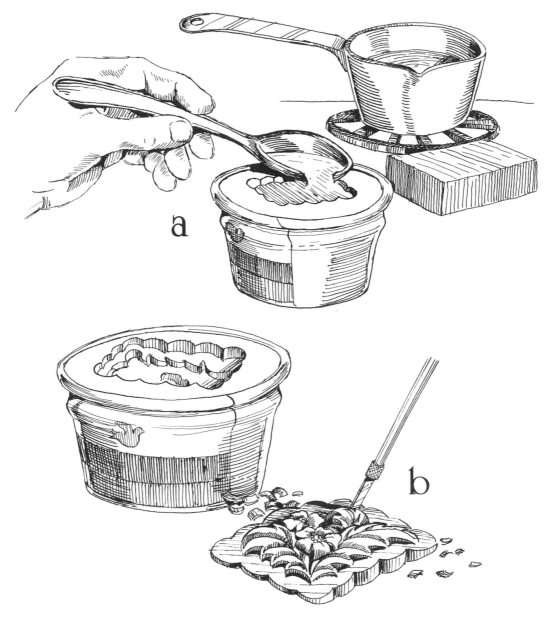

Fig. 3.8   a. Ladling molten wax into the mold. b. Refining the wax model.

residue which will adhere to the surface of the wax may be removed by turning the tap of the kitchen sink full blast on the surface of the wax.

Finishing Touches

It would be naive to imagine that a perfect wax model could be produced from these really quite primitive methods. Chances are there will be imperfections on the surface of the piece: pitting, bits of embedded plaster, areas which have not filled in completely, obscured or obliterated details, holes, or nodules. All these imperfections should be corrected before the wax is to be presented to the caster. Basically, there will be only two distinct types of flaws: those that must be cut away, and those which must be filled in.

The flaws which must be cut away are easily repaired with an X-Acto knife, a file or even sandpaper. These flaws are generally those which either are raised up from the surface of the piece—as nodules are—or else are small, entirely superficial surface scratches or pockmarks. Both of these may be set right without any real difficulty, if you keep in mind one rule which applies to all finishing processes, from the wax model to the finished metal item; in order to achieve a smooth, glass-bright finish, work from the roughest possible abrasive gradually up to the finest. In the case of the nodule, a knife will cut it off; a file will take it down to the surface level; then different grades of sandpaper ranging from 2/0 to 6/0 will blend in the spot with the surrounding area; then, last, a vigorous polishing with a piece of felt, first saturated with lighter fluid (lighter fluid dissolves the surface of the wax very very slightly), then applied dry. This process does not take as long as it sounds; the total surface of the wax buckle should not amount to over six square inches.

Surface pitting requires slightly more care, especially if the extent of the damage is sizeable. Here the knife is again used. Only this time, the stroke employed is not a slicing one, with the blade held level to the piece; it is a scraping one, with the blade held at a 45-degree angle and dragged across the surface under very light pressure (Fig. 3.8b). This scraping action is readily controlled and therefore perfect for removing imperfections from spots which might perhaps be inaccessible for any other tool. But, a heavy hand may result in an unpleasant wavy texture appearing across the surface of your piece. A light touch and a sharp blade are your best insurance against this happening. The scraping operation should be continued until all sign of pitting has been removed from the surface of the wax. A fine 6/0 sandpaper will smooth away the distinctive marks left by the knife. Finish by buffing with a felt cloth.

Details which have become either softened or obliterated may be sharpened with a few carefully considered cuts of the knife. When working with the knife, cut away as little as you can with each stroke until you become familiar with the material. Wax is not wood; it has no grain to push against, to crack suddenly apart with any hasty cut. It offers very little resistance to the blade but, if you turn the knife while cutting, it might chip away in fractures. In fact, before you even try to touch up your model, you really should practice on a piece of scrap wax. You will find that a combination of cutting and scraping should suffice to restore any detail that has been lost. Then simply proceed with the abrasives, rolling the sandpaper around a toothpick or nail in order to create a disposable tool which can reach into out-of-the-way places. Finish by buffing with a felt cloth.

Even if there are no imperfections in the wax, some finishing will be necessary in order to bring forth a high lustre on the surface. For this sort of light finishing work, either the finer grades of sandpaper are employed or else the entire surface of the piece is rubbed with a mixture of pumice and water. Pumice is volcanic ash. Cabinetmakers use it in its powdered form for final smoothing; it is available from either a hardware or paint store. Just mix it with water until you form a paste, and then rub vigorously with a thin cloth until the entire surface is smooth. Those areas that cannot be reached with the cloth can be smoothed with a pipe-cleaner dipped in the paste. Then buff as before, first with the wet felt cloth, then with the dry one. When you are done, you should—literally—be able to see your face reflected in the wax.

Imperfections which are deep in the surface of the piece—deep pitting, large air bubbles, embedded bits of plaster—are somewhat more difficult to eradicate. For this job you will have to add wax with an alcohol lamp and spatula.

Applying new wax to a wax carving is one of the essential acts of the model-maker. The piece which does not require it is a very rare one, so the operation must be mastered completely right from the very outset. Nor is it a particularly difficult job, once the underlying principle has been comprehended. *Hot wax does not bond to cold wax.* The natural impulse of most beginners, being unwilling to endanger their carving by going near it with a hot tool, is to drip the molten wax onto the solid block from a height of several inches. Superficially, the wax appears to have bonded; however, a few minutes work with the file will result in the new wax just falling off. The hot wax, coming into sudden contact with the cold wax, hardens very rapidly when it hits the block. The result is tantamount to a piece of cold wax dropped onto the cold block; no permanent bonding is possible. The surest way to determine whether your new wax has, in fact, bonded to the old is to shine a light directly onto the applied globule; if it shines back with an appreciably lighter shade of color than the block, then it has not bonded.

The proper method of applying wax is to hold your spatula directly over the flame with one hand. (Note that the flame basically may be divided into three parts: blue nearest the wick, colorless in the middle, and orange at the top. The spatula should be held into the colorless section of the flame where the heat is most intense.) The other hand should, if it is at all possible, be holding a long thin piece of wax, one end of which is resting in the cup of the spatula. The result should be a little pool of molten wax collected in the spatula (Fig. 3.9a). The stick of wax is then taken away from the flame and put aside. The free hand now should be employed to hold the wax model steady while the molten wax is applied.

71

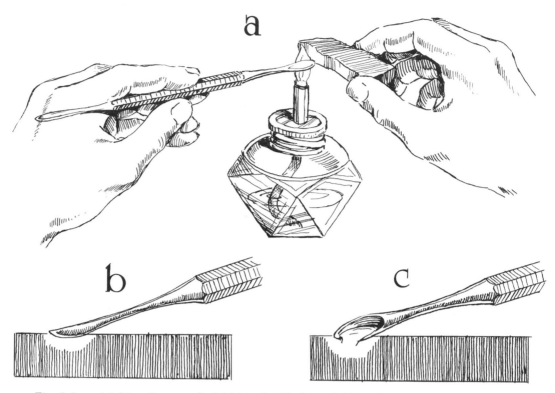

Fig. 3.9 a. Melting the wax. b. Melting the block. c. Adding the molten wax.

The procedure for applying the wax is very simple. Both sides of the spatula are used. The concavity, of course, is used for holding the molten wax. The convexity on the bottom is applied directly onto the surface of the wax block (Fig. 3.9b), melting the surface where the new wax is to be bonded. When the solid wax begins to melt underneath the spoon, the spatula is tilted so that the molten wax contained in the cup of the spoon is poured directly onto the hot wax below (Fig. 3.9c). This brings hot wax into contact with hot wax, and the bond created in this way is a permanent one. By controlling the heat of the spatula, the height of the deposit may also be controlled; the lower the heat, the less the wax will run, and the higher the deposit. If you are careful, your pockmarks may very readily be eliminated, their places taken by a series of tiny bumps and ridges which may then be easily removed by abrasives.

The only deep-seated surface defect which cannot be corrected in this way is an embedded piece of plaster, or any other foreign body trapped below the surface of the wax. These foreign bodies *must* be removed before the piece is presented to the caster, because, in the burn-out process, when the wax is evacuated, there is a possibility that whatever has become entrapped has a much higher melting point than the wax. Therefore, it will not burn out, remaining instead within the cavity of the investment where its form, unfortunately, will be forever immor-

72

talized in the metal. This, of course, is especially true if the foreign object embedded in the wax is a piece of investment.

Removal of foreign bodies must be performed surgically. The knife must be dug into the surface of the wax and the object either cut away or pried out. Smaller objects may be picked away with a thick carpet needle. The resulting hole must be filled with molten wax, and the details recarved.

Forming Buckle Hardware

Once the surface of the piece has been polished to your liking, turn your attention to the intended function of the model: its use as a belt buckle. While the front of the piece is bowed out gently to conform to the average stomach, the back is still absolutely flat (Fig. 3.10a). This is because the molten wax seeks its own level as it fills up the cavity of the mold. In order to make the back conform to the contour of the front, you should use a large half-round wax file.

Working the rougher half-round surface, cup the buckle in one hand—so as not to mar the surface finish inadvertently—rest that hand firmly against the bench pin, and begin to file (Fig. 3.10b). Always work from the center outward and, applying slight pressure but allowing the file itself to do most of the cutting, push the file forward. After you have completed a stroke, do not pull back on it; the backward stroke will not cut well and cannot really be controlled. The result will be an uneven, wavy surface. Instead, working only on the forward stroke, lightly form the back to match the curve of the front. When the piece has been reduced to a uniform 3-millimeter thickness, stop and apply sandpaper until all sign of the file marks has been eradicated.

The buckle's hardware, as I call it, consists of a bridge to hold the end of the belt and a hook to secure the buckle into a hole (Fig. 3.10c). Both of these pieces are easily crafted from ⅛ inch (3mm) sprue wax.

The bridge must be slightly wider than the belt which is to be used, and slightly smaller than the width of the buckle so that it will not be visible when worn. In general, the widest belt available is little more than 1½ inches wide, so the interior dimension of the bridge should be 1⅝ inches (4.2 cm) across, maximum. Of course, if you intend to wear a narrower belt, you would reduce the size of the bridge accordingly. The creation of this piece is one of the simplest jobs you will ever confront as a wax model-maker. Cut off a piece of sprue wax ¾ inch (19 mm) longer than you wish your bridge to be. The sprue wax, as you will discover, is an extremely malleable material. Simply bend down ¼ inch (7 mm) of the rod at each end so that both angles are at 90 degrees; measure the distance between the two posts to double-check. For the hook, just cut a slight taper on one side of a sprue rod; cut off a 13-millimeter section and bend it slightly.

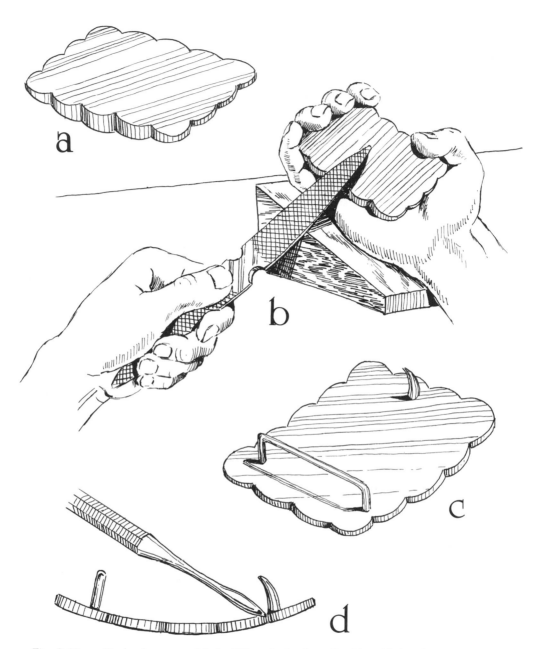

Fig. 3.10 a. Back of wax model. b. Filing the back. c. Buckle with hardware added. d. Attaching hardware to buckle.

Heat up the spatula now and test it on a scrap piece of sprue wax. *Always test each new type of wax before you use it for your model.* You will discover that it runs at a much lower temperature than the green carving wax. Joining waxes with different melting points requires some care. Touch the bridge and hook down, first marking the points of contact on the model, and melt the green wax directly under the sprue wax, allowing the heat of the molten carving wax to melt the sprue wax in turn. This technique of bonding two waxes of different melting points—by melting the higher first and allowing the hot wax to melt the lower—will give an excellent, permanent bond in almost every instance where the situation is encountered. (Fig. 3.10d). If any open spots remain at the juncture of the two waxes, fill them in with sprue wax.

The technique of pouring wax, although it is the most precise and the most versatile way to make a wax impression from a plaster mold, is not the only one—and in many cases it is not even the preferred one. If, for example, you have a smaller piece to produce, an earring or a pendant, and your design is rather simple in its forms, having no undercuts or really tight detail work, there are two alternative methods for filling the mold with wax.

Mold-A-Wax

The first of these utilizes a material called Mold-A-Wax, also put out by Ferris. Mold-A-Wax comes in two varieties: the red which is quite soft, and the black which is somewhat harder and becomes flexible at a higher temperature. Both of these waxes, though, have the same properties. Unlike the carving wax, which has to be melted in order to take on the configuration of the mold, Mold-A-Wax is simply cut off the block in an ⅛ inch (3 mm) slab, made flexible by immersion in warm water and, after it has been stretched out thin between the fingers—to about 2 millimeters—is pressed directly into the glycerine-lubricated mold (Fig. 3.11a). For this buckle, the softer red Mold-A-Wax is preferred; under slight pressure, it will conform readily to all the contours of the mold. In this way, you need not worry about hollowing out the back of the model; there is no liquid wax which must find its own level in order to fill up the entire mold. By simply pressing the softened wax, which has a consistency not unlike the clay which we had used to carve our original model, against the walls of the mold a uniformly thick wax model will be created, with a hollow in the back. This, of course is particularly useful if you intend to cast your piece in a precious metal and therefore must be concerned about the cost. (The poured wax may also be hollowed out, but the techniques and equipment employed are far more sophisticated and will be discussed fully in the chapter on green wax carving.)

However, removal of Mold-A-Wax is not as simple a job as with the carving wax. It is quite soft, and easily distorted with excessive handling. By putting the mold into the refrigerator for a few minutes, the wax will harden sufficiently (and contract slightly too) for removal to become much easier; if everything has gone well, the wax can just be eased out. If not, the plaster will have to be chipped away slightly until the model can be removed. If the wax begins to soften in the process, another few minutes in the refrigerator will harden it again.

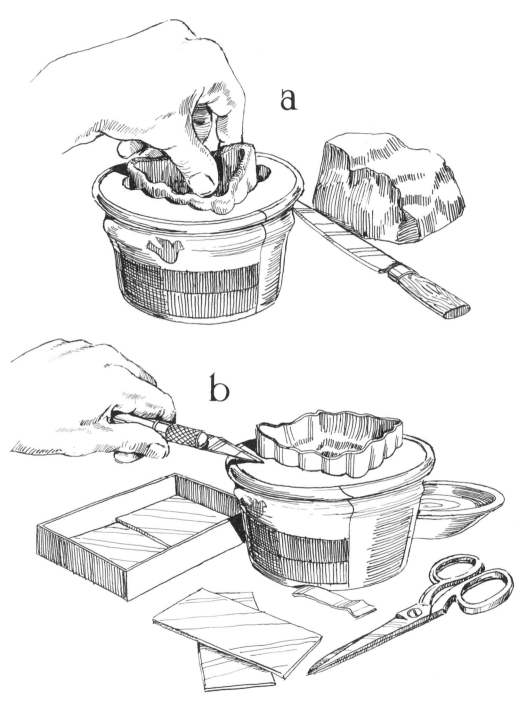

Fig. 3.11 a. Using Mold-A-Wax for model. b. Using sheet wax for model.

This method, while significantly simpler than pouring molten carving wax into a mold, has some very serious drawbacks which might render it unacceptable in many cases. The wax is so soft that it cannot be filed or even sanded; it may only be carved with a knife dipped in glycerine and, even at that, very fine details cannot be cut into it. The pressing process itself, while able to take on much of the detail of the original, can never substitute for a process whereby molten wax actually runs into every part of the mold. Nor can imperfections readily be eradicated; the wax melts at such a low temperature that any application of heat might seriously damage the model. In short, for anything other than very simple, rough-hewn pieces, or for approximate prototypes to be reworked through other techniques in their final form, this method—though easier than poured wax—should be your second choice.

Sheet Wax

More limited still, yet at the same time more acceptable for a finished model, is the application of sheet wax to the plaster mold. Sheet wax is exactly that, thin sheets of wax that had originally been designed for use in the dental trade, for taking impressions of teeth, and which are now regularly used by professional wax model-makers for specialized work (a section has been set aside later in the book for a complete discussion of this useful material). Like the other types of wax, sheet wax comes in a variety of grades, from very flexible to quite hard. More important, though, sheet wax is available in a wide range of thicknesses from 6-gauge down to as thin as 30-gauge. (For a complete equivalent chart for wax gauges in millimeters, consult the Appendix.) Depending upon the overall dimensions of the piece, choose either 16-gauge (1.30 millimeters), 18-gauge (1.02 millimeters), or 20-gauge (0.81 millimeter).

Selecting a flexible grade of wax, first immerse it in warm water. Some sheet wax is brittle at room temperature and, in order to be worked, must be softened with heat. When the wax becomes flexible, press it into the well-lubricated mold, just as with the Mold-A-Wax, starting from the deepest spot and working upward along the sides, trimming off whatever excess might rise above the rim (Fig. 3.11b). Sheet wax does not generally have as much give as Mold-A-Wax. Therefore, the type of model on which it can utilized is limited to gracefully curved planes which are fairly free of ornamentation—a fairly accurate description, after all, of most modern jewelry. You will find that, after the sheet wax has been warmed, it will conform nicely to the impression of the mold. The only things you must watch out for when handling sheet wax—here as well as elsewhere—are, first, that the surface of the wax, which is as smooth as glass when removed from the pack, may very easily be marred irreparably when heated, especially by fingerprints and, second, that the wax cools rapidly, becoming brittle again and very easily broken. However, if you are careful when pressing the wax into the mold, a very clean model should be the result. Not only will the model be clean, since the sheet wax never does become so malleable that it will pick up every last little imperfection in the investment, it will also be of a thickness acceptable by commercial standards. Since most mass-produced jewelry manufactured today does not exceed 1 millimeter in thickness, a model constructed of 18- or 20-gauge sheet wax falls well within the economic limitations of the industry.

As you have probably observed, model-making from molds is a very flexible process, capable of being adapted and altered according to needs and tastes. Not only may the wax be changed and adapted, but the plaster mold may be altered as well, before you ever introduce the wax. For example, if after you have pried out the clay model, you observe obvious rough spots in the impression, it is an easy matter to sand them away or, if they are inaccessible, to use a cotton swab rolled in pumice paste. Any holes or sections which you might wish to obliterate may be eradicated with a little ordinary spackle, available at any hardware or paint store. All sorts of interesting textures, not possible to achieve in a clay model, can be cut into the plaster mold. A nubby texture or a texture which suggests granulation is easily done with a round burr either attached to the flexible shaft machine or set into a mechanical pencil holder. Raised letters, almost impossible to cut evenly on clay, may be cleanly incised into the plaster—providing you cut them in backward so that they will be reproduced correctly. In fact, any type of raised detail—veins in a leaf, porcupine quills, sun's rays—may be nicely accomplished by incising the pattern into the plaster. When the wax is poured in, it will convert all these incisions into sharp raised surfaces, almost impossible to create in any other way.

Nor is experimentation with wax and plaster the only way in which the basic process may be adapted. Original models may be fashioned of any substance at all—wood, stone, Styrofoam—as long as it is well-lubricated before you add the plaster, porous substances requiring more lubrication than non-porous ones. You need not even create your own model. A sea shell might strike your fancy, or an especially beautiful mineral specimen, or a plastic toy, an ornate piece of antique jewelry, a piece of bark. Simply place whatever piece you have selected to reproduce down on the glass plate. If there is any air space between the flat glass surface and the back of the piece—and very few things come equipped with flat backs—that space must be filled in before the plaster is introduced. If it is not filled, the liquid plaster will run through the spaces, sealing off the back. In order to make a proper mold from an irregularly formed object, you must first plug all the holes, which is best done with clay (Fig. 3.12).

The result will be a plaster impression that will contain not only the form of the model, but the totally functional blank walls that will permit the level of the wax to rise and fill the cavity completely. The model will come out of the mold bearing the imprint of these blank walls; this excess which must be cut away with a file or a knife before the piece can be cast. In this way, almost anything at all may be reproduced through a remarkably simple process that is able to capture every nuance of the original with fidelity.

FULLY FORMED SCULPTURE

The problems confronted while creating a bas-relief are approximately mid-point between a two-dimensional drawing and the truly three-dimensional sculpture. Within its fixed borders, a bas-relief extends outward into space, giving the illusion of complete three-dimensionality, but it is only an illusion. A sculpture has no fixed borders; its external form changes with each shift in perspective. You cannot ignore any angle of a sculpture; there is no proper front and back.

With all of my own fairly extensive art background, the single most essential lesson I ever learned about sculpting was from my Cub Scout manual, while doing a whittling project. All subsequent knowledge of sculpture has only augmented what I learned then, and even though I used a small pine wood block as my medium, the same principles apply to whatever material you might wish to carve.

First, you should have a good idea of what you are going to carve; play-as-you-go sculptures are best created after you have studied many basic forms. Even the most abstract of Picasso's sculptures are end results of carefully considered studio studies. Naturally, the more flexible your material, the freer you may be without fear of fatality. The worker of marble cannot expect his medium to admit of many mistakes. The worker of wax—as well as the modeler of clay—has much more leeway; if a section has been botched, new material may be added. However, even the wax model-maker should approach the work as if sculpting marble.

Clay Model

For this project, you need two drawings: one which shows a front view and one which shows a profile. A third drawing which shows a top view would be a great help, but it is not absolutely necessary. If you are working from photographs, there is a chance that only one view of your subject will be available. If that is the case, then select something which is familiar to you so that, from a single photograph, you can

Fig. 3.12 Making clay bases for irregularly shaped objects.

reconstruct the entire form. Reduce the two views to the proper size if necessary and press an outline tracing of the most characteristic view against one side of your clay block (Fig. 3.13a). Carefully, so as not to distort the clay, shave the excess away with a knife until only the flat silhouette of the figure remains (Fig. 3.13b). Using the second drawing as a guide, cut away clay to form the second silhouette (Fig. 3.13c).

Next you select and define the major planes. Determining the angle and direction of these planes is not as clear-cut as in the first project, but with care, you should encounter no difficulties. Simply study the original photograph and cut in the large movements, working all around the piece (Fig. 3.13d). The best way to work a sculpture is to keep every part of it at the same stage of completion; do not carve secondary movements until the principal ones have been established. Keep the angles sharp; the same rules apply here as in bas-relief. Do not round off your corners or carve in any detail work until you have completed *all* of the major movements, appraising your piece from every angle. Once the piece is acceptable any way you turn it, you may begin work on the final touches, adding clay where it is needed, smoothing, sharpening detail until you are satisfied.

Investment

There are three ways to make a mold from our model, four if you want your piece to be solid. In the latter case, you simply employ the glass plate method explained in the first project and pour the plaster over the entire piece just as you have carved it, with the base down. For many reasons, however, this is the least acceptable method of producing a mold. Unless your piece is quite small, the chances of porosity are very great in a solid casting, since thicknesses exceeding 5 millimeters are extraordinary for average casting procedures. Also, if you plan to cast in any type of precious metal, the cost could be prohibitive.

A variation of this method, which would also allow you the luxury of one-piece casting, would entail hollowing your finished wax model out from the bottom, removing as much material as possible. However, this is an extremely difficult job. The flexible shaft tool is the only implement capable of accomplishing it, and even *it* cannot be controlled well in very tight narrow spots. One miscalculation and you might easily bore through the wall. And even if you were to produce a fine job in the wax model, the rubber mold made from it would demand such a deep core that distortion of the final piece would almost be a certainty. It would be more advisable, in this case, to take the solid block of wax, score a line completely around the length and, with your finest jeweler's saw, split the wax into halves that can be hollowed out fairly easily.

Better still are the other methods, all of which basically reduce your fully-formed sculpture to two halves—each, in effect, a bas-relief—that will be cast separately and joined in the metal. The first of these, and

80

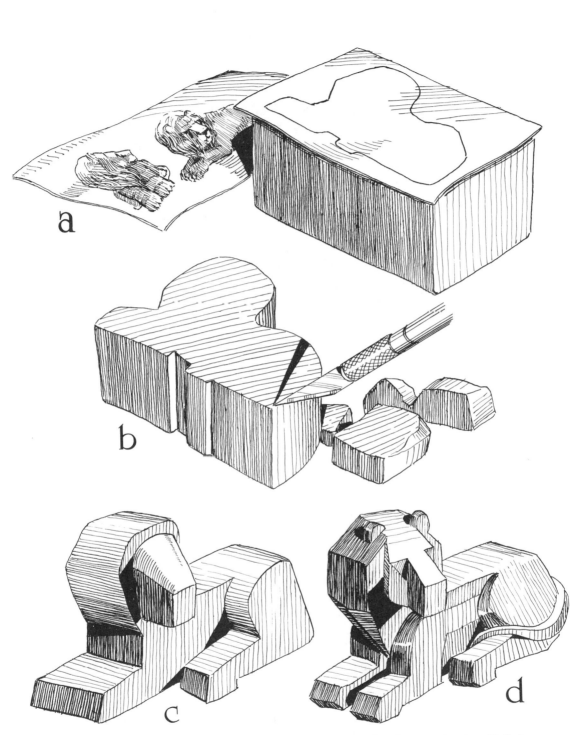

Fig. 3.13   a. Lay outline against clay block. b. Silhouette of sculpture cut out. c. Defining the second silhouette. d. Defining major planes.

the best for most models, is also the simplest. All you have to do is split your clay block in half before you even begin to rough-shape it. Insert a piece of a fairly thick acetate, available at any art supply store, between the two halves; press the two halves together again and you may begin (Fig. 3.14a). A bit of planning ahead is necessary however. If you are not careful, you could send your separating line straight through the most intricately carved sections of your piece. Determine first, before splitting the block, those areas which will hold the broadest planes and insert the acetate sheet there. Remember, your two sections need not be equal in size; ideally, they need only be flat at the point of contact. If you have correctly accomplished this, you may very readily split your clay model into two sections along the acetate insert after it has been completed; place the flat side of each section down on the glass plate and proceed as if each piece were a bas-relief (Fig. 3.14b).

Another method involves splitting the clay after the major shaping is complete, but before the final details are added. Take a very sharp X-Acto knife and, working slowly and carefully, define the separating line completely around the piece. Then, gradually increasing pressure on the blade, make the cut deeper and deeper—taking care to work around the entire piece, keeping your incision at a uniform depth until you have successfully separated the figurine into two halves. The burr that is raised by the knife cut is easy to remove with the edge of the blade. More difficult to correct is the unavoidable distortion that will result from the pressure involved in dividing the piece. You will have to fit the halves loosely back together in place in order to assess the damage. Then, either by adding clay or by remanipulating the material, try to reform the piece to its original shape. Once you are satisfied that this has been accomplished, separate the two halves again, place them flat side down on the glass plate and add the finishing details.

The last method should be reserved for fairly elaborate pieces which would be deformed irrevocably by the straight-slice method. Here you will not actually be splitting the clay model physically; the splitting will occur while making the plaster mold instead. Again defining your separating line with the X-Acto knife, cut down to an approximate depth of ¼ inch (6 mm) all around. Then, cutting your acetate into pieces of about 1 inch (25 mm) square, insert the pieces into the slit, so that each acetate piece overlaps its neighbor slightly (Fig. 3.15a). Set the piece aside and, taking your original tracing, press it against a fresh block of clay; then cut the outline of your piece into the new clay, making sure that the outline is ⅛ inch (3 mm) larger in all dimensions than the original carving had been. Cut straight down until you have either scooped out a basin which is deeper than the profile of your model or else have cut through the clay completely, leaving a hole which bears the external contours of your piece (Fig. 3.15b).

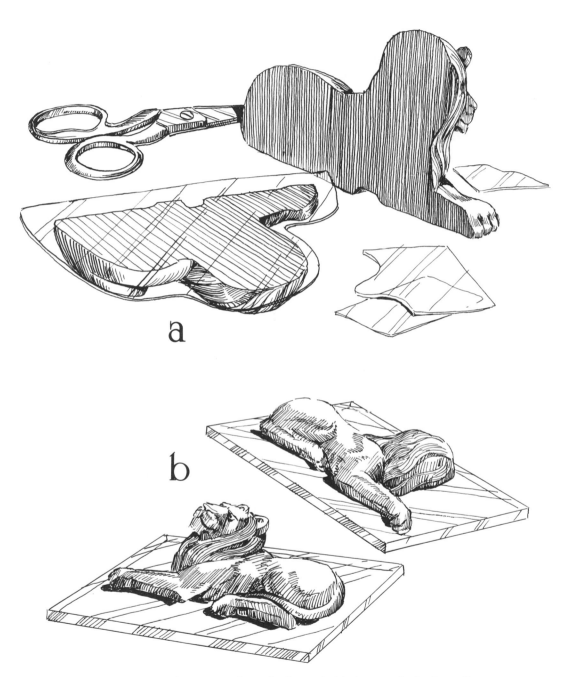

Fig. 3.14 a. Inserting the acetate sheet. b. Separated halves ready for investing.

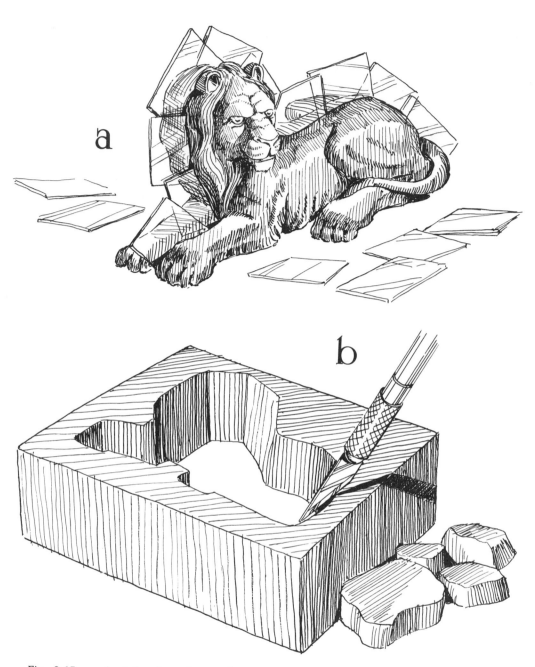

Fig. 3.15   a. Acetate pieces inserted along dividing line. b. Cutting outline into clay block.

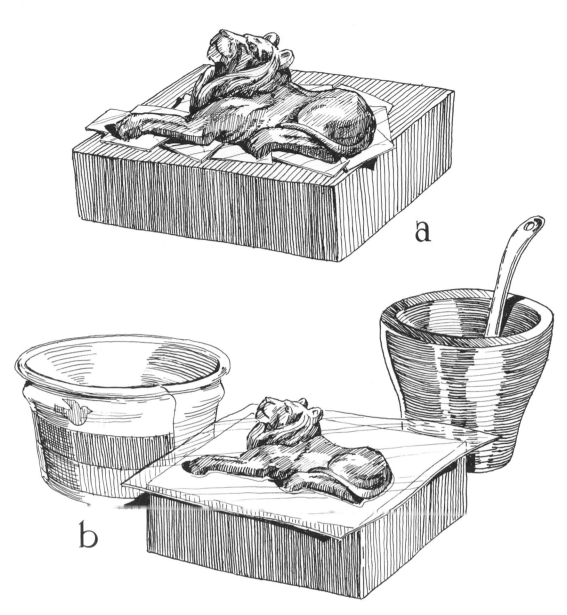

Fig. 3.16 a. Setting the clay model into place. b. Clay model ready for investing.

Carefully lay your figurine into this space, suspending it over the opening by means of the acetate sheets (Fig. 3.16a). Taking the tracing for the third time, cut out the outline of your model—again ⅛ inch (3 mm) larger in all dimensions—from a sheet of acetate and lay that acetate sheet down over the model so it rests on the clay block. Lubricate the model and the acetate sheet; set the cardboard flask in place on top of the acetate, and you are ready to pour the plaster (Fig. 3.16b). Once the plaster has set on this first side, simply invert your sculpture, making certain that the acetate sheet adheres to the plaster rather than to the clay base. Remove the clay base altogether—the plaster mold will serve nicely as a base—set another flask in place, and repeat the process. When both halves of the mold have set completely, split them apart. You will have two perfectly fitting molds into which you may pour or press your wax, as you will, and then simply proceed with the finishing techniques that you have already learned.

You will find that, the more you experiment with both the aesthetics of the actual sculpting and the techniques of mold-making, the more pleasure you will derive and the more excellent your pieces will become. You can also experiment with mold-making materials as well. Jewelry supply houses carry a special kind of very fine sand which may be packed around a solid model to make quite a satisfactory mold. Cuttlebone, also sold in jewelry supply houses, is a highly porous material which, under pressure, compacts to a solid wall, taking a very fine impression from a solid object. Simply press whatever model you have directly into the material and, when you remove it, you will have a mold. You may also vary the texture of your piece by adding foreign substances to the investment slurry: sand, fine gravel, pine needles, anything small and hard which will alter the surface texture of your mold; the final wax, of course, will bear the impression of this texture.

Keep in mind, in this context as well as in every other aspect of wax model-making, that making a good model is by no means a static occupation. Do not imagine that once you have perfected several techniques, or even all the techniques that will be described in the subsequent chapters, that you will have come to the end of your learning process; if that happens, much of the fun of model-making will be over. Always be on the alert for new materials, new tools, new approaches to perfecting your craft. Some will work; some will not, but in either case, you will continue to find excitement and the pleasure of discovery.

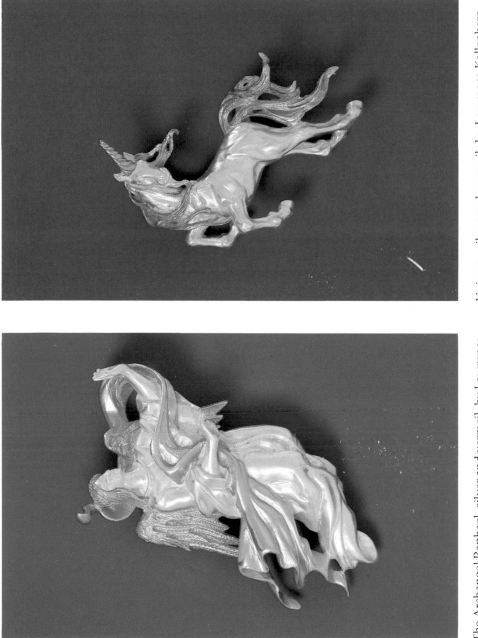

The Archangel Raphael, silver and vermeil, by Lawrence Kallenberg.

Unicorn, silver and vermeil, by Lawrence Kallenberg.

Jewelry box, silver and walnut, by Lawrence Kallenberg.

(Top, left and right) winged scarab earrings, vermeil; (top center) King Tutankhamen pendant. (Below) Double Crown of Egypt necklace, vermeil. All by Lawrence Kallenberg.

(Top, left) feather ring, 14 kt gold; (right) diamond ring, 14 kt gold. (Middle, left) shell motif earclips, 14 kt gold; (right) brooch, 14 kt gold. All by Lawrence Kallenberg, courtesy of Diplomat Jewelry. (Bottom) earclips, 14 kt gold, courtesy of Diplomat Jewelry.

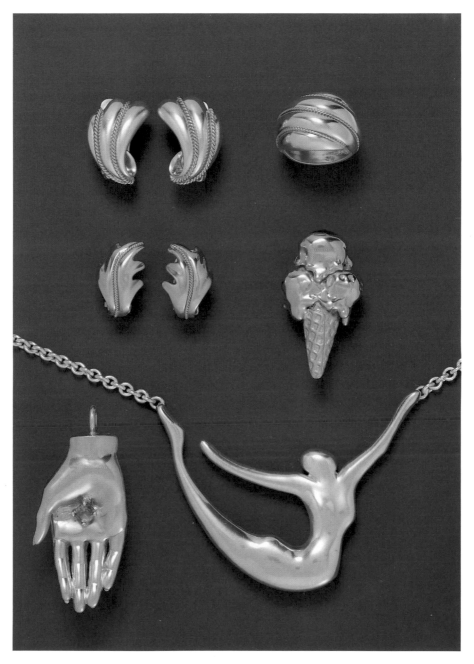

(Top, left) silver and gold earclips; (right) silver and gold dome ring. (Middle, left) leaf earrings, 14 kt gold; (right) ice cream cone pin, tri-color 14 kt gold. All by Lawrence Kallenberg, courtesy of Diplomat Jewelry. (Bottom, left) hand pendant, 18 kt gold and emerald, by Lawrence Kallenberg. (Bottom, right) silver figure neckpiece, by Victor Goldberg.

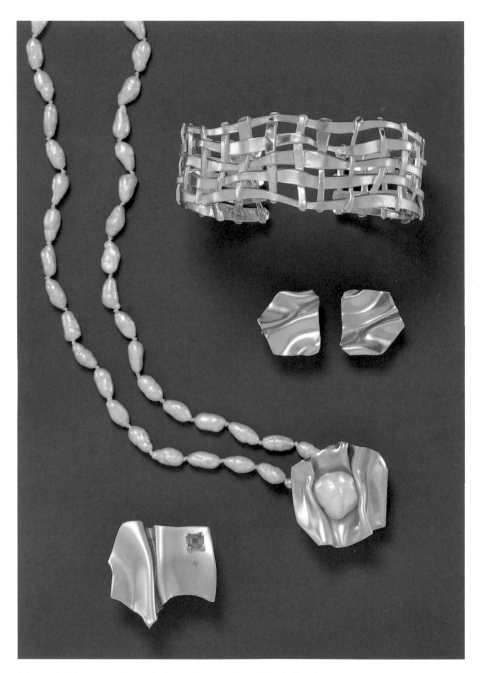

(Top, right) woven bangle bracelet, 14 kt gold; (below) earrings, 14 kt gold; pearl necklace, 14 kt gold. (Bottom, left) sapphire pin, 14 kt gold. All by Toby Davis.

(Top, left) horse ring, 14 kt gold; (right) double lion and diamond pendant, 14 kt gold. (Middle, left) monkey ring, 14 kt gold; (right) Moses pendant, 14 kt gold. (Bottom) lion pendant, 14 kt gold. All courtesy of Maurice Katz.

The Resurrection, silver figure on geode base, by Lawrence Kallenberg.

Chapter 4

Wax Carving—Part One: Blue and Purple Wax

CARVING the wax is the essential wax-working technique. Everything else you might learn here may be considered as additions or refinements or shortcuts. If you are able to master carving, then all other approaches to forming the wax become secondary. Everything which one might be able to accomplish by utilizing the more esoteric approaches can be done by the skillful carver, not so quickly perhaps in some things, but every bit as precisely. At least three-quarters of all tasks which the average model-maker is called upon to perform require only carving and another large portion of his jobs requires carving in conjunction with other techniques. Carving is the mainstay of the wax model-maker's craft.

It is important to understand at the outset that all wax cannot be carved. In fact, relatively few types of wax can be carved successfully. Most wax is either too soft or too brittle to be worked successfully using the conventional methods. Only wax which has been specially formulated may be carved properly. The criteria by which a wax may be judged carvable or not are five: hardness, durability, flexibility, an evenly dense consistency, and high melting point.

A carving wax must be hard enough to sustain the finest detail work imaginable, detail work so fine that it often requires the use of high magnification to see it well. Good carving wax should have a hardness approximately equivalent to a medium hardwood—such as walnut or maple—only wax, of course, is completely free of grain. It should be able to be inscribed with a pin, leaving a clean sharp line without any chipping and without any burr being raised. It should be able to be cut cleanly with a knife, filed as one might file metal, and even be worked with the electric flexible shaft unit. The fact that the wax can be worked with a tool driven by a high-speed motor, capable of building up to 1400 revolutions per minute, necessitates a very high melting point; the heat of friction is enough to melt away most waxes. Good carving wax melts at a temperature exceeding 220°F, which is roughly 70°F higher than the average casting or build-up wax.

Durability and flexibility are absolutely essential if you intend to work professionally. Many waxes will snap at thicknesses of 1 millimeter or even greater. Many waxes will deform when being worked to unusually thin gauges. A good carving wax should be able to hold its shape even if you are grinding your wall down to 0.3 millimeter, not so unusual in these times of soaring gold prices. You should be able to hold the piece in your hand, sure that it will not crack no matter how thin it is and no matter how intricate might be the details you wish to carve into it.

Last, the wax should be of a uniform consistency. Model-makers cannot afford to come upon sudden irregularities in the density of their material. All detail work must be uniformly sharp. All walls must be uniformly thick. A wax model-maker often gauges the thickness of his piece by the uniformity of its color when it is held up to a light; an irregular spot will show a different color when the light passes through it, confusing the model-maker who might mistake it for either an excessively thick spot or for one that is excessively thin. Nor should any foreign bodies have found their way into the wax. Often the dye which is used to color the wax will not dissolve completely in the original melt, leaving chalky particles embedded in the wax. If you are unfortunate enough to come upon one of these particles in an area where you have projected a good deal of detail work, you will have to correct the problem surgically.

There are two major wax producers that are well known in the jewelry industry: Kerr and Ferris. Most of the materials which shall be discussed in this book will be produced by either one of these two companies. If I recommend one brand or the other, it is my own personal preference that I am voicing. It might, however, be beneficial were you to experiment with many different products, familiarizing yourself with the unique properties of each, until you have ultimately selected the product that is best for your own particular type of work. Most professional New York model-makers prefer Ferris carving wax.

FERRIS CARVING WAX

Green Wax

Ferris carving wax comes in three types: green, purple, and blue, each dye representing a group of distinct properties. The green, which is the most popular of the three, is a very hard substance able to sustain the most elaborate, most minute detail work you can carve into it. It is able to be polished to a shine which resembles glass. It can also be ground down to thicknesses less than 0.2 millimeter, the absolute minimum

88

thickness you can achieve and still have reason to expect a sound casting. Moreover, at even this minute thickness, the wax—no matter how large or how small your piece might be—will never deform in any way. It is an extremely rigid material, compounded to have only the minimum amount of flexibility needed to insure that it will not crack under your fingers while you are working it. It is this very rigidity, so necessary in the production of a delicate and precise model, which limits the use of Ferris green wax to pieces of rather small size (1½ inches or 38 mm maximum for pieces which gauge under a millimeter), with a basically flat orientation; larger pieces with highly convoluted surfaces will be subject to cracking and fissuring if green wax is employed. For most model-makers, however, this presents no problem. The limitations of green wax are the limitations of the jewelry industry itself, where it is very rare to find a piece which is larger than 1½ inches (38mm) and where polishing considerations virtually prohibit truly elaborate twists and turns except in the finest and most expensive pieces.

Green wax melts at roughly 220°F. When it melts, it almost immediately becomes fluid instead of first going gradually through a viscous phase. And when it melts, it runs like water, setting very quickly to a flat shiny surface which is slightly more flexible than the original block wax had been.

This product, of all the waxes that I am familiar with, is the greatest pleasure to work. It may be carved with a knife, although I have found that taking away large pieces in this fashion is an extremely tedious and dangerous business; the material is so rigid that, although it has no grain, it does have a tendency to crack when large sections of it are hewn off. For green wax, I have found, the use of the knife is limited to either a scraping motion, which smooths the surface of roughness and irregularities, or a very precise chiseling of extremely fine detail work. The rough hewing is usually accomplished with a spiral saw blade which readily cuts through even large blocks, leaving a trail of wax powder. However, for production purposes, the most important feature of the green wax is the fact that it may be filed or worked with the flexible shaft tool at very high speeds without any clogging, distorting, or melting of the material. This means speed and precision. Indeed, this wax may be worked much as one might work metal, except with far greater ease and flexibility. This is why carving waxes have supplanted metal as the medium of choice for making original models.

Purple Wax

But green wax is not the only type of carving wax that is employed in the industry. Many model-makers prefer the medium-grade purple wax because of its versatility. Indeed, for an all-purpose material, I have found nothing better than Ferris purple wax. It is a more flexible wax than the green, so it may be carved much more readily with a knife—the danger of unexpected fissuring is still present, but to a lesser extent. Because of this flexibility, it is the ideal material for larger pieces, miniature sculptures and figurines, and for pieces which display a good deal of open work and twists and turns. It will rarely crack, even over a fairly extensive surface area. It may be worked with a file and ground with a flexible shaft machine; however, the tools cannot be as fine as those used on green wax. The material, because of its increased flexibility, does not fall away into a fine powder as does the green wax, but rather produces distinct particles which have a tendency to clog up a finer tool.

The melting temperature of purple wax is also slightly higher than the green, around 230°F, and when it melts, it first becomes viscous before it really becomes fluid. The consistency of it also changes after having been melted. Like the green wax, it becomes more flexible, but here the difference between the block wax and the wax that has been melted is truly significant; the purple wax becomes highly flexible and cannot really sustain any elaborate detail work after it has been melted. That is why, if I choose to work in purple wax, I make my repairs by adding green wax instead of purple (in a later chapter, you will discover that it is an accepted practice to bond waxes of different consistencies and melting points in order to obtain maximum utility).

The purple wax, despite its versatility, has its shortcomings, the major one being its relative inability to sustain sharp details on very small pieces when compared to the green wax. By "very small pieces" I mean pieces which may best exhibit their detail through a 10-power magnifying lens. A general rule for carving waxes is that the more flexibility the material has, the less its ability to hold fine detail work. The purple wax is moderately flexible and is able to be worked admirably in ninety percent of all the jobs you might encounter. However, do not expect needle-sharp lines to be incised into it; do not expect to polish it to a glossy surface; do not expect to grind it down to thicknesses less than 0.5 millimeter without deforming it slightly—and even a slight deformation is enough to render a carefully executed fitting unusable. In short, purple wax is not a substitute for the harder more rigid green wax; it has its own clearly defined sphere of utility which includes most larger pieces of jewelry and almost all miniature sculpture. Note as well that, in those sections of a sculpture where a great deal of precision work is required—a face and hands for example—a piece of green wax may be welded into place on the purple wax body without anything being affected in the final burnout.

Blue Wax

The third grade of wax is designated by a blue dye. Blue wax is so flexible that a piece of it, ⅛ inch (3 mm) thick, after a short immersion in boiling water, may be bent permanently 180 degrees to form a semicircle. Of all the types of wax available, Ferris blue most nearly approximates a good whittling wood: white pine with no knotholes and no grain. It is the perfect wax for carving with a knife. Instead of powder being the residue, as in the case of the green wax, or flakes as in the case of the purple, blue wax actually falls into thin shavings. No matter how big a piece you might carve away, if your knife is sharp enough, you run very little danger of inadvertent splitting of the material. An assortment of knives and chisels, such as a sophisticated wood-carver might employ, are the best tools with which to fashion your models. And the results, if you are careful, should be equal to the finest boxwood carvings, and, more likely, significantly superior.

Blue wax is primarily used because of its flexibility and the characteristic way that it reacts to melting. Unlike the other two waxes, blue wax—which melts at approximately 240°F—never really runs. It always remains more or less viscous in its molten state, allowing the model-maker maximum control over the application of new material onto the old (for a complete discussion of the uses of blue wax in this context, see Chapter 6).

In its block form, when cut into slabs, it is significantly more flexible than the medium-grade purple, rendering it highly useful for pieces which are fairly thin and have a great deal of openwork—anything which could crack were a more rigid material to be employed. The blue wax, even if you take it down to 1 millimeter, will not crack under the pressure of your file; however, it will deform. It is never to be used where precise fittings are intended, only for individual pieces that require little raised detail and for pieces that are best produced by a combination of carving and build-up techniques.

Blue wax may be filed fairly readily if you employ tools of a medium-coarse grit, nothing finer than a cut-2, and work slowly. Impatient scrubbing, even with a coarse-cut file, will result in clogging; so dense and flexible are the particles created that they will compress into the teeth of your tool to be removed only with a wire brush or file cleaner. For this reason, use of the flexible shaft machine is not recommended, except with the very coarsest burrs and under the slowest speeds you can manage on the rheostat.

BLUE WAX MONOGRAM

Blue wax is perhaps the easiest to handle of all the waxes and, therefore, it will provide a very good introduction to the carving process. The first project will be a raised monogram.

Tools and Materials

    Pound block of Ferris blue wax
    Hacksaw
    Jeweler's saw frame

Spiral saw blade
Package of number-4 piercing saw blades
Metal scribe or long needle
8-inch wax file
Knife-edge escapement file, cut-2
Round escapement file, cut-2
Half-round escapement file, cut-2
Barette escapement file, cut-2
Few sheets of sandpaper, number-2, number-4/0
½-inch knife-edge felt buff (hard)
Felt cloth
Tracing paper and Venus pencil, 3H
Rubber cement
Alcohol lamp
Spatula
X-acto knives, number-11, number-4

Monogram Design

Cutting a monogram is usually the job of the metalsmith; he scribes the pattern onto a piece of metal plate, either gold or silver, drills starting holes in the appropriate places, and saws out the design. This method is very precise, since the metal is completely rigid even at very thin gauges, and may be sawed directly through the contours of the outline without fear of producing any really severe undercuts. Whatever irregularities might be created by the sawcut are easily corrected with a file. However, this method leaves something to be desired: dimension. Had the metalsmith merely employed a die-stamping machine, there would be little essential difference between the machine-made product and the one made painstakingly by hand. Not so with a wax carving. Here, to the basically flat design, raised thicks and thins are added, providing interest on the surface of the piece as well as in the outline contours.

To begin a monogram, you must first find letter forms which appeal to you and then you must redesign them so that they fit together harmoniously. A good, inexpensive reference book is put out by the Speedball Pen Company, and it is available in many art supply stores. Other, more complete books are also available. These books present you with a complete alphabet, both upper and lower case, in many different style letter forms, from the simplest block letters to the most elaborately flowing scripts.

Select a style that boasts at least some variation in thickness; lay your tracing paper over the three letters you intend to use and copy them—leaving sufficient space between the tracings to cut them into three individual sheets. Although each individual letter might be interesting, it is actually in the juxtaposition of the three letters that the success or failure of your design will lie. Monograms are generally letters arranged to fit within the boundaries of a distinct imaginary geometrical shape: usually a circle or an oval. The initial of the last name is usually larger than the other two and is almost invariably placed in the center, with the first name initial placed to the left of it and the middle name initial placed to the right.

Separate your three letters so that each is on a different piece of tracing paper. Draw—on a fourth piece of paper—the exact shape of oval or circle into which you would want your monogram to fit. The length of this oval will determine the height of the center letter. Either by eye, or by the grid method of reduction or enlargement, make that letter the correct size, tracing it into its appropriate position in the oval. Then, approximating the height of the smaller letters according to the available space in the oval, reduce or enlarge these two accordingly, each on a separate piece of tracing paper. Then set the oval with the central letter in place on top of first one letter, then the other, shifting and moving the various elements around until a pleasing design emerges. Very few letter arrangements will naturally combine well; it might take some time and some reshuffling of the actual letter forms until you have created a successful monogram. Transpose the design onto a piece of tracing paper with a hard 3H pencil so that every contour is razor sharp.

Blue wax, like both the green and purple varieties, comes in several different shapes and sizes. The most economical of these is the five-pound block, which should last the average model-maker well over a year, but the most popular is the one-pound block which measures $3\frac{9}{16}$ inches by $5\frac{3}{4}$ inches by $1\frac{7}{16}$ inches. Ferris also puts out a one-pound block, packaged in transparent plastic, with measurements that more nearly resemble a cube ($3\frac{9}{16}$ inches by $3\frac{9}{16}$ inches by $2\frac{3}{8}$ inches). The weight and the price of these two are the same; it is up to each individual model-maker to determine which proportions are more useful. Ferris carving wax is also available in boxes of pre-cut slabs which range in size from $\frac{1}{4}$ inch to $\frac{3}{32}$ inch thick. Naturally you pay extra for this convenience. For the professional model-maker, whose time is best spent in the actual fabrication of the model, shortcuts actually represent a savings; however, for the beginner, who should learn the long way around before utilizing shortcuts, it is perhaps best to begin with the block and saw from it the exact size piece necessary to do the job.

Sawing from a block of wax can be a tricky, if not a difficult job. Like so many other procedures concerning wax, it should be done slowly and deliberately until you have become familiar with the material. If you are accustomed to handling a saw, most likely you are used to working it on wood—or if it is a hacksaw, as used here, you have geared your stroke for metal work. In neither case is the stroke appropriate for wax, which is a much softer material than either. Your control over the cut must be much more decided, otherwise you will find your saw veering off to one side or another instead of slicing straight down. This possibility is further

93

increased by the very thickness of the block itself, which makes control over the direction of the cut more difficult the deeper you go.

In sawing a block of wax—or anything else—it is best to clamp it in a bench vise to steady it or, failing that, to secure it to the bench with C-clamps: not too tightly incidentally, or it will split. Mark the path of your cut *on all four surfaces* before you begin to saw; then, making the tension on your hacksaw as taut as possible, begin to make your cut straight across the block. The rocking motion which facilitates the cutting of wood is undesirable here, so is a very frenzied sawing motion which will heat up the blade and, consequently, melt the wax either into the teeth of the saw or else back into the very cut you have been trying to make. A slow, level cut in which you exert pressure only on the forward thrust is ideal. Go down as far as you can on this first side until you observe that you are beginning to lose absolute control over the saw; remove the block from the vise, give it a quarter turn, and begin on a fresh side until you are forced to shift sides again. In this way, no single cut becomes a major obstacle and you should be able to slice off a fairly uniform slab without very much difficulty. A word of caution: when you get to the last small piece of wax which is still holding the center of the slab onto the block, saw very slowly and lightly, perhaps even exerting pressure on the backstroke instead of on the forward one, to insure that you slice your piece off evenly; if it snaps off at this point, you will end up with either a knob or a cavity in the center of your slab.

Once you have successfully removed the slab from the wax block, you should then level it off with your large wax file until it is a uniform thickness. The motion of the file is not unlike the motion of the saw: forward. Take the wax slab and lay it flat on the bench pin, making certain to hold it steadily and comfortably with your left hand; then, with the file in the right hand, place the flat side of the file onto the slab and push. The action should be straight forward, slow and deliberate, allowing the teeth of the tool to do most of the work without exerting excessive pressure (Fig. 4.1a). Do not exert pressure on the backstroke; the teeth cannot do their work properly, and the tool will have a tendency to wobble. Do not scrub back and forth furiously; the result will be an uneven surface.

When the piece has been filed on both sides until it is level, and has been reduced uniformly to the desired thickness (in this case no more than 2.5 millimeters), take your barette file and smooth the top until no heavy file marks show.

Using rubber cement, brush the glue onto both the reverse side of the tracing and onto the smooth side of the slab; wait until both surfaces have dried and then just simply press the tracing onto the wax. It is a good habit to try to conserve your wax. Do not smack the tracing onto the dead center of the wax so that no other part of the slab is salvageable; place it in a corner, as close to the edge a you can, while still allowing

94

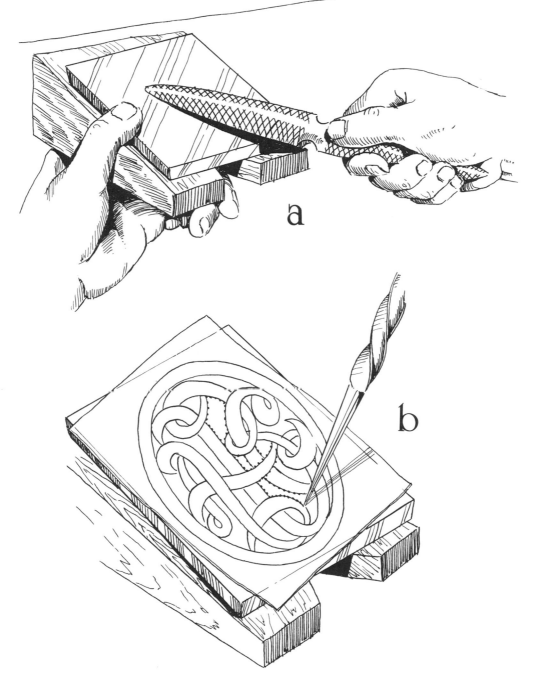

Fig. 4.1   a. Filing the wax slab. b. Outlining the design with pin holes.

yourself margin for error. Ordinarily, this simple bonding would be sufficient to hold tracings; however, for the really precise work of a monogram, you must take further precautions. Take the point of a scribe or even a long pin and push through the tracing, just outside of all the borders of the pattern, so that a system of closely spaced dots outlining all the intricacies of the monogram is impressed into the wax (Fig. 4.1b). Then you can either leave the tracing paper in place, assured that it will not slip as you begin to saw it, or else you can remove the tracing paper altogether and use only the dots as your guidelines (or else, you can connect the dots and begin your work with an incised linear pattern).

Sawing Wax

Proper use of a saw is one of the most important things a beginning model-maker can learn. If the saw is correctly handled, chances are very good that a neat job will follow; however, haphazard sawing is certain to cause you extra work and, despite the fact that wax can be repaired easily, the job is never as precise as the first time out. At least half of a good sawing job depends upon proper choice of a saw blade and proper loading of it into the frame. For this job, you will need two different blades: a spiral blade and a number-4 piercing blade. The spiral blade will be used for sawing out the rough external shape of the pattern; the piercing blade will be used for the finer sawing within the pattern itself, where extensive filing and carving are not really possible.

Begin by selecting the spiral blade, the narrowest one they make, opening up both locks in the saw frame and laying the blade in. Note that it makes little difference in which direction the blade is facing; it has been designed to cut with equal effectiveness in all directions. The only thing which is really important when loading a spiral blade is that it be stretched as tightly as possible across the frame; any sag in the blade will produce an inexact cut, different at every point along the slice.

The most frequently used method of loading a blade into a saw frame is to loosen both locks, turn the frame so that the opening faces upward, set the blade in place, and tighten the screw farthest from the handle. In order to achieve maximum tension on the blade, the sides of the frame must be compressed so that, when the blade is finally locked in place, the action of the sides as they spring open to their natural position will make the blade taut. Most jewelers place the far side of the frame against the edge of the bench, set the edge of the handle either against their shoulder or breast bone, and, while exerting forward pressure with their body, tighten the second screw in place (Fig. 4.2a). An alternate method, which depends upon the size of your hand, is simply to grasp the saw frame in one hand and squeeze the sides of the frame together with your fingers, tightening the screw as you do so.

The bench pin, as I have already mentioned, is an absolute necessity for fine model-making work; however, before it can be used, it must be

96

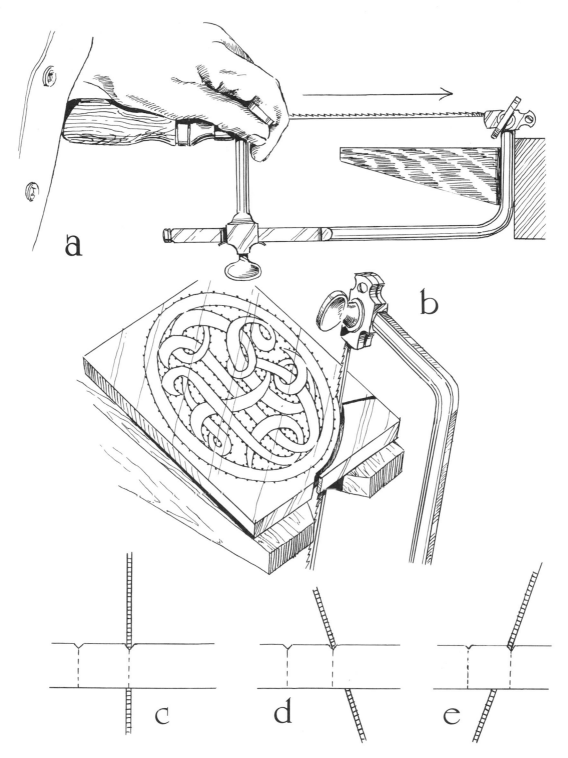

Fig. 4.2   a. Tightening the blade in a saw frame. b. Sawing on the bench pin. c. Saw blade at 90-degree angle to wax. d. Proper overcompensation of the saw blade. e. Undercutting, which cannot be corrected.

altered slightly. Each type of work, actually, demands its own specially shaped bench pin. For model-making, a bench pin is always placed into the bench flat side up (the inclined side is used for heavy filing), and rapped into its slot with a heavy piece of wood. If it is too big to fit into the slot, file a little from each side until you can hammer it in place. Under no circumstances should the bench pin wobble; it must be rock steady. But you should not glue your bench pin in place; it is not a permanent part of your bench; the beauty of a bench pin is that it may be shaped to fit each individual job and then be discarded when it has become too small to be serviceable. Once the bench pin has been set in place, take your hacksaw and cut out a small V from the front. This V should not be greater than one inch on either of its arms. Nor should it be placed dead center, but rather off to the right side of the bench pin so that you retain a fairly broad surface on which you can rest your work comfortably. This V cut is utilized primarily for sawing. When the wax slab is set on the bench pin, the cut-out V will allow sufficient room for pierce-sawing through the wax, while the surrounding unaltered area will provide support to insure against inadvertent cracking or slipping (Fig. 4.2b).

You should saw the outline of the piece first—although this is not a hard and fast rule; often it is preferable to saw out the inside piercing first. In this case, the piece would become entirely too delicate to sustain the heavier stroke required to define the external contour. The most important thing to remember when sawing is that the blade be straight up and down, 90 degrees from the plane of the wax (Fig. 4.2c). Even the slightest variation will cause an irregular cut. On a piece of metal plate 1 millimeter thick, this is not nearly as important as when working with the much thicker pieces of wax, where—although you might be following the contour exactly, the reverse side will show vast distortion. At the beginning, if you must err, discipline yourself to incline the bottom of the saw away from the outline; this will allow you ample room on the underside to correct irregularities with your file (Fig. 4.2d). If you lean the saw the other way, you will undercut and never be able to set the damage right (Fig. 4.2e). In short, try for perfection—but make your assault from the safe side.

Always exert pressure on the down thrust when sawing on the bench pin. With the piece of wax held firmly onto the flat of the bench pin begin to make your cut—always working *outside* the line, never directly through it. Always allow yourself ample margin for error, especially when working with the spiral blade which cuts in all directions and is, therefore, somewhat difficult to control. Do not attempt to cut sharp corners with this blade; expect to do most of the precise work with the files and knives. In this way, proceed around the entire pattern, always keeping the same even stroke with your saw and maneuvering the wax around with your left hand, like feeding wood into a jigsaw. In fact, if

98

you can mechanize your right hand altogether, both in sawing and in filing, keeping the same angle, pressure, and length on each stroke and allowing the opposite hand to position the work against the stroke, you will find that your work will be significantly more controlled.

After you have succeeded in rough-sawing the external contour of the monogram, proceed directly to sawing the pierce-work within the pattern: a much more difficult and exacting job. Remove the spiral blade and insert, in its place, a number-4 blade. Unlike the spiral blade, the piercing blade has teeth which face in only one direction. When inserting the blade, it is essential that these teeth face backward toward the handle, instead of away as is the case with almost all other saws. The teeth should always face in the direction of the cut and, in jewelry work, the cut is always straight down with pressure exerted on the backstroke.

Before doing any interior cutting, you must drill a hole in each of the areas to be cut away. The best way to put holes in the wax is to put a twist drill, somewhat thicker than your sawblade, into your flexible shaft handpiece and drill a hole through the center of every projected opening in your monogram (Fig. 4.3a). If you do not have a flexible shaft tool, the next best thing is to heat a long pin over your alcohol lamp and slowly pierce the center of each opening with it, lifting out the wax that will adhere to the pin. This second way is slower and less exact than the drilling and somewhat hazardous when working with very small openings; the heat of the pin might melt away too much and you will have to patch later. A third way is to scratch an opening gradually with the point of a knife until daylight appears. Do not take a scribe or any other pointed tool and attempt to jab it through the wax; even such a flexible wax as Ferris blue will crack under the pressure.

Only after you have punctured every hole in your design should you begin to saw. And now, before you can tighten your blade completely, you must first thread it through one of the holes in the wax. In order to tighten the blade properly, just push the wax piece as far up toward the far lock as possible so that the weight of it will not bow the blade and make tightening it difficult. Then proceed as you did with the spiral blade (Fig. 4.3b).

Sawing with the number-4 blade is slower but much more precise than sawing with the spiral blade; you are able to control your cut better and, therefore, are able to come closer to your line—a good idea, since filing interior contours requires much more painstaking work with the file than working outside contours. Note as well, that when doing this fine pierce-work, your V-shaped cut should be utilized; in this way you can hold your work absolutely steady, braced on either side of the path of your cut. If you are careful and work slowly, wax should not clog the teeth of the sawblade; if it does, just scrape it out on the spot by running your file cleaner against the direction of the teeth. When sawing these interior shapes, do not try to execute really sharp turns or get into corner

99

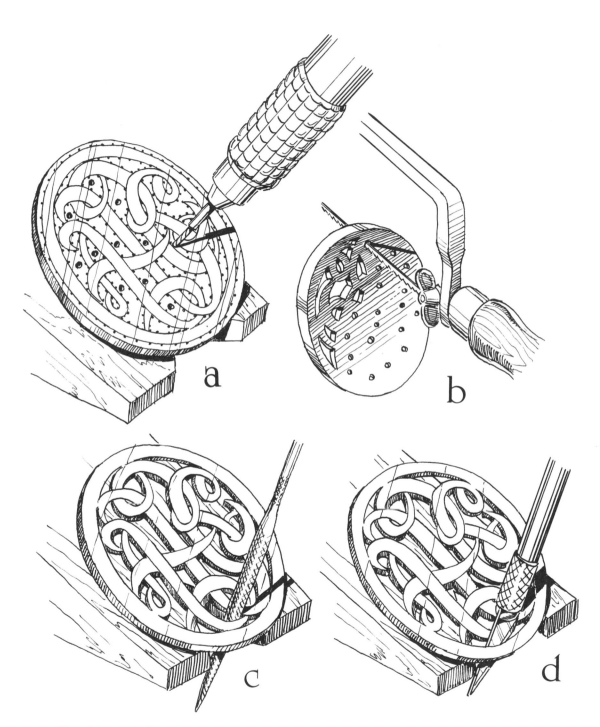

Fig. 4.3   a. Drilling holes to start pierce-work. b. Pierce-sawing the wax. c. Filing the model over V-shaped cutout. d. Refining details with knife.

100

angles; these nice points are much more readily accomplished later, with a file and knife.

Shaping Details

After all of the holes have been satisfactorily sawed out of the wax monogram, the more precise shaping work must now be done with files. There is no secret to selecting the appropriate file for any given job. Almost every outside contour can be formed with a barette file; the only exception is a rounded concavity, which requires the use of a half-round or round file. For most inner contours, a combination of a half-round and a tri-corner will do admirably, with perhaps a little assist from a knife-edge and a round file. Again, do not concern yourself at this point with those really sharp little corners; that is a job for an X-Acto knife.

Proper use of the file, although dependent on the particular job you are doing, is a very simple thing to master, if you just remember to push and not to pull, and if you allow the file itself to do most of the work. Do not press down hard with your tool; your control over it will be diminished. The angle at which you work, however, depends entirely upon the effect you wish to achieve. In order to get sharp edges, running at 90 degrees to the surface of the piece, you must position yourself directly over the piece and work your file straight down, utilizing the outside of the bench pin when working the outside and the V-shaped cut when working the inside. File the outside first, while the filigree work inside is still firm enough to allow you ample freedom of movement without fear of inadvertent pressure causing cracking at the center. Always allow yourself as little overhang as possible when filing (Fig. 4.3c), so that the wax flexes as little as possible under the pressure of your stroke. File slowly and carefully right up to your line, always checking the reverse side of your piece to make certain that your cut is true. When you near the line, lighten the pressure on your tool so that the marks of the file become quite faint at this last stage in the filing process.

When you have finished the outside, begin on the inside, selecting the thickest sections of your pattern to work first, always respecting the delicacy and fragility of your material. Only after you have properly shaped all the thick sections—even if it means leaving one shape incomplete to start on another—should you approach the intricate twists and turns. Remember, we have selected blue wax for this project because of its flexibility and toughness; yet, at this stage, the slightest mishandling will crack it, leaving you with a ticklish repair job. Always brace your work firmly, either on the bench pin—which is preferable—or else between your fingers, gripping any delicate projections firmly so that they are not endangered and shifting the angle of your stroke so that it remains at 90 degrees to the surface plane of the wax.

101

Next, you must refine the details with a knife. With your number-11 X-Acto blade, work gradually into the corners, cutting away small pieces instead of attempting to remove the entire piece with just two cuts. If necessary, use your smaller swivel knife blade and scrape the excess away. Never cut down from the surface of your piece as if you were cutting a slice from a chunk of cheese; always place your blade into the opening and, again with the blade at 90 degrees to the surface of the piece, cut into the corner (Fig. 4.3d). When you have completed the silhouette of the monogram, the most important aspect, you may begin work varying the surface plane.

Here it is best to allow the silhouette itself to determine the highs and lows of your surface. Remember, the beauty of the monogram is largely dependent upon the intertwining of the letters; at any point where one letter overlaps another, the surface should be higher, to impart the illusion of a double thickness. Conversely, those areas in your pattern which exhibit the more delicate scrollwork should be at a lower level. Since the overall thickness of your slab is less than 3 millimeters, the variation between high and low points is not great; however, if properly modulated, even a small difference can be quite significant, if not down-right dramatic.

Begin by scribing in all points of overlap. With your knife, first cut down along the line which separates the two letters; then, very carefully working toward the cut, gradually lower the level of the bottom letter (Fig. 4.4a). Repeat this procedure at every juncture until you have defined all the levels of your monogram.

Next you round off the shapes, either with a file or with a knife. The safer way is with the file. Simply go around the entire pattern, both inner and outer contours, with a file. Only this time, instead of working at 90 degrees to the surface, work at 45 degrees, first putting a bevel on the entire piece and, then, rounding it off (Fig. 4.4b). Do not take the curve down to the base level of your monogram; always leave a little bit of straight wall so that, in polishing the back in the metal, you do not come up with knife edges. If you feel more comfortable working with a knife, use a number-4 stencil knife and scrape around the corners of the edge until the desired rounded effect has been achieved (Fig. 4.4c). I have found that a combination of knife and file is best for doing this type of work: the file for whatever standard geometric forms you might have to render and for those sections of the design which demand only the lightest of touches; the knife for any undulating form and for work which may be done quickly without aesthetic or technical loss.

The file or knife marks now have to be eradicated along with any inadvertent angles. A piece of very fine sandpaper rolled into a tube or folded in half to produce a thin cutting edge should do the job nicely. When all surfaces have been refined to your satisfaction, the piece may be polished.

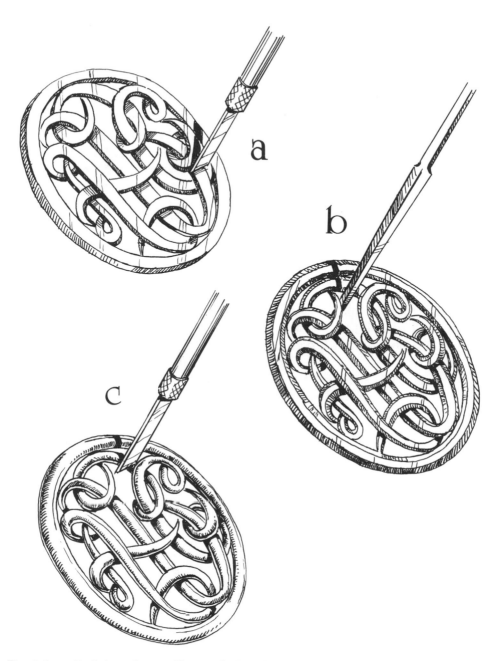

Fig. 4.4   a. Defining planes of letters. b. Beveling edges with file. c. Rounding corners with knife.

Perhaps the best all-purpose polishing instrument I have yet discovered is an implement familiar to every polisher in the jewelry industry: the felt buff. These are compacted felt wheels of various diameters which, when used in conjunction with finer abrasives, produce a high gloss on metal. Since you are working on a miniature scale, use only the smallest felt buffs, those intended to be screwed into a special holder, called a reinforced mandrel, and used on the flexible shaft machine. These miniature buffs come in different sizes, different hardnesses, and different shapes; however, the only ones which you will ever really need are the hard, flat 1-inch wheel, for polishing the broader surfaces, and the hard, knife-edge, ½-inch diameter size, for the more intricate spots, both available by the dozen from jewelry supply houses. With these simple tools, you should be able to smooth every kind of surface you will ever confront, regardless of what type of carving wax is employed. Just hold the tool between your fingers and rub it over the surface you wish to refine. Do not attach it to the flexible shaft machine; it will melt even the sturdiest carving wax. The buff has not only an abrasive action but a burnishing one as well; it compresses the surface of the wax slightly, producing a very smooth, slightly reflective finish which is not nearly as dramatic on blue wax as it is on the harder green.

Be very careful when using the buffs, which require pressure in order to work. At this stage, the very delicate piece is not able to withstand much pressure. Lay the model down flat on the bench pin and work your knife-edge buff over it in short deliberate strokes. Do not endanger your piece by working it in the air—even if such a procedure might facilitate polishing. It is better to polish only what can be done in absolute safety; postpone polishing frail pieces until you get the metal model from the caster. Try, however, to work the felt buff into those areas where a file could not fit: corners, junctures where one plane overlaps another, incised sections—even if you have to alter the shape of the buff with the X-Acto blade. It is easier to clean up the wax than it is to clean up the metal. Use discretion in trading off ease with safety and, when you have finished with the felt buff, a light buffing with the felt cloth will complete the job. The piece is ready to cast.

Purple Wax Pendant with Stone

Purple wax, I have found, is the perfect material in which to carve miniature sculptures and figurines, but its use is not limited to art objects; it is extremely useful in making jewelry pieces which demand high relief, open-work, and a fair amount of detail; in short, almost all representational jewelry is best fabricated from purple wax: animals, plants, human forms, flowers—anything which seeks to imitate a natural object. For the purple wax project, you will try a fairly standard piece of representational jewelry: a pendant about 1½ inches (38 mm) in length, in which two highly detailed figures, mirror images of each other, flank a central stone. Serpentine dragon figures are ideal for this type of project; they can be made to twist and turn in any which way according to the artist's whim and still be recognizable.

104

Tools and Materials

  Pound block of Ferris purple wax
  Hacksaw
  Jeweler's saw frame with spiral and piercing blades
  Metal scribe or a long needle
  Half-round needle file, cut-2
  Half-round escapement file, cut-3
  Barette escapement file, cut-3
  Knife-edge escapement file, cut-3
  Fiberglass brush
  Sandpaper, number-2 and number-4/0
  ½-inch knife-edge felt buff (hard)
  1-inch wheel felt buff (hard)
  Felt cloth
  X-Acto knife, number-11
  X-Acto knife, number-4 stencil
  X-Acto swivel stencil blade set in a mechanical pencil holder
  X-Acto holder with gouging blades
            or
    Flexible shaft unit or Dremel tool with assorted round burrs
  Degree/ligne gauge
  Tracing paper
  Venus pencil, HB and 4H
  Alcohol lamp with spatula
  Binocular loupe
  Cabochon stone, 28 mm by 20 mm approximately

You will see, if you compare this list to the list required for carving blue wax, that, although the materials are essentially similar there are several basic differences. The first is that there is a much greater reliance here upon knives rather than files. This has nothing to do with the inherent difference between purple and blue wax, but with the difference in the demands of the individual projects. The next dissimilarity you will discover is that the cuts of the files are finer and that instruments for the use of magnification have been included. This is because more detail-work can be done with the harder, less flexible purple wax than with the blue. This is also the reason for including, at this point, the mainstay of all professional model-makers and jewelers: the flexible shaft tool.

Design Work

In order to make preliminary sketches, before ever touching a pencil to tracing paper, you need a stone to determine the correct proportions for the model; you do not want your ornament to dwarf the stone, or the stone to be an overpowering element. On a purely technical level, aesthetics aside, you need the stone in order to determine the size of the setting, the height of the prongs, and, particularly, the height of the carved model relative to tbe height of the stone.

For this project, a cabochon stone—which is smoothly domed on the front and perfectly flat on the back—is best. Almost every stone, with the exception of the diamond, is available in this cut but, in the larger sizes especially, it is most popular for the less expensive minerals, which would not be displayed to their best advantage were they to be faceted. These minerals are primarily either opaque, such as jasper or onyx, or else they exhibit highly distinctive or decorative markings, such as moss agate. At this stage, you hardly have enough skill to work on the very minute scale demanded of most pieces of jewelry; therefore, it would be best to select a fairly large stone as the focal point of the design, at least 25 millimeters in length, to allow yourself ample room to experiment with the wax.

After the stone has been selected, creating a design around it is a fairly simple thing to do. No matter how baroque an element might be, if its mirror-image is placed beside it, a symmetrical ornament, instantly recognizeable as decorative art, will result. Trace the outline of your stone onto a piece of tracing paper, place another piece of tracing paper on top of the first, and doodle a pattern of serpentine shapes around the stone until you come upon one which pleases you, remembering that the piece is to be ultimately worn around the neck. You must then define your forms so that the suggestions of the original abstract design become the actual coils and features of the snake or dragon. It is unnecessary to render both halves of your pattern; in fact it is preferable to concentrate your efforts toward clarifying, stylizing, and refining a single serpent. After that has been done to your satisfaction, simply fold your tracing paper in half, so that the outline of your stone is divided straight down the middle lengthwise, and trace what you have drawn on the other side. When you unfold the paper, your design will be ready for final criticism, all problems solved.

However, unlike the monogram, where the tracing was simply transferred onto a thin slab of wax, there is a more efficient approach to working our representational piece—even though the first approach is applicable here as well. In this case, it is better to fashion each of the three elements (the setting for the stone and the two serpents) from individual pieces of wax and to join them afterwards with a hot spatula. The advantages of this are obvious; you will be able to concentrate fully on forming each unit without having to worry about the fragility of the other two; you will be able to neatly finish areas which would be inaccessible were you to attempt the piece as a whole; you will be able to achieve exact mirror images which would be extremely difficult and time-consuming if you were to approach your model in any other way.

You must decide at this point whether the piece will be one-of-a-kind, or whether you intend to make a rubber mold from it and put it into production. If the latter alternative is the case, you must allow for shrinkage, fashioning your piece about ten percent larger in the wax than you intend the finished product to be. This becomes extremely tricky, especially when fitting a stone into a setting. If you use your stone as a model, the finished setting will be too tight. Therefore, you might facilitate matters by using as your model a stone which is approximately ten percent larger than the stone you plan to use in the cast piece. Either that, or else you must compute the approximate shrinkage using only your eye as a gauge. This is a very difficult part of wax model-making; only experience will really teach you to compensate correctly for shrinkage. At this point, you will be confronting too many new problems to allow your attention to be distracted by things which really are the domain of the experienced professional.

Stone Setting

Approach the pendant as if it were to be a unique piece. The first problem will be to make a setting for the stone. In almost every piece of jewelry that you will be called upon to produce, the best approach is always to begin with the purely functional elements, those elements which demand absolute precision, around which the design must be structured, before attending to the decorative aspects of the piece.

A simple setting basically consists of two sections: the seat, upon which the stone will rest, and the prongs which will hold the stone in place. There are several ways to create a setting in wax. The most simple would be to cut the seat to the exact dimensions of the stone from a $\frac{1}{16}$-inch (1.6 mm) slab of wax, saw out a central hole and file the entire piece until it is smooth; then add the four prongs individually, using a tweezers to hold each delicate prong in place while bonding the units together with a fine heated spatula (Fig. 4.5a). Simple as this is however, I would recommend that the beginner carve the complete unit from a single piece of wax; it is much more time-consuming, but easier and more precise.

On a piece of wax, approximately 1.5 millimeters higher than the dome of the stone, scribe the exact outline of your stone (Fig. 4.5b). Lay the stone aside and, retaining the proportions of your original inscription, scratch an oval about 2.5 millimeters larger than the original contours of your stone; scratch another oval, about 3 millimeters smaller than your stone, inside the first outline, so that there are three ovals marked in the wax, one inside the other. Using your spiral sawblade, taking care not to undercut, saw along the outer line and file it smooth. This shape will be retained only in the extreme outer dimensions of your prongs.

After you have filed the outer contour, you must mark out the position of the prongs. There is no hard and fast rule about the positioning of the prongs, except that you must temper mathematical rules with common sense. Ideally, the prongs should be placed at the "corners" of the stone, which will only work for square or emerald-cut stones; otherwise, a good method is to imagine your oval stone inside a rectangle with the extreme edges of the stone touching the sides of the box. If you connect the two sets of opposite corners with two diagonal lines, the points where these lines transect the outline of the stone suggest the placement of the prongs.

Naturally, however, this formula will not work on irregularly shaped stones or stones which are extremely long and thin. After you have completed your measuring, mark off 2.5 millimeters for each prong, extending your line from the original outline marking of your stone to the outer edge of the wax. Using a barette file, cut away the area between the prongs until you reach your contour line (Fig. 4.5c).

Fitting the piercing saw blade into your frame, and working across the wax—rather than in the usual vertical way—cut down two parallel lines beginning at the inner corners of the prongs until you reach a point about 2.5 millimeters from the base; now, shift the position of the wax so that the usual sawing procedure may be employed, and simply saw parallel to the base, leaving 2.5 millimeters of material for the seat, until you have reached the other saw cut and the discarded piece pops out (Fig. 4.5d). Repeat this operation at right angles, and your prongs will be defined (Fig. 4.5e).

Now simply use your barette file to refine each prong and to level off the seat of the setting, testing the fit of your stone as you do so. When everything is clean and the stone rests snugly in the setting, turn the setting over and saw out the shape of the remaining inscribed oval. After you have filed the inside clean and, depending upon the desired thickness of your setting, have reduced the dimension of the seat by filing away the undersurface, the setting is complete and ready for the application of the design motifs (Fig. 4.5f).

Mirror-Image Dragons

Making mirror images requires a very simple technique which will save you a good deal of time endeavoring to fashion exact proportions utilizing just your eye, either alone or aided by any number of calipers and gauges. It should be especially useful later, when you begin to make left and right halves of earrings or cuff links. To begin, make an exact tracing of only one half of your design unit. Make certain that all problems have been thought through on the rough sketches before you ever touch the wax. Special care should have been taken especially to insure that the configuration of your motif fits neatly around the setting that you have just made; nothing should hamper the working of the prongs; the design elements should physically touch as much of the setting as possible so that the final piece will be sturdy. Once all of this has been settled, trace your design and rubber cement it onto a piece of wax which is roughly two and one-quarter times thicker than the intended final

108

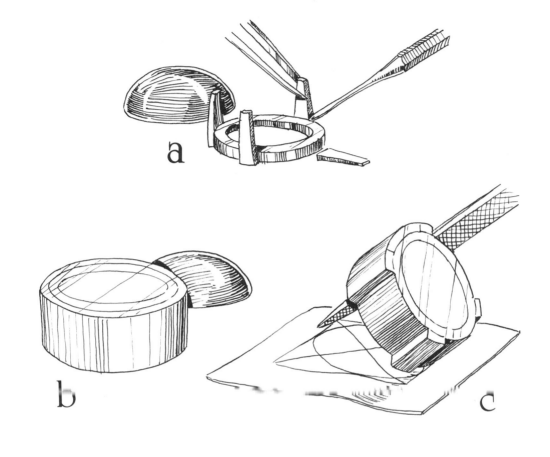

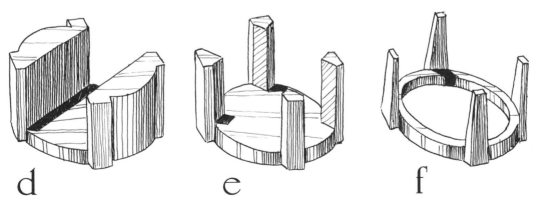

Fig. 4.5   a. Assembling a setting. b. Scribing outlines on wax. c. Filing the outer contour.
d. First sawcut. e. Second sawcut. f. A completed setting.

thickness of your piece. Then proceed to saw out the outline with a spiral blade, using extreme caution to cut straight down; the thicker the wax, the more difficult it is to keep the top and bottom proportions the same and the more care you must exercise in the sawing. After sawing, file your wax until it is as equal, top and bottom, as you can make it. Then, scribe a line midway around the entire depth of the piece; change to the number-4 piercing saw blade and slice the wax exactly in half (Fig. 4.6a). Open the two halves as if opening a clam, exposing the two inner surfaces, and scratch an identifying mark on each half (Fig. 4.6b). These marked surfaces—where any discrepancy which might exist between the two halves of your piece is at an absolute minimum—will be placed facedown on opposite sides of the setting, their contour will become the final external outline of the piece. All subsequent work on the design should exclude altering this outline by limiting itself to the formation of the top surface only. Work on the baseline of the piece should only be in the realm of refinement, small detail, and polishing. Any real alteration should be done *now,* while the two halves can still be brought into apposition for checking. One thing that must be checked at this point is the fit of each half around the setting. If there is a misalignment, if parts intended to touch do not touch, if there are aesthetic failings, if the bases are not level, do the fixing now by either adding wax where it is required or by removing it where it is not. Remember, these three units must be joined later and any mistakes which you allow to pass at this stage will haunt you then, when you will have to modify pieces that have been painstakingly carved. Only after you have made certain that the three pieces go together, both functionally and aesthetically, should you lay your setting aside and begin work on the two facing serpents.

It is good practice to work both pieces simultaneously—despite the temptation to stay with only one segment until you have completed it. In this way, each step from the roughing out of the basic shapes and movements to the final polishing may be checked for symmetry. You also run no danger of your second piece becoming so superior to the first that the first has to be redone to come up to the standards set by the other—as is often the case if you approach these units as two separate pieces.

Begin by roughing out the basic movements of the piece. Unlike your work with the monogram where the surface plane was actually flat, here you must be concerned with depth—highs and lows, as well as thicks and thins. Logic will dictate, in most situations, the arrangement of these planes. Clearly, the serpent will be thicker at the middle than it will be at the tail; where it faces forward, the plane will be higher as well. It is up to each individual to interpret the surface movements in accordance with a personal sense of aesthetics; however, one rule must be observed. The lowest depth should not be lower than the base of the stone as it rests in its setting. Ideally, no part of the seat of the setting

110

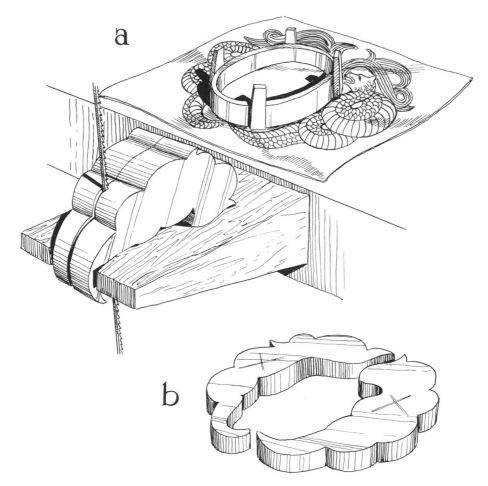

Fig. 4.6   a. Splitting a wax piece. b. Marking the matching halves.

should be glimpsed from the side; it is a purely functional element in the design and, as such, should be hidden from view as much as possible.

Begin to shape out the largest planes with the half-round needle file, bringing the two pieces together to insure uniformity. Soon, however, you will discover that a file is simply inadequate to define all the intricacies of the pattern. A file is best used on designs which are basically geometric; for natural forms, the flexible shaft tool and the knife are best. Here, you should start with the basic number-11 X-Acto knife.

With the first cut, you should be able to notice the difference between this material and the blue wax. It does not slice as cleanly as the blue; instead it falls away in rather irregular flakes, leaving a characteristic pock-marked plane. Therefore, you must vary your approach to the wax. You cannot happily whittle this material, as you had with the softer blue; you must make smaller strokes which—instead of the straight cut previously employed—describe a sort of shallow U shape: entering the wax,

111

cutting a sliver out, and rising up toward the surface again. In this way, you can avoid the possibility of inadvertently splitting or chipping the wax.

Any really deep cuts could also result in fissures. It is best to use your number-11 blade at a relatively flat angle and take small slices out of the wax until you have reached the desired depth. The number-11 blade is a versatile tool. At this stage, you should be cutting with the broad edge of the blade; much later on, you will use the point to clarify the inner contours and to incise details into the surface of the wax. Once, however, you have determined the largest planes of your piece (Fig. 4.7a), you should lay your number-11 blade aside and take up the smaller, less steeply angled number-4 stencil knife.

This blade, which closely resembles an angled chisel, has a two-fold use; it is used to cut in deep notches and to separate and define abutting shapes (Fig. 4.7b). It is also used as a scraping tool. In this latter capacity, it is drawn backward across the surface of the wax—instead of being pushed forward as it is in its usual cutting operation—held at about 75 degrees to the surface plane. In this way, nuances are delicately modeled into the piece, and the sharply defined cuts left by the number-11 blade are softened into rounded contours.

The first step in finishing up a piece fabricated with a knife is to smooth out the irregularities. On many pieces, a file cannot reach into all the places that the knife has gone; moreover, a file can very often impart a dead, mechanical aspect to a piece that had looked alive in its rough form. You will discover that each type of tool creates a piece which has a specific "look," and the free-flowing shapes formed by the knife are nullified when worked over by the file—just as the precision of a filed piece would be totally destroyed were you to use a knife on it. However, there is a tool which accomplishes the work of a file—removing irregularities, making forms undulate gracefully—but does not undermine the snap of the knife cut. I borrowed this tool from a stationery store: a fiberglass typewriter eraser (Fig. 4.7c), an item which sells for around $2. It consists of a tube of plastic with a small rectangular opening on one end and a screw mechanism on the other. Attached to the screw mechanism is a stiff fiberglass tassel fixed in a metal base. A turn of the screw will push the bristles through the opening, creating a brush made of glass. Depending upon how far out the bristles project, the cutting surface will have more or less flexibility. Run the edge of the fiberglass bristles lightly over the surface of the piece; the brush will adapt itself to the shape of your model, and scratch away all sharp angles. Two words of caution, however: if you press too heavily on this tool you will scour the surface so severely that it will require another scraping with the knife to eradicate the scratch marks; also, the bristles break under pressure. They are glass and, if they get into your fingers, they can be very painful and difficult to remove.

112

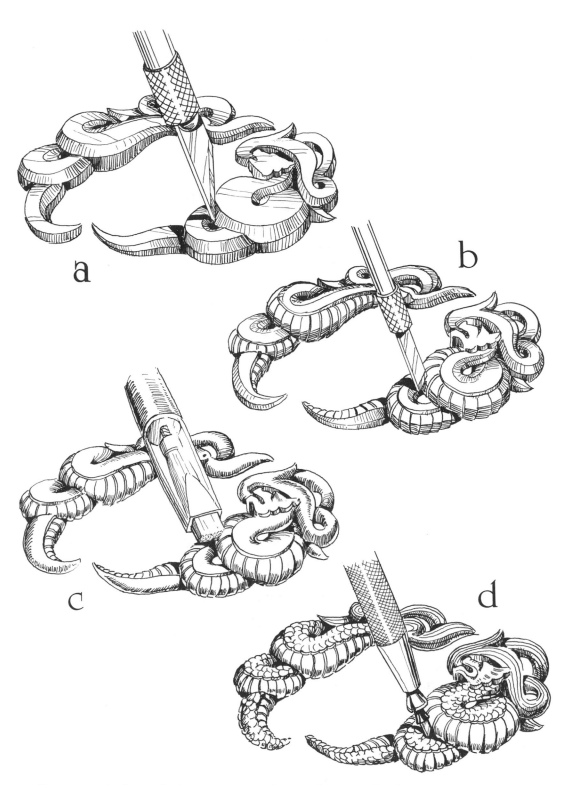

Fig. 4.7   a. Defining the large planes. b. Cutting the major details. c. Removing irregularities with fiberglass brush. d. Finishing detail work.

113

After you have smoothed the surface with the fiberglass brush, a rolled up piece of sandpaper should be sufficient to prepare the piece for its final operation: the incising of the individual details.

Fine detail work is the province of the model-maker. A good model-maker can invite scrutiny of a piece under a 10-power loupe and still elicit admiration for his craft. But it *is* craft. The real artistry of a piece lies in its movement, in the juxtaposition of its forms, in its very three-dimensionality. Fine detail work is merely an incredibly precise and highly sophisticated type of texture. All it requires of the model-maker is a sharp eye, a sharp knife, a steady hand, patience—especially patience—and strong nerves.

Begin again with your scribe. Lay your detailed drawing beside the model and copy it lightly onto the wax with the scribe. If you do not have enough confidence yet in your abilities to do this, paint the entire surface of the wax with Pro-White non-crawl water paint and first draw the details in with a 4H pencil. After this has been accomplished to your satisfaction, trace over the drawing with the point of the scribe. After you have washed off the paint, the lines of the scribe will remain to guide you.

Begin, as usual, with the largest details; in this case with the dragon's head. It is usually good practice, when doing detail work, to work first on the sturdiest areas of the model, leaving those places which are fragile or which project out from the main body for last. These sections are apt to become yet more fragile after having been worked and, should they break off, the repairing will often obliterate a good portion of your hard-won details. For this, you will need your swivel knife blade set into the mechanical pencil holder, and very good vision.

A model-maker is only as good as his eyes. Before even attempting to cut in the details, you should be certain that your eyes are up to the job. Most eyes, even those with perfect vision, will require assistance at this stage. Magnifying lenses come in a very wide assortment of styles and powers. There are the large magnifying glasses, the doublets and triplets, the individual eye loupes, binocular loupes, lenses which can be mounted onto eyeglass frames, standing magnifiers, even microscopes. There are, however, three things which you should bear in mind when shopping for a lens; do not get one which boasts a stronger magnification than the job demands. There is no sense in putting more strain on your eyes than you have to—and any increase in magnification renders you more dependent upon the lens. Magnification, in fact, ranges from 1½-power up to 5-power for most binocular models, with 7- to 10-power being fairly standard for single eye loupes, and 50-power not unusual for microscopes. Actually, for most jobs, 2- or 3-power magnification is more than adequate.

A lens should also allow you complete freedom to use both hands. Obviously, any hand-held magnifying glass will never be functional; nor
114

will a lens whose depth of field is so shallow that there is not enough room between the lens and your model to allow ample work room. And last, as well as perhaps most important, you should stay away from single eye pieces. In order to function with maximum efficiency, both eyes should focus on the piece. Not only will distortion of the detail work result if you use a single eye loupe, but your eye will soon begin to hurt. The single eye loupe was not intended for prolonged use; it was designed to inspect pieces at close range in order to detect imperfections. Instead, you should obtain a binocular loupe which fits over the head like a visor (Fig. 4.8) and allows both eyes to focus on the piece.

Binocular loupes come in a variety of styles and varying degrees of magnification. Most have provision for interchanging lenses to vary the magnification in accordance with the job at hand. Attachments which are used in conjunction with the lens may also increase magnification but, I have found, these are at best imperfect substitutes for replacing the lens completely with one that offers higher magnification. Nor are binocular loupes the only magnifying instruments which fulfill the criteria. If you are really serious about your detail work and wish to invest a sizeable amount of money to insure the precision of your craft, the ideal instrument is a dissecting microscope. These microscopes have individual eye focus so that the correct paralax is maintained; the piece may be held easily under the lens and worked with no difficulty or eyestrain whatsoever. Depending upon the scope you purchase, you can obtain magnification ranging from 7-power all the way up to 80-power. It is a wonderful luxury, of which I have often availed myself, but it is by no means essential to the production of a clean, sharp model.

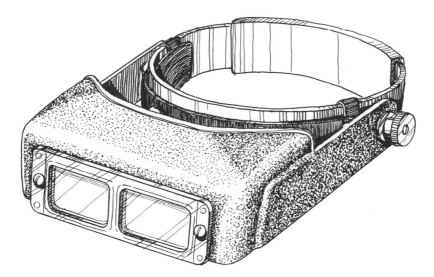

Fig. 4.8   Binocular loupe.

Whatever magnification you choose—if you decide to choose any at all—it will only make your work easier to see. The actual doing depends upon the control you have over the instrument. Working details is fairly much the same as working the larger areas—you worry about planes and the modulation of shapes—only here everything is miniaturized. The knife blade is ⅛ inch; the detail is even smaller; and your stroke must be so controlled and so short and so light that it might not even travel a full millimeter across the surface of the wax. Yet its track can very easily be seen, even without magnification.

To make your job simpler, further miniaturize your collection of cutting tools. Do not rely on the swivel blade alone, but have a complete assortment of tiny implements at your disposal. I have found that the mechanical pencil holder is not limited to holding swivel blades; it is also an excellent device for holding any number of small sharp instruments that may be used to carve details into the wax. The best source for these instruments is the box of burrs that you might have purchased for use with the flexible shaft machine. The ³⁄₃₂-inch shafts fit perfectly into the pencil and may be easily removed when you want to change burrs. The cutting points, as you will see if you examine the profile, can be of great assistance in shaping the details. Cone-shaped burrs may be used to incise sharp V-shaped channels; cross-cut cone squares are very useful for smoothing out tiny forms; and the tiny round burrs—some so small that they are barely visible to the naked eye—are just as useful set into the mechanical pencil holder as they are when snapped into the flexible shaft handpiece. Depending upon their size, they may be used to cut and define a line, clean up inaccessible places which might have become abraded, or carve out a concavity. Remember, however, when using the flexible shaft burrs, that they have been designed for rotary cutting. If you take a round burr and simply stand it straight up, trying to make a cut with the point, the results will probably be irregular. Hold the burr at an angle and make the cut with the edge, perhaps even turning the tool slightly as you use it.

Other implements, such as dental picks, sewing needles, wax carvers, or even tools that you might have fashioned yourself on a grinding wheel from an old nail or a thick paper clip may be utilized here. There is no one type of tool which will do every job every time; common sense and experience will show you the right tool for each job.

Be prepared, even with the best magnification and cutting implements, to spend many hours working on the details of the model. The scales of the serpent alone—an uncomplicated enough job, requiring only one semicircular incision into the wax and one or two scrapes to define each scale—becomes a major project when you have over one hundred scales to do and each scale is less than 2 millimeters across. Remember, there is no trick to doing tight detail work, only endurance.

116

After all the details have been carved into the wax, the surface of the model is polished. Unfortunately, the methods used when working on larger pieces no longer suffice. The felt buff cannot be used except to polish the high points; any pressure on it will soften the details until they are obliterated. Better is a piece of hardwood, itself smoothly finished, which may be used as a burnisher to put a shine on each individual plane of your detail work. Then a light buffing with a felt cloth should finish off the job nicely. If any detail still remains unpolished at this point, wait until you get the metal model back from the caster and polish it then, when there is less danger of eradicating hours of precise and painstaking work just to make something shine.

Hollowing

All that remains to do is to lighten the weight of the dragons somewhat. Ideally, this is done by hollowing out the backs with a flexible shaft machine. However, save this approach for the work on green wax, when professional techniques will be stressed, and use, instead, only hand tools for this job. The tools I would recommend here are a set of miniature gouges, such as X-Acto puts out, a round burr fixed into the mechanical pencil holder, and the fiberglass brush.

The object here is simply to scoop out as much material from the back of the wax model as you deem necessary without harming the front surface of the piece. Aim for a fairly uniform thickness of 1.5 millimeters, with a border on the back also measuring 1.5 millimeters wide. This might seem very slight but, in reality, it errs on the side of being overly thick; however, considering that we are working with rather unsophisticated equipment, and working with it for the first time, this gauge will be adequate for now.

To begin, scribe a uniform 1.5-millimeter border around the entire back surface of each dragon. Under no conditions should you go beyond this border when doing further work on the piece; it will serve both as a guide for regulating the thickness of the rest of the model and as a secure base for the finished model. Taking a small rounded gouge and working very slowly and lightly, start to scoop the material away from the very center of the piece (Fig. 4.9a). I need not overemphasize the importance of care at this stage; overzealous use of the gouge will completely destroy all the work you have invested in the model. You can crack the piece or you can cut completely through to the front surface from the back, leaving a hole where some finely wrought detail work had been. Work slowly and check the thickness of your model constantly.

There are two ways of checking thickness. The first is with the degree/ligne gauge. Just press the legs together so that the jaws open; center the piece between the jaws and *slowly* relax your pressure so that the jaws close on the model. The measurement will be easily read on the

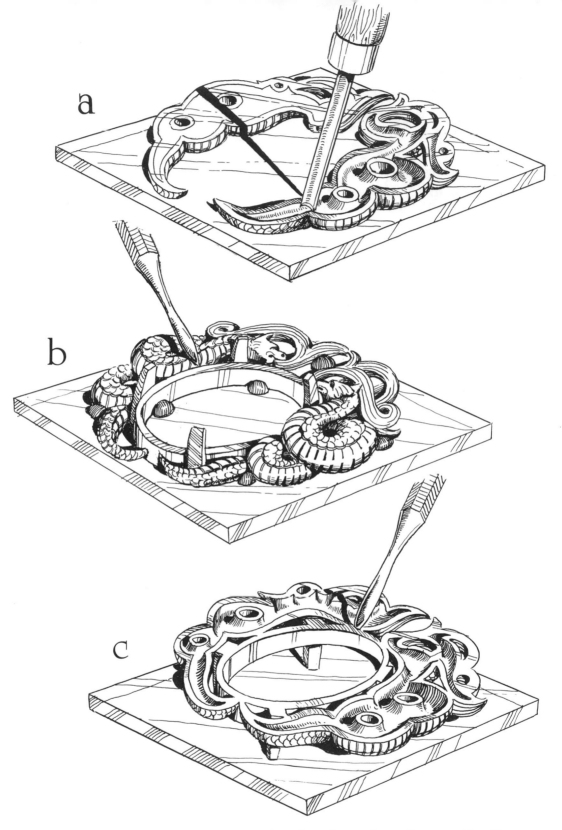

Fig. 4.9 a. Hollowing out the backs. b. Tacking the units together. c. Permanent bonding.

gauge. Be careful to close the jaws slowly; if you snap them shut, you will surely scratch the surface of the wax or even crack it. This method, however, is generally used in conjunction with another, less time-consuming, more flexible one.

The wax, as you know, is dyed a certain color, whether it be blue, or green, or purple. The color is consistent throughout the entire block, but it is not opaque. Depending upon the thickness of the slab and the intensity of the light source, the same wax will appear just barely translucent and very richly colored in thick pieces while, in thin slivers, it will be almost colorless and actually transparent. This range in color is what the professional model-maker uses to gauge the thickness of his model. He knows that at 1.5 millimeters, light passing through the wax will create a particular tone of purple; he knows this because he has carefully measured his piece with the degree/ligne gauge. Once the desired thickness—and its distinctive color—have been determined, all that remains is to achieve that same color throughout his piece. Places which are too thick will show a darker hue; places which are too thin will show lighter, and must be built up. In this way, without having constant recourse to your measuring gauge, you may fairly accurately ascertain the thickness of your piece.

You will notice, however, as you work with your gouge, that, while the back of the model might have been scooped out uniformly, you still see, as you hold your piece up to the light, many areas which are dark in comparison with the desired thickness. This is because the front surface is not uniform but has various highs and lows. The lows will be the correct thickness but the highs will require more work. So you must switch to a small round burr set into the mechanical pencil holder. Carefully scrape out the wax wherever it shows dark until the entire piece exhibits a fairly uniform color; then apply the fiberglass brush with the bristles well extended. In a few moments you will have smoothed out most of the irregularities and, at the same time, will have imparted a uniform texture to the back. The three units are now complete, and all that remains is to join them and bring them to the caster.

Joining Pieces

The process of joining pieces of wax is a very simple one; however, anytime you expose your model to extreme heat you must be aware of the potential danger. Begin by laying out your pieces on a glass plate or any other perfectly level surface. A bit of clay pressed lightly against the outer edge of each dragon on the glass will insure against inadvertent shifting of the elements as you join them. The first step now is to tack the pieces together so that you can turn the model over to join it permanently from the back.

Select abutting areas which have the least amount of detail work and, taking a little wax on the end of your smallest spatula, touch the

119

hot tool to the place where the two pieces touch, depositing the wax in the crack (Fig. 4.9b). Remember, this is a temporary joint, so you need not concern yourself with a complete bond; what you should aim for instead is to deposit as little wax as you possibly can on the surface of the piece. This application of wax will have to be worked and refined so that no crude shapes intrude into your finely wrought detail work; the less wax you use in tacking, the less work you will have to do later.

Permanent joining of different pieces, whether the pieces have been originally designed for bonding or even if they have been accidentally broken off and require repair, is a job which must be approached methodically. First, the different sections must all be tacked in place before any permanent work is to be done. In this way, you can be absolutely certain that all the units fit together properly before you devote your attention to the purely technical job.

There are two methods of joining pieces together through the use of heat: one is to bond from one side only—as you will do here for the dragon pendant; and the other is to bond from both sides. This latter method is the usual way in which a model-maker repairs pieces which have been accidentally broken, and which still require additional work. It is important for us to know how to repair broken pieces since there is not a model-maker in the world who is immune to catastrophies of this nature. I am not talking about surface nicks or chips which can be repaired by a globule of wax bonded to the surface; I am referring to a complete fracture where a large piece has broken off the main body of the model.

To repair such a fracture, you must first tack the unit back into place (Fig. 4.10a). Once you are secure in the placement of the section, bury your hot spatula two-thirds of the way down directly into the crack so that the break is bonded first at the center of the block of wax (Fig. 4.10b). The object of all repairs of this kind is to expunge totally all sign of the break. This can only be accomplished if all wax on either side of the crack is totally reworked. After you are certain that the center is bonded, take some molten wax on the heated spatula and, again, bury it into the crack, adding the new wax to the wax which has melted down from the sides of the crack. Repeat this operation as often as it is necessary until, instead of a fissure line on the surface, you have a ridge of wax (Fig. 4.10c). Turn the model over so that the underside of the break is exposed and, once again, bury your heated spatula two-thirds of the way down into the crack, directly into the layer of wax you have just created; in this way, there can be no doubt that all vestiges of the break, as well as all entrapped air pockets, have been removed and that you again have one solid unit (Fig. 4.10d). Fill up the rest of the crack on the first side until another ridge is created (Fig. 4.10e). File down both ridges level with the surface, and proceed as if nothing had ever happened.

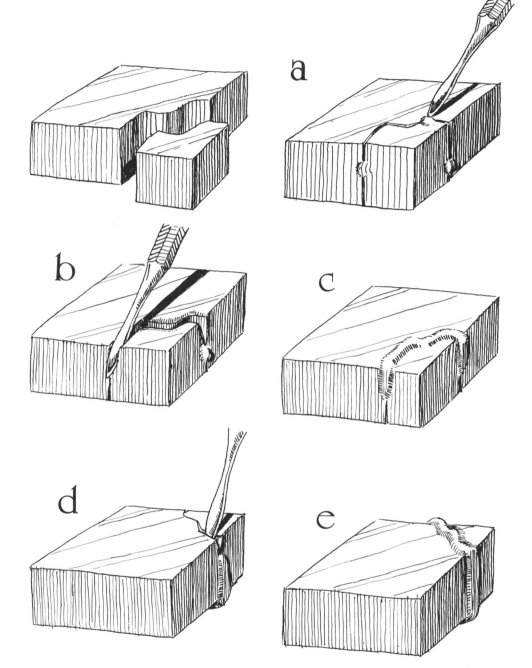

Fig. 4.10   a. Tacking pieces together. b. Bonding the first side. c. Bonding, half-completed. d. Bonding the second side. e. Completed bond.

This method is the most drastic type of bonding; all material around the juncture has either been replaced or altered. However, in the case of a break, such extreme measures are necessary, especially if you intend to do further work on the piece.

In those situations where the bonding of different units represents the final stage in the completion of a model, a less drastic type of joining will do nicely. After you have completed tacking the pendant sections together from the front, turn the piece over to join it permanently from the back (Fig. 4.9c). No further work—save for the unavoidable reworking of details that might have become obliterated in the tacking operation—is to be done on the front of the model. Joining the units from the back is no great mystery; simply bury the hot tool as far as possible into the joint, without breaking through to the front of the model. Once the deepest possible spot has been melted closed, proceed as explained above on fractures; add a bit of wax to the tip of your spatula and deposit it as you melt the joint around it. When the newly applied wax forms a ridge above the level surface of the back, stop and file the entire back smooth.

You must now clean up whatever wax might have inadvertantly spilled over. First clean the back, scooping out any excess that accumulated. Then finish by carefully picking away the wax that you used to tack the units in front.

Repolish the surface wherever it is necessary and your model is finished. After it has been cast, have a loop soldered on (or else make one yourself from a thin wax rod; see Chapter 8), polish the model, have the stone set, buy a chain for it and you will have created a truly lovely piece of jewelry.

At this stage in your progress as a wax model-maker, the finished product, no matter how exquisite it might be, is of secondary importance. It is what you have learned, the experience you have gained, which should be your main concern. Whether your model has turned out to be good, mediocre, or even absolutely terrible, is really of little consequence at this point. Whether you even bother to cast it at all or, rather, decide to toss it into the melting pot, you still will have extracted from it something of great value: the experience of having made it.

Chapter 5

Wax Carving—Part Two: Green Wax

OF all the materials employed in the production of a wax model, not one is even remotely as essential to the jewelry industry as Ferris green wax. It is the mainstay of almost every wax model-maker I have known. Some model-makers, in fact, use no other wax. Indeed, in almost all spheres of model-making, this wax has—in just the last twenty or so years—replaced metal as the preferred material for making models of all types, from the most precise kind of fittings to the cleanest abstract forms. The experienced professional can work this wax with about as much precision as metal—and in one-tenth the time. The green wax is also able to do things impossible in metal; the grace, alone, which is possible through the use of wax, is enough to convince anyone of its superiority as a model-making material. And it eventually will be cast into metal anyway, so even those things which properly are the domain of the metalsmith—prong settings, galleries, hinges, interlocking parts—may be quickly brought to a relatively refined stage in the wax and then finished off in metal.

Ferris green wax, like the blue and purple waxes, is produced in a variety of sizes and shapes, from the big five-pound block to the one-pound blocks to the boxes of assorted slabs. It is also available in ring tubes: tubes of wax, approximately 6 inches long, basically circular in orientation and bored through to accomodate a size-4 finger. Considering how little they weigh, ring tubes are quite expensive; but they represent a considerable savings in time. For a professional, the ring tube is well worth the additional expense. If he had to rough out the shape from a solid block and then bore it, it would take at least fifteen minutes; here in thirty seconds with a saw the rough shape is ready to refine.

Ring tubes are available in four basic profiles (Fig. 5.1): the solid cylinder, which I would not recommend for rings—there seems no point in the extra expense if you still have to bore the hole yourself; the center-bored tube, which is really only useful for wedding bands and rings which require a uniform shank; the off-center-bored tube, which is regularly used for most smaller rings and for shanks to be used in stone rings; and the flat-sided tube—available in three thicknesses (1 inch, 1⅛ inches, 1¼ inches). It is the flat-sided tube which most model-makers select; with it, you can make almost any sort of ring from the most enormous dome to the most dainty shank—and, unless you have a special order for eight or so wedding bands, it is best to keep the most versatile shape in stock.

Depending upon dimensions of the rings, each tube will yield from five to ten usable sections, a very good investment since, easily, one-third of all jewelry is comprised of rings. It is appropriate that this chapter on green wax, which is devoted to techniques used regularly in the jewelry industry, should begin with the creation of a ring, in fact, one of the most successful of all ring styles: the diagonal dome ring.

Diagonal Dome Ring

Tools and Materials

Green wax ring tube (flat-sided)
Jeweler's saw with spiral blade
Eight-inch wax file
Half-round needle file, cut-4
Ring mandrel
Hollow scraper
Pro-White paint
3H Venus pencil

Fig. 5.1 Ring tubes.

124

Scribe
Tri-square escapement file, cut-3
Fiberglass eraser
Few sheets of sandpaper, 2/0, 6/0
½-inch knife-edge felt buff, hard
Felt cloth
Flexible shaft unit
Round burrs, numbers 20, 10, 4, 1, 0
Degree/ligne gauge
Mirror

Of all jewelry, a ring is perhaps the most difficult to produce well. Other ornaments—pendant, necklace, pin, even bracelet—are all worn loosely, so an occasional slight protrusion or cleft is admissible. A ring, however, must be worn snugly; the least variance from the basic circlet will render it unwearable and thus unusable as a piece of jewelry. Therefore, all functional aspects must be completed first; worry about the aesthetics later.

Determine the width of the ring at its widest point, mark off this measurement (about 2.5 cm) on the ring tube and saw off the section (Fig. 5.2a). Generally, it is best to use the jeweler's saw with the spiral blade set in place, sawing all around the tube gradually instead of attempting to cut cleanly through; in this way you are assured of a straight cut so that there will be no waste—either on the section you intend to use now or on the next one to be cut from the tube. If you prefer to use a hacksaw, make sure that the tube is cut flat-side down; undue pressure on the shank will snap inches off the tube, as will any inadvertent twisting of the blade as you use it. Remember at all times that green wax, unlike the blue and purple waxes, is quite brittle and apt to break if you are not careful.

Sizing a Ring

You must size the ring before beginning to work the design into it. Sizing a ring, like all matters in which shrinkage is a potential factor, is determined according to whether the piece is to be unique or to be used in production. For those rings which are intended for a particular customer, simply make the wax a quarter-size smaller than the correct ring size; this will allow you to polish the inside of the shank smooth in the metal and arrive at the proper size. For rings which are to be reproduced in quantity, the model-maker generally makes his wax "stock-size": size-6 for women, size-8½ for men. In order to have the finished cast piece come out stock size, however, the model-maker must take into account not only the increase in size which will occur through polishing, but the reduction in size through shrinkage. Generally, a ring intended for stock is made three-quarters of a size larger than the size intended; 7-scant for

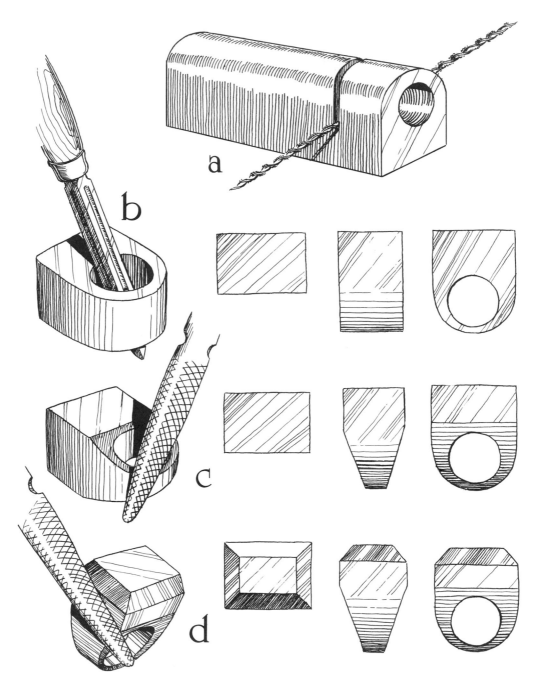

Fig. 5.2   a. Sawing section from ring tube. b. Opening the bore with hollow scraper.
c. Shaping the shank. d. Beveling the top surface.

126

women, 9-full for men (there are no quarter-sizes in jeweler's jargon, only exact and half sizes; sizes between are designated either "full" or "scant").

In order to begin, you need a measuring device to gauge ring sizes. The standard tool used for this purpose is a ring mandrel (see Chapter 6, Fig. 6.5). Ring mandrels come in several styles: the solid steel mandrel which is used by jewelers to hammer rings a size or so larger; the plastic mandrel which is used only to measure the rings; and the hollow steel mandrel which I would recommend for your purposes here. It is light, relatively inexpensive, accurate, and you can do sizing in wax directly on it: a task which is cumbersome with the heavier solid mandrel and impossible with the plastic one. (Some jeweler's benches, incidentally, come equipped with holes bored to accommodate the ring mandrel: a nice luxury which allows you to use both hands in working the wax.)

The tube is already bored to fit a size-4 finger; your job is to open it to a 7-scant. It is not easy to file a perfectly circular opening. For the professional, for whom time is money, the easiest, most precise method of getting the wax to stock size is to buy a ½-inch rotary wood file from a hardware store and bore out the hole with it. Unfortunately, the shaft for this useful tool is too thick to fit into your Faro handpiece; a number-30 chuck-style handpiece is needed. Of course, the same method can be used with the largest cylindrical burr in your tool box; it will take longer, but if you are careful you should have the same successful results.

However, I have found that the surest way to make a precise circle is to use the half-round part of the large wax file, working the file under even pressure and turning the ring after each stroke, then working the ring from the other side after completing one full turn. When the shank is about 1½ sizes smaller than intended, take up the hollow scraper, which is ideal for opening up the shank of the ring. Unlike a file, it does not leave marks. Simply place it inside the opening of the ring and, using an action which resembles peeling a potato, scrape the wax away lightly until you are a half-size away from completing the job (Fig. 5.2b). The final touches can be done with a very fine half-round needle file or with 4/0 sandpaper rolled around a ½-inch dowel. One complete turn around the ring should be sufficient to smooth out whatever marks the hollow scraper left and to open up the ring the remaining half-size. Double-check the finished opening on the ring mandrel, both for size and for roundness. Do not press the ring down in place since even this brittle wax will expand under pressure; you will not get a true reading—and you might scratch the shank, if not break it. Instead, ease it down the mandrel until it rests lightly with its bottom edge on the designated spot.

Shaping the Shank

Generally, before any work is done on the crown (top) of a ring, the shank is formed. The reason for this is simple; the ring must be com-

127

fortable to wear. If you begin with the crown, you might arrive at proportions which would render the shank too thick and, therefore, bulky between the fingers. In correcting this mistake, there is a good possibility that the aesthetic integrity of the ring would be destroyed. Too much bad jewelry is mix-and-match, with crowns arbitrarily soldered onto shanks, regardless of how terrible the two look together. All too often the shank is considered a purely functional element, something which enables the ornament to be worn; but a ring shank is seen and, therefore, must be considered part of the design.

To begin, you must determine how thick the shank is to be, and how wide. Unless the ring is intended for a customer with very large knuckles, the shank should nowhere exceed a thickness of 2 to 3 millimeters, the thinest point being in the back and gradually thickening as it approaches the juncture with the crown. So begin by rough-filing the shank of the ring from the back and working your way around to the sides. Leave a healthy thickness, say 4 millimeters, on all sides except, of course, the thickest side designated for the crown. Ideally, the crown should not exceed the outer diameter of the circlet. Even at this rough stage, you should taper the shank gracefully up toward the front of the ring. If the crown needs reduction, the shank can always be reduced in turn.

After the thickness has been shaped, turn your attention to the side view, the width. From this angle, the ring is still unformed, top and bottom describing two parallel lines. Leaving the crown section untouched, and beginning at the front edge of the bore, begin to file your material away at an angle so that the top and bottom will form two converging lines (Fig. 5.2c). To make certain that the two lines form equal angles, scratch a mark midway across the width in the very back of the shank. File the wax to within 4 millimeters of the mark on either side so that the width of the ring, at this stage, will be 8 millimeters.

Shaping the Crown

Only after the function of the shank has been attended to, should you approach the main aspect of the model. First determine how high a dome you want, file down as much material as you need to reach that height, then file a uniform bevel around the entire top of the ring (Fig. 5.2d). Then round out the entire dome, blending the form of the crown gracefully into the shank. This rounding-out is perhaps the most important of all the steps; if the basic dome is clumsy, or flat, or lopsided, no amount of detail work can make the ring acceptable as a commercial model. *A model should be as perfect as possible at every stage in its creation.* In rounding out the dome, more work is done with the eye than with the hand, more time is spent in checking than in filing. Do not attempt to finish one side and move on to the other; rather, work around the ring, three strokes on one side, three strokes on the other, then check.

128

Use your large wax file, taking long even swipes. Do not scrub the file back and forth to take down the material quickly. If your stroke looks graceful as you are working, the results will tend to be graceful. When you are satisfied that the basic shape has been successfully formed, that it blends well into the shank, that it is symmetrical no matter how you view it, lay the large file aside and take up either the fiberglass brush or the hollow scraper—whichever you feel more comfortable using. Lightly scrape the tool across the entire surface of the ring—both crown and shank—until all file marks have been eradicated and all minor irregularities in the symmetry have been smoothed away (Fig. 5.3a). You have just created a basic dome ring which requires only polishing and hollowing to be ready for production. However, our project is to make a diagonal dome ring; therefore you must take the model one step further.

Incising the lines diagonally across the surface of the dome demands planning. Good design requires a definite relationship between the external form of an object and the details with which it is adorned. Simply scribing in lines that are uniformly spaced, as might be your first impulse, does not take into account the fact that the ring itself is higher and wider in the very front and slimmer and flatter down the sides. The lines, then, should be more widely spaced at the front and gradually come closer together as they approach the shank on either side. This is more difficult to accomplish than uniform spacing, but much more pleasing to the eye.

Depending upon your self-confidence, there are several ways to arrange the pattern of diagonal lines on the dome. You can, of course, do it freehand, but at this stage in your development as a model-maker, I would suggest that you take as many precautions as possible. To avoid marring the surface with scratch marks, first paint the entire dome with Pro-White or any other non-crawl water paint (available at art supply stores), and do the marking lightly in pencil. Start from the center and work your way down both sides concurrently; indicate the spacing with dots, the widest apart being at the center and the most closely spaced at each end. Do not go beyond the midpoint of the shank; excessive figuring too far down on the shank will render the ring uncomfortable to wear.

Once the spacing has been determined, the lines themselves are drawn. A straight line drawn across the dome is fairly easily accomplished; however, it is also fairly graceless. In this case try for an extended S shape which rises from the shank, crosses the crown diagonally, and disappears down the other shank (Fig. 5.3b). There is no rule for the arrangement of these lines. Begin at the middle, in order to arrange the general shape of your diagonal; then, working one line to the left and one to the right of the center mark, define the entire pattern, relying more on your eye and good taste than on absolute mathematical symmetry. After the pencil lines have been drawn, scribe them into the wax, and wash the paint off.

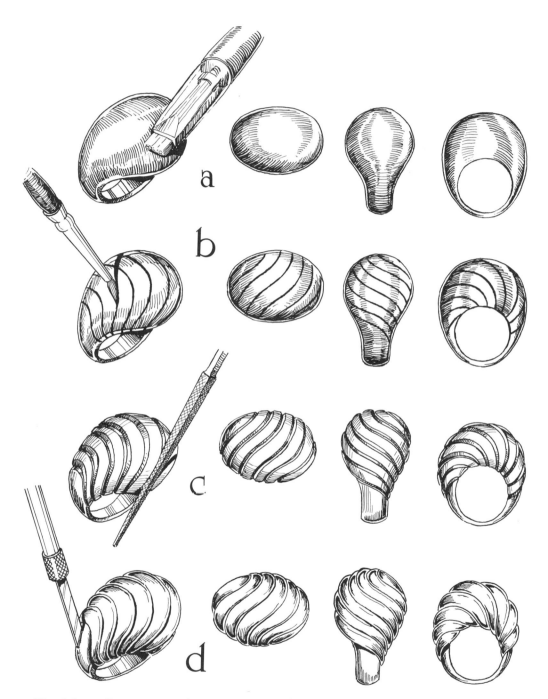

Fig. 5.3 a. Removing surface irregularities. b. Drawing the pattern onto the dome. c. Incising channels with a tri-corner file. d. Shaping shank so diagonals appear to wrap around it.

130

Working now with a tri-corner file, always beginning from the center, cut a V-shaped channel through each diagonal line. Try to cut the entire channel with just one or two graceful strokes, instead of many short uncertain ones. The flow of your entire design depends upon the grace of each line. Do not cut the channels deeply; one or two light strokes per line will do at the outset. Your objective is to make a series of ridges, the highest being on the top, and the lowest being down toward the shank; therefore, the cuts must be deepest at the very top of the dome. You will know you have achieved the proper depth when the sloped sides of each ridge are the same width as the top (Fig. 5.3c). When this proportion has been achieved on every ridge, using either a number-4 stencil knife or a fiberglass brush, round off each ridge.

Now you must define the juncture of crown and shank. As it looks now, the shank is on the same level as the last ridge, making the entire section appear clumsy. In order to render this part of the ring graceful, the shank should be scraped down, so that the ridges appear to be wrapping around the shank (Fig. 5.3d). To complete the illusion, round off the edges of each ridge, so that the design does not end abruptly where it touches the finger. Shape the shank so that it truly becomes one with the crown, doming it slightly at the sides and bringing it down to 1 millimeter in the back; sand it, and polish it with the knife-edged felt buff, making sure that a uniform border is maintained on both edges.

Hollowing Out a Dome

Hollowing out the inside of a ring—or any piece of jewelry for that matter—requires as much technical consideration as the formation of the outside, and probably more skill. It is an essential aspect of jewelry-making, for both economic and functional reasons. Most fine jewelry is cast in gold and silver; therefore, the model-maker must be concerned not only with the aesthetics of a piece, the relative ease of producing it in quantity, and its ultimate comfort when worn, but with the cost in metal. For most orders, he must try to shave down as much material as possible from the inside of the model in order to give the illusion of heft without the cost. Many ladies' rings are actually no thicker than 0.6 millimeter in the wax model. Thanks to the wonderful properties of gold, these models can be produced without mishap; however, the model-maker, working with almost no margin for error, must always be aware of the exact thickness of any given wax.

There is also a purely functional aspect to hollowing out the back of a piece of jewelry. In many cases, a very heavy ornament is simply inappropriate, while—at the same time—the design calls for a large piece. Such is frequently the case with earrings. Often style demands extremely large forms, but the very nature of an earring prohibits any sort of weight. Therefore, earrings have always been rendered as thin and as light as possible. Similarly, brooches, which have the tendency to pull and tear

131

the fabric of a dress by sheer gravity, should be made fairly light. You are also less likely to encounter porosity in a piece which requires less metal.

In order to grind a piece of wax down to 0.75 millimeter (your goal here), the jeweler really has no recourse but to use the flexible shaft unit; all other methods—gouging, melting, scraping—are either too primative or require too much physical pressure on the wall of the piece to be safe and effective. Hollowing requires the light, steady touch which only the flexible shaft unit can provide. It is a sizeable investment, but if you intend to produce professional quality work, there is no way around it.

The flexible shaft unit must be hung from a pole or pipe secured into the top of the workbench (see Chapter 2, Fig. 2.12). A pipe approximately the correct height is sold at jeweler's supply houses. Should you be unable to obtain one, three feet of one-inch diameter brass pipe—available in plumbing supply and good hardware stores—threaded into the appropriate sized drilled wall plate, and equipped with a hook on the top, will do nicely. Do not hang the motor from the ceiling by means of a chain; the excessive movement will undermine all attempts at precision in carving. Do not hang the motor from a bracket on the wall; the angle of the shaft will be too steep, and gravity will make manipulation of the tool difficult. Set the pole into the top of the bench so that the base is as much out of your way as possible and the bottom of the shaft—minus the handpiece—rests to the right of the benchpin on a level with the top of the bench. The pole will have to be bent, so that the base is well out of your working space, toward the very back of the bench, while the motor hangs forward. Secure the pole with three wood screws; and attach the rheostat behind the bench so that the foot pedal is conveniently placed. Snap the handpiece into the shaft, making sure that the metal rod that projects from the shaft engages completely in the hollow C-shaped tube in the handpiece.

Before you attempt to work on a model which has taken many hours, it is good practice to test the equipment on a spare piece of wax. Insert a round burr, number-8 or larger, into the handpiece. (If you have a Faro model, do not push the burr in as far as it will go; it will become quite difficult to remove if you do. Instead, insert the burr three-quarters of the way and close the handle slowly. Be careful: the handle has a very strong spring mechanism which can close on your finger. If you have a number-30 model, open the chuck by turning the key counterclockwise until the opening is sufficient to accomodate the burr, then, reversing the direction of the key, tighten it in place.) Step down lightly on the foot pedal; if it slides around under the bench, buy a small rubber mat for traction. Try to vary the speed of the drill, just by altering the pressure of your foot.

The highest speed—the one you attain by flooring the pedal—should be used only when grinding down very large areas with a very large burr. No matter how well-oiled your motor, shaft and handpiece might be, there will always be some vibration. The fewer the rotations per minute, the less pronounced will be the vibration. Since the slowest speed will cut the wax as effectively as the highest, opt for the procedure which will allow you maximum control over the tool.

I have found that the best grip to use on the flexible shaft handpiece is the one with which one naturally grasps a pencil or pen, especially if you have the narrow Faro-style handpiece. The only difference is that, in writing, the stroke generally moves away from you, while in carving with the drill, the stroke moves toward you. The burr rotates counter-clockwise; if you attempt to push the tool, the teeth cannot grip into the wax properly and the possibility of losing control becomes great.

This tool was designed for use on metal. Think how much lighter your touch must be on wax, which can be scratched with a fingernail. Control must be maintained at all times, both in the foot pressure on the rheostat and in the pressure of your hand on the wax. Part of the secret in controlling the handpiece rests also in how well you have braced your arm and hand. The elbow should be braced on the armrest; the hand should be braced on the bench pin. If possible, at least the little finger should also be utilized as a brace, pressed against the front of the bench while the rest of the hand directs the tool.

When you feel that you have practiced long enough on the scrap, you may begin work on the wax model. There are two ways to hollow out a ring: you can take your finest piercing blade and saw through the shank at the midpoint of each side, exposing the inside of the crown to the burr without obstruction (Fig. 5.4a), or else you can hollow the piece just as it is. For now, I would recommend the latter method. There is always the possibility of the crown becoming slightly distorted when worked to 0.75 millimeter, making rejoining with the thicker shank inexact. Also, it is good practice to learn how to manipulate the handpiece from every angle—not just straight down.

Before beginning, you must arrange a proper light source to determine the approximate thickness of the wax. This light source must be behind the wax—not the entire time, just when you approach the desired thickness. Most model-makers can gauge the thickness of a piece by noting the color of the wax when light passes through it. This procedure has one drawback: if the light must be behind the piece, then it also must shine directly into your eyes. Hollowing out a wax model is tedious enough without straining your eyes.

One solution to this problem is simply to set a mirror up on your bench pin so that the light from your bench light reflects from it through the piece. Another solution is to drill a ½-inch hole into your bench pin at a 45-degree angle so that a small pocket flashlight can be set into the opening. For my own work, I have designed an illuminated bench pin (an idea which a fellow model-maker suggested to me) which I hope to

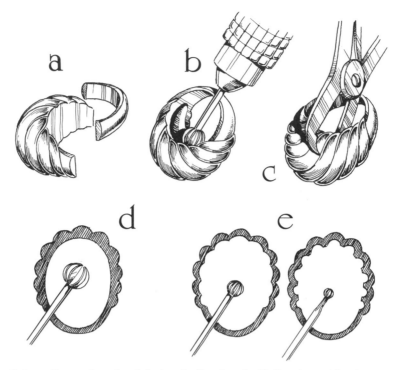

Fig. 5.4 a. Removing shank before hollowing. b. Hollowing with a large round burr. c. Measuring thickness with a degree gauge. d. Cross section of ring. e. Improper and proper hollowing.

market in the near future. With it, the bench pin becomes the light source so that you can work the piece from the back as naturally and as easily as if you were modeling the front.

To begin, load your largest round burr into the flexible shaft handpiece. Always use the largest burr possible in any situation; the result will be a smooth, uniformly thick wall. With this round burr, try to remove all material from the inside of the crown to the midpoint of the shank, where the cut should end gracefully in a rounded taper (Fig. 5.4b). Work slowly and carefully, checking the thickness of the piece regularly by lightly closing the jaws of the degree gauge into any diagonal groove on the crown (Fig. 5.4c); when the gauge uniformly reads 0.85 millimeter in all grooves as well as the wall of the shank where you have hollowed it out, stop and change burrs.

If you look through the crown, you will see an alternating pattern of light and darker green lines which will match the pattern of the diagonal lines on the front surface. The lighter lines represent the grooves where you have already approximated the correct thickness for the piece; the darker lines represent the ridges which are still thicker than the rest of the piece. In order to bring the thickness of the ridges into consonance with the rest, you will have to rely on matching the color throughout the
134

piece. Before you even begin to work, it is a good idea to envision the piece in cross section (Fig. 5.4d). The grooves represent the thinnest sections, while the crests of the ridges are the thickest. In order to make everything a uniform thickness, you must reduce the crest and the sides of the ridge to the same gauge. If you rely on one steady light source shining directly through the piece, the crest and the grooves will reach the correct thickness, but the walls of the ridge will become much too thin (Fig. 5.4e). In order to overcome this phenomenon, you must check the color from several angles.

Select a burr which will leave enough wall on the sides of the ridge while scooping out the desired thickness under the crest. Depending upon the variety of the surface pattern you may have to employ several, or even many, burrs. This is slow and painstaking work, but so essential that I have yet to meet a model-maker—or any other person knowledgeable in the jewelry business—who will not scrutinize the inside of a model for at least as long as he studies the outside surface. Try to work with the burrs for as long as you can, taking down the material to within 0.1 millimeter of the desired thickness. When the light shows uniform color throughout the entire inner surface, stop and take up the fiberglass brush. Brush the inside of the piece lightly until all sign of the burr marks is removed, and an even, lightly textured surface remains.

Texturing

Many model-makers do not go beyond this point in the wax, waiting for the metal model to come back from the caster in order to polish the inside smooth or to texture it further. Texturing is much more safely done in metal; however, some customers prefer that the piece, texturing and all, be done entirely in wax. Texturing is necessary simply because of economics. It takes time and several operations to bright-polish the inside of a ring; pit-marks are liable to show; imperfections due to improper working of the wax are liable to show. Texturing eliminates all of these; one buffing and the inside is done—and the piece is lighter also.

The standard ring texture consists of a pattern of closely spaced tiny craters created by touching a small round burr momentarily to the wax. Depending upon the level of precision you wish to attain, this texture may be as even as a golf ball or as irregular as scrambled eggs. But you must be really careful of going too deep with the burr; one bit of extra pressure can drive it completely through the wax. Adding unnecessary time onto your labors. A very light buffing over the outside surface of the piece with a felt cloth will finish up the piece.

SIGNET RING

While each year produces a wealth of new designs for ladies' rings, there are, unfortunately, only a few men's styles which have attained respectability; these are the signet ring and its variants, and the basic gypsy mounting designed to accomodate a fairly large cabochon stone. It is, however, amazing to note just how many variations of these two basic models exist. The signet ring is available with a round-shaped top, an oval-shaped top, a square top, a cushion-shaped top, a cushion-square top, an emerald-shaped top, hexagonal and octogonal tops, to name only the more traditional forms. The shanks also exhibit great variety. They can be flat, angular, domed, carved with any number of beasts or devices, textured or bright. The combinations of signet shape and shank style possible make this a very versatile model, which has been popular for over a hundred years and will, no doubt, be popular for a hundred more.

The other ring which is the mainstay of the man's ring market is the gypsy ring with a stone setting. Like the signet, this ring is also available in a wide variety of shapes—depending upon the stone selected and the style of the shank. Both rings are very simple to make; in fact, the gypsy ring is basically a signet ring with its seal replaced by a stone.

Therefore, for this second project, you will first make a signet ring, and then make a stone mounting from it. Before beginning you must decide what kind of stone you ultimately will set into it. For men's rings there are basically three types of stones: flat or slightly cushioned stones, cabochon stones, and faceted stones—in that order of popularity. Opaque stones are almost invariably contained in the first two categories. Lapis, bloodstone, onyx and sardonyx are the most popular stones for men's jewelry; and, whether the cut is flat or cabochon, whether the shape is round or square, all these stones are perfectly flat underneath. It is with the undersurface that the model-maker is primarily concerned. Faceted stones are usually associated with ladies' jewelry, because the prong setting, by permitting light to reach the faceting, highlights the brilliance of the gem. However, certain faceted stones—the garnet, ruby, and aquamarine in particular—are traditionally used in men's rings. A faceted stone does not have a flat underside; like an iceberg, most of it lies below the surface when the stone is set. It should be obvious that a faceted stone will, of necessity, require much greater depth of seat than a cabochon or flat stone—if you do not want the point of the pavilion (the underside) to puncture the wearer's finger.

For this ring, use a typical oval stone, a cabochon 16 by 12 millimeters to determine the size of the mounting. First, however, you will make a basic signet ring, using the size and shape of the stone as a guide; the top of the ring, the seal, should measure approximately 19 by 15 millimeters when it is finished, allowing a 1½-millimeter border around the stone.

Tools and Materials

> 28-millimeter section of flat-sided green wax ring tube
> Cabochon stone, 16 by 12 millimeters

Eight-inch wax file
Barette needle file, cut-3
Hollow scraper
Fiberglass brush
Sandpaper, number-2/0
Wheel felt buff, hard
Flexible shaft unit
Burrs: round, numbers 20, 10, 2
       cylinder, numbers 6, 2
       cone square, number 10
Calipers
Degree/ligne gauge

A signet ring is a very simple piece of jewelry. But you will often discover that the simple pieces are the most difficult to make. When a piece has many components, or individual details, the eye is so continually distracted from one element to the next that a critical appraisal of the underlying geometry of an oval, or a circle, is avoided. In a very simple piece that contains no such detail, the least variance from precise symmetry becomes obvious. Therefore, you must approach this ring, not as an artist, but as a technician, relying more on measuring devices than on your eyes. You will be making what is called a "master model."

Master Model

In the jewelry business there are, basically, three types of models. The first is the unique piece which technically is not a model at all, since no rubber mold is made from it. It is cast, cleaned, polished and sold as a one-of-a-kind piece. The second type of model is the one which is almost the standard assignment for all wax model-makers: the model which is intended for reproduction in quantity. This model is created with the understanding that it will never be worn, but that finished pieces will be made from its rubber mold. In making it, the model-maker must take into consideration the shrinkage factor, the realization that details will be softened in the rubber mold, the possibility of distortion, ease in polishing the piece in quantity, and many other factors involved in mass production. The third type of model is the master model and, as its name implies, it is a model from which other models are made. It is usually a fairly simple piece which, when reproduced by rubber mold, is altered either in the casting wax by the model-maker or in the cast metal reproduction by the jeweler to create dozens of variants on the basic pattern, each variant then becoming an original model from which the finished jewelry is reproduced. The master model, then, will undergo a double shrinkage; first, when it is reproduced to make the basic structural model; then, when that altered model is reproduced to make the finished piece of jewelry. It will undergo a double distortion, as well, and a double softening of detail; therefore, when the model-maker is forced to confront the prospect of producing a master model, he knows that everything must be as absolutely precise and as sharp as possible. He knows, also, that he must account for that double shrinkage factor. In short, he must do a good deal of thinking ahead.

Planning Dimensions

A fortunate model-maker will receive a very good, detailed rendering from the designer. The rendering, if it is really precise, will show the ring from the front, from the side, and from the top. If there are no further instructions, it is to be assumed that the dimensions which are shown on the rendering are the dimensions intended for the finished piece, *exactly*. Unless you enjoy a good rapport with the designer, do not presume to alter any aspect of his sketch in the model—especially if he has provided you with three views of it. If something seems incorrect or inappropriate to you, question him before beginning; otherwise proceed according to his blueprints. The first thing that you must do is measure the height and width of the seal, the width of the shank at its thinnest point, the thickness of the shank, and the height of the crown (Fig. 5.5a). Note these dimensions either very lightly on the sketch or, preferably, on a piece of tracing paper. Keep in mind that these are the dimensions of the *finished* piece. You are making the grandparent of the finished piece: the master model, and, before you can even begin to work on the wax, you must revise all these dimensions to compensate for the double shrinkage which will occur. Therefore, if the seal measures 19 by 15 by 5 millimeters on the drawing, you must make your model about twenty percent larger than you intend the finished piece to be—not ten percent as in previous projects.

The twenty percent shrinkage is in total volume—and you must be concerned only with the external dimensions. You cannot arrive at the correct adjustment by adding twenty percent on to the measurements; the resulting volume will be far too great. Nor is there a precise mathematical formula, since you are not dealing with geometric forms, but with irregularly shaped objects. Therefore, the adjustment must, of necessity, be approximate. I have found that an addition of 0.5 millimeter for each 10 millimeters in any given dimension of a model should allow ample room for ten percent shrinkage. This rule, of course, is only approximate, especially since the larger a piece is, the greater will be the amount of shrinkage proportionally. Therefore, if you were making a standard model, the measurements would be increased to about 20 by 15.75 by 5.5 millimeters. For a master model, you must further increase the proportions to approximately 21 by 16.5 by 6 millimeters: measurements which should more than make up for the shrinkage factor.

138

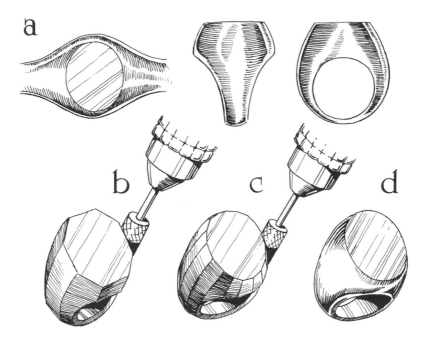

Fig. 5.5   a. Different views of a signet ring. b. Angling the wax. c. Rounding off the corners. d. The completed model.

Carving the Signet

Begin your signet by sawing off a section of flat-end ring tube, about 28 millimeters wide. Size it as before, taking into consideration the double shrinkage. Therefore, intending size-8½, you must make it size-10 (three-quarters of a size larger, twice); when the model is finished it should look like a well-proportioned ring intended for a large man. For the shaping of this model, you have a choice of tools. You may work with a large wax file and smaller needle files as you did before, or you may use the flexible shaft machine.

The flexible shaft machine, far from being confined to hollowing out models where only a rotary motion can accomplish the task, is literally able to substitute for almost any implement in your toolbox—the only exception being your very finest knives, files, and buffs. In the practiced hand, it can grind down material as smoothly as a file, and it can do it with more grace and much more speed. A change of burr and a line as sharp as a knife could produce is inscribed into the wax. Of course, this takes time and practice, but once you have mastered the use of this tool, you will be loath to exchange it for any other.

The first tool you would ordinarily have reached for would have been the coarse wax file, in order to remove large sections of wax quickly and give the ring its rough form. Instead, use your largest, number-20 cylindrical burr; working systematically, define the planes of the piece, just as you would do with a file. A word of caution; the danger in working

139

with the flexible shaft does not lie in the fact that the instrument is difficult to handle; it lies in the fact that it can be too easy. There is practically no resistence to the cutting implement; because of the great speed of the tool, there is always the temptation to eliminate steps, to grind the material away carelessly, and to begin the final shaping of the piece before the basic proportions have been achieved correctly. Therefore, you must deliberately slow down the work pace until you are accustomed to the power of the tool.

With the large cylindrical burr, first angle the piece symmetrically (Fig. 5.5b), then round off the corners until the basic rough shape of the ring is formed. The strokes which should be employed are different for the two parts of this operation. For the angling, try to sweep the tool deliberately over the surface, as if you were peeling a potato, maintaining an even, fairly heavy pressure until the proper proportions have been achieved. For the rounding, the stroke should be much lighter, barely touching the surface of the wax. These strokes should work away the sharp angles in several directions until a rounded, although fairly irregular, effect is the result (Fig. 5.5c). At this point, the large burr should be exchanged for a smaller number-six cylinder and the surface again worked and refined until the proportions begin to approach the set of measurements. Change the burr again, to a small number-four crosscut cone-square, and play it lightly over the wax, until you come to within 1 millimeter of each of your measurements.

Now you should return to your set of files to finish the job. With files, you will be able to work more slowly, thereby attaining the correct dimensions without the danger of grinding away too much material. The file's cutting surface is broader, so the flat signet on top can be leveled in a few strokes. The cutting surface is also finer than the burr's, requiring less finishing work with sandpaper. And when you come right down to it, you have more control over your cutting implement. Once a model has been formed and fairly well finished by the flexible shaft machine, it is almost always advisable to do the refining and finishing operations by hand. After the file, finish by using the fiberglass brush, then sandpaper, then the felt buff, and finally a felt cloth. Hollow the inside to 1½ millimeters; and the basic signet ring is complete (Fig. 5.5d). If, however, the ring is to be converted to a stone setting, the hollowing out should not be done until later.

RING WITH STONE SETTING

Stones generally come in standard sizes—12/10 millimeters, 16/14 millimeters and so on—but these dimensions only pertain to the measurement across the widest and longest parts of the stone, called the girdle. The height of a cabochon, however, is in no way dependent upon the length and the width of the stone. Nor is the depth of the pavilion, in faceted stones, really based upon the dimensions of the girdle. The

140

height of a stone is related more to the dimensions of the rough stone from which it is cut. Obviously, even in a quest for uniformity the lapidary will not polish away perfectly good gemstone; it is enough that he has to conform to certain standard widths and lengths. Therefore, two stones, both having the same measurements across the girdle, may vary in weight by several or even many carats. It is the stone-setter who must compensate for the dissimilarity between one stone and the next, shaping his mountings to fit each individual stone; and the model-maker must help by allowing as much freedom of play as possible. When designing a mounting for a faceted stone, the seat should be deep enough to accommodate even the most bottom-heavy stone. Most stones will be lighter but they may certainly be accommodated in the same mounting—and the illusion of depth will make them appear more substantial. Similarly, the seat for the flat-backed cabochon stone should be deep enough to grip the most highly domed stone; the mounting may always be ground down to fit stones which slope more gently.

Cabochon Setting

To convert the basic signet ring into a ring mounting; you must be sure that the height of the crown is able to sustain the depth of the stone below the girdle. For a cabochon stone, on the finished ring simply allow 2 millimeters for the bezel to grip the stone and another 2 millimeters for the thickness of the seat (Fig. 5.6a). Translated into the master model, the height of the crown should gauge at least 5 millimeters.

With a scribe, outline the dimensions of the stone directly onto the flat shield of the signet, aiming for a uniform border of 1 millimeter on the finished piece—which means almost 2 millimeters on the master model (Fig. 5.6b). Then, with a number-4 cylindrical burr, cut straight down into the shield until you have removed as much material as is required to define both bezel and seat. Reline it by scraping all inner surfaces carefully with a number-4 X-Acto and polishing with a felt buff cut to size. Then, in order to lighten the weight of the ring as well to aid the setter in maneuvering the stone, insert the same cylindrical burr into the center of the seat and grind away a hole until only a 3-millimeter border remains (Fig. 5.6c). Finish off the bore with a half-round file (Fig. 5.6d).

The only real difficulty in making such a mounting lies in gauging the dimensions of the opening itself. Unique pieces are the exception; the opening on the model should be *exactly* the dimensions of the stone, so that when the piece is cast, the stone will fit snugly into the mounting, and the setter has but to burnish the metal over it. If, however, the piece is intended for reproduction, shrinkage must be considered. Make the opening *slightly* bigger than the stone which is to fit into it. To test the size of the opening, place the stone into the wax mounting. Shift it around with your finger; a slight play will be sufficient to account for shrinkage.

141

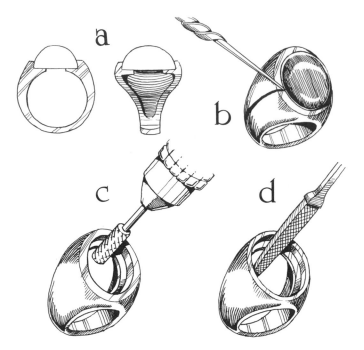

Fig. 5.6   a. Cross section of cabochon setting. b. Scribing the stone's outline. c. Creating the bezel. d. Finishing touches.

For master models, where shrinkage is a real factor, you should actually be able to see a thin border separating the stone from the lip of the mounting. As in most cases where shrinkage must be determined, only experience can really guide you. However, if you must choose between extremes, make the opening rather too tight than too loose. The stone setter can always grind away the metal to make his fit; he cannot add it.

Faceted Stone Setting

As for the mounting of the faceted stone, it naturally would require a much higher crown than a cabochon stone. If the stone is 16 by 12 millimeters, you should allow a height of at least 9 millimeters in order to accommodate the pavilion of the stone as well as to allow the setter enough material to push over the girdle. A fairly safe guideline is to allow half the length of the stone for the pavilion plus 1 millimeter for gripping the stone. Therefore, adding in shrinkage, the master model should allow 11 millimeters.

Once the height of the crown is computed, the rest of the operation is as simple as cutting the bezel for the cabochon stone—simpler, because you do not have to worry about cutting a seat for the stone; the stone-setter will do all that. We have only to provide a modified funnel-like hole which will be cut entirely through the crown (Fig. 5.7a). The measurements for the top opening should be gauged according to the guide-

142

line established for the cabochon stone. The hole, though, instead of being cut straight down in perpendicular walls as with the previous mounting, should become smaller the deeper it goes. Such a cut conforms to the general orientation of the stone's pavilion, and it also allows the setter the freedom to compensate for minor irregularities in the size and cut of a stone; a stone which is slightly smaller will simply be set down deeper into the hole. The angle should be about 65 degrees. First drill straight through the crown with a 3/32-inch twist drill (Fig. 5.7c). Then change to a number-10 crosscut cone-square and carefully open the center hole. The angle of the burr will naturally help form the correct angle for the setting (Fig. 5.7d). Finish off the hole with a half-round escapement file, cut-3 (Fig. 5.7e).

This type of mounting is much simpler to accomplish than a cabochon mounting; it is also more versatile, since it can accommodate not only faceted stones but cabochon as well. The stone-setter simply has to cut his seat with an inverted cone burr and the stone is fitted. Obviously, faceted stones cannot be set into mountings intended for cabochons. Why then even bother at all with strictly cabochon mountings? There are several reasons. Aesthetically, the very high crown might serve to dwarf a low cabochon or flat stone. Practically, a very high cabochon set into a very high crown makes a very unwieldy ring for a man to wear except on state occasions (theoretically, a man will select only one ring and wear

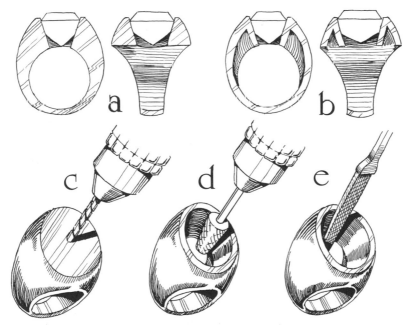

Fig. 5.7 a. Cross section of faceted stone setting. b. Setting after hollowing out. c. Drilling to start hole. d. Defining the slope of the walls. e. Finishing with a half-round file.

143

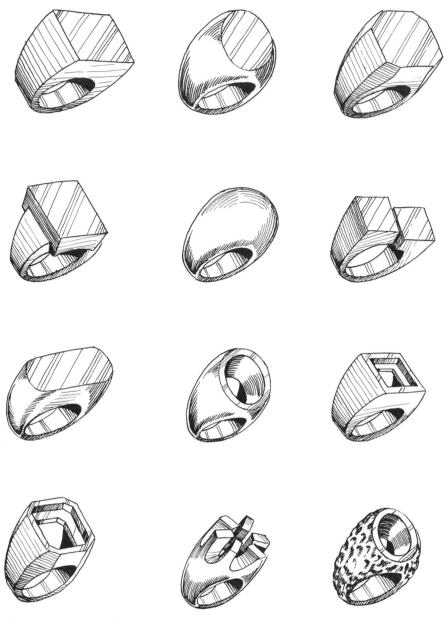

Fig. 5.8 Wax ring blanks.

it every day for a lifetime, while a woman is thought to have an assortment of rings, one to fit each occasion or mood). Also, the extra height in the mounting means more gold, which today means more money without any appreciable display advantage.

Of course, like all pieces of jewelry, the faceted mounting may be hollowed. But when hollowing the inside of the ring, the walls of the

144

hole must be kept intact—to at least 1.5 millimeters—in order for the setter to do his job.

The concept of the master model might be rather a complicated one to grasp at first, because so many of the measurements must be approximated. It is, however, an example of the problems which a model-maker must confront if he is to make a contribution to the industry. Admittedly, few people are called upon to make master models; almost every model which is completed is intended only to be used for the reproduction of a single style piece—but that single piece may be reproduced a thousand times.

Blanks

There is a shortcut available for model-makers who wish to make a standard model ring of a certain style. Jeweler's supply stores carry blank wax which has already been formed for you—with even the correct shrinkage factor figured in!

A blank is a wax which has been reproduced from a master model such as you have just made. Unlike the waxes intended only for casting, which are pulled from rubber molds, these waxes are reproduced in much more expensive metal molds—and are intended for carving. (Carving wax requires much more heat in order to flow than casting wax, therefore the necessity of a much more durable mold.) There are many basic styles of blanks from which to choose (Fig. 5.8), and considering the savings in time, they are actually not very expensive at all. Purchase a few styles—all the dog-work has already been done—and you may allow your imagination free rein in forming all sorts of wonderful and novel designs and patterns. However, it is not by chance that I have made mention of blanks, remarkable time-savers though they are, at the very conclusion of my discussion of wax carving. They are short-cuts and, in order to really appreciate a short-cut, you must first learn the long way around.

Chapter 6

Wax Build-Up

UP until now, I have presented the process of building up the wax only as a curative measure: to repair a piece which has been broken or accidentally filed away. However, many beautiful effects can be achieved by the judicious application of heat to wax. In order to examine the techniques involved in this process, you must first become familiar with the materials available.

SPATULAS

Spatulas come in a variety of shapes, each intended for a specific function and, if the assortment appears bewildering, there are two factors to be considered: the thickness of the metal and the shape and placement of the tip in relation to the shaft (Fig. 6.1).

In comparing the shape and direction of the tips, notice that they are either basically round or basically pointed. The round tips are used for building up larger areas, while the pointed ones are intended for detail work. Those whose tips veer off at an angle from the shaft are highly specialized instruments designed to deposit wax in difficult to reach nooks and crannies. Considering the expense of a spatula, these specialized tools are rather a luxury. I have found that they never quite fit anyway, and I am forced to make my own tool. Most model-makers save their broken or bald files for this purpose; play a torch over them until they are red-hot, allow them to cool gradually, and they are ready for shaping. If you have no spare files, a cheap screwdriver will do, or a large nail set into a wooden dowel. A hammer on an anvil will very quickly flatten and rough-shape the metal, and a few minutes at the grinding wheel will provide just the tool you need to take care of just that job.

146

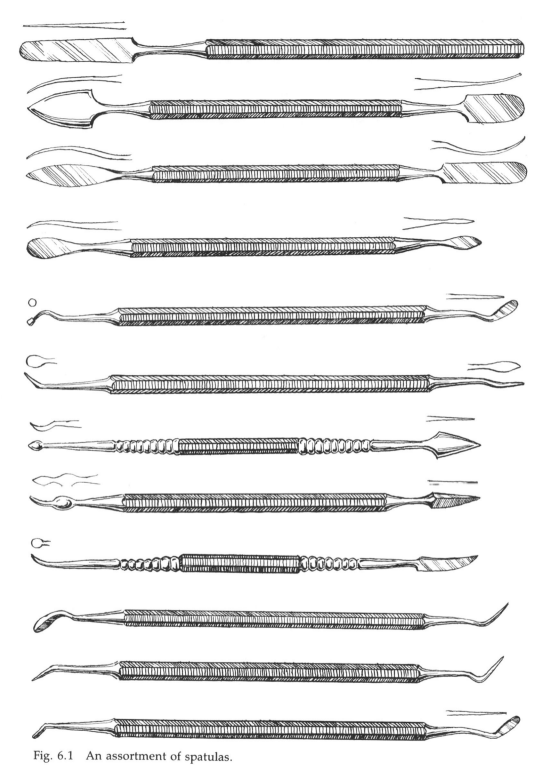

Fig. 6.1　An assortment of spatulas.

147

The second factor to be considered when selecting a spatula is the relative thickness of the metal. The thinner the metal, the more quickly it will heat and melt the wax but, conversely, the less long it will retain its heat. Very thin spatulas are most useful for spot touch-ups or building up fine details. The thicker spatulas not only build up large areas quickly, but also scoop away excess material when knife, file, or drill are not feasible tools. The level of heat may also be controlled, in some measure, when using a thicker spatula. However, for absolute control over the heat level, the perfect tool is the electric spatula.

There are several electric spatulas on the market. They are called Precision Waxers or Miniwax Welders; Kerr puts one out, as does Walter W. Giles Co. The Precision Waxer is a simple tool: no more than a sophisticated soldering gun with a thermostat which controls the heat of the interchangeable tips (Fig. 6.2). Ten minutes of experimentation with this tool will familiarize you with the relative melting points of the various types of wax you have at your disposal. Simply adjust the thermostat from its lowest to its highest setting and note the effect upon the wax.

Because the Precision Waxer is quicker and more controlled than the older method, it is preferred by most professionals in production situations, especially when dealing with waxes that melt at much lower temperatures than Ferris green. It has, however, several drawbacks: the initial expense, which is in the $60 and up price range; the care which is required to maintain the machine; and the fact that, when pin-point accuracy is demanded, the Precision Waxer is less than precise.

Waxes

Wax build-up, as well as requiring a greater array of spatulas, demands a greater variety in the wax that you use. The types of wax which may be filed and worked with an electric drill are relatively few; however, all wax may be melted, at different temperatures and with different results. Generally the preferred building types melt at relatively low temperatures when compared with the carving waxes. The two primary types are Kerr set-up wax, which comes in sheet form, and any standard casting wax.

Both of these will melt at low temperatures: but the set-up wax will remain soft and pliable for a much longer time than the casting wax, which will set to its original hardness quite quickly after melting. Neither wax can be filed with anything resembling ease; after a few swipes with the file, all the teeth will become so clogged with wax that only a wire file cleaner will be able to restore your tool. Neither wax can be worked with the flexible shaft; the heat from the friction will melt the wax and spray you with hot globules. When set, neither wax may be cut with a knife; both will shatter like pottery. You are dealing here with a very unwieldy material that demands a deft hand, if not a great amount of artistic ability, to work properly.

148

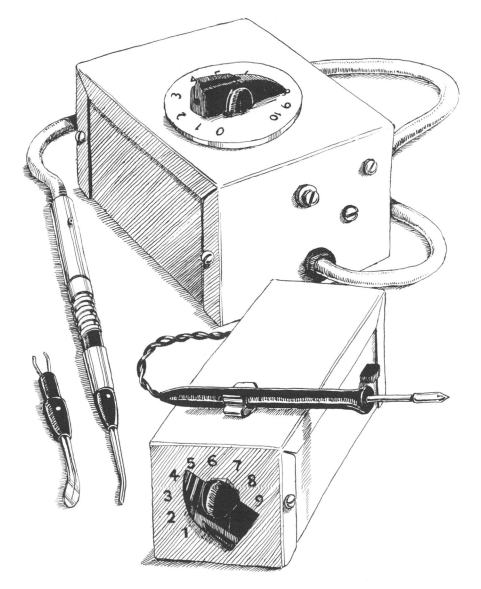

Fig. 6.2   Electric spatulas.

There are two alternatives that can also be used: Ferris blue wax and Kerr Perfect wax. The latter of these is used in conjunction with the softer waxes and will be considered later in the chapter. The former, Ferris blue, was used for the monogram in Chapter 4. Ferris blue is so pliant that a strip $\frac{1}{16}$ inch thick by 6 inches long by 1 inch wide, when immersed in boiling water, may be bent 180 degrees, retaining its new shape when cool. Like the other Ferris waxes, it may be filed and worked with the flexible shaft; however, in this case, only the coarser files and burrs are advisable. A file with a fine cut will soon clog with the stuff. The ideal

149

tool for working this wax is a knife. It carves beautifully and, even if the detail is not as precise as you might wish, extraordinarily graceful shapes can be achieved simply by carving it as you would carve a bar of soap. It is the one well-known brand of carving wax which may be readily adapted for the build-up process. While the green and purple waxes will flow like a liquid when heated, forming a flat surface, the blue wax is considerably more viscous. It will not run. Its flow can be controlled, and it will set in peaks. In short, it differs from the standard build-up waxes in only three respects; it melts at a much higher temperature, when set it contracts appreciably from its molten state—which waxes that melt at lower temperatures do not; and, when set, it may be carved.

FREE-FORM PIN

The first project is a relatively simple one; yet, from it, you will familiarize yourself with the nature of the material and the ways of approaching wax build-up.

Tools and Materials

Glass plate
Few sheets of Kerr Set-up Wax
Spoon-shaped spatula
Alcohol lamp
X-Acto knife, number-11
Glycerine (or Microfilm, or Waxlube)
Tracing paper
3H pencil
Modeling clay

Begin by doodling, by making outline drawings of pleasing shapes no bigger than 1½ inches (38 mm) in any direction. It is always a good idea, incidentally, when designing, to work on tracing paper. In that way, if a design is not quite right but almost, you simply slip a piece of tracing paper over it and make your modifications right there instead of having to begin a brand-new sketch. When you have arrived at a drawing whose proportions are pleasing, place it on the work table, put the glass on top of it, and smear a thin coat of wax lubricant onto the glass. This coat will prevent the wax from sticking to the glass with the resulting breakage of the piece when it comes time to remove it (Fig. 6.3a).

The set-up wax will melt readily, and for this piece you will need two distinctly different consistencies of wax. The first of these will be a very fluid one. Fill up the larger spoon of the spatula with liquid wax and allow it to run onto the glass, covering the drawing underneath completely to the outline (Fig. 6.3b). If you go beyond the specified borders, cut away the still-warm wax with an X-Acto knife—or else, retain the accident as part of the piece. Accidental effects are perfectly

150

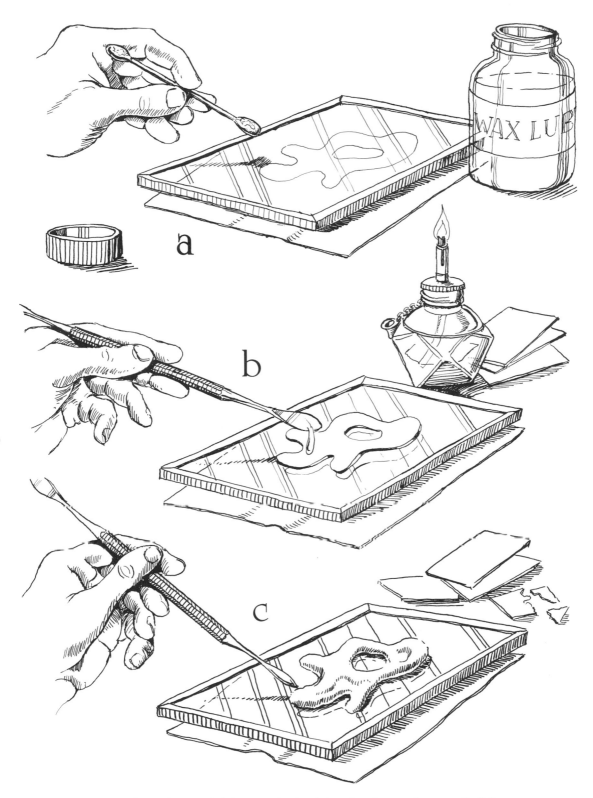

Fig. 6.3 a. Coat glass with lubricant. b. Applying first layer of wax. c. Building up a wax shape.

acceptable in model-making, provided that they become *part* of your arsenal of techniques and not the only approach. Clearly, the sketch under the piece of glass is not absolutely essential to the finished piece; however, it does provide an underlying order to your efforts, disciplining and, to some extent, controlling the spontaneity inherent in the technique.

After the wax layer has cooled, the result should be a thin, fairly flat sheet, through which the original drawing should still be visible. This first step has merely transferred the two-dimensional sketch on paper to a basically two-dimensional piece of wax; now begin the true work of the model-maker: the modulation of a form in space.

Melt the wax until it flows, but to a more viscous consistency than the first application. Using the smaller spoon of the spatula, very slowly begin to add wax (Fig. 6.3c). Every once in a while, turn the glass around or shift the light source in order to get a different point of view on the piece. If an area is becoming too clumsy, cut it away with an X-Acto knife before it cools completely. Vary the consistency of the wax for different textures. There are only two guidelines you should bear in mind. The piece should not be too high, since hollowing with the flexible shaft is impossible, and the edges should be at least 1 millimeter thick to prevent knife-edges in the final casting. This latter is easily accomplished by allowing the undercoat to flow slightly beyond the borders of the sketch and then, when the piece is completed, cutting back to the correct size with a knife (Fig. 6.4a). If the edge obtained in this manner appears too harsh, bevel the edges slightly; in the final polishing, a gentle curve will be produced.

There are several ways to hollow out the piece—none truly effective. You can use a heated spatula as a scoop, keeping a pan of cold water nearby in order to cool the wax off quickly and, thereby, prevent distortion. Or conversely, keeping a pan of very warm water nearby to keep the piece flexible, you can scrape out the inside with a round-edged knife, a small gouge, or a heavy round wax burr inserted into a mechanical pencil holder or pin vise. Both methods will lighten the piece somewhat, but most of the hollowing out must be done in the metal casting. Too much handling of the wax will leave a texture of fingerprints and grime which is almost impossible to remove. However, there is a very simple method of creating a hollow behind the piece. It does curtail some of the spontaneity of working with the wax but, in return, a great deal of unpleasant labor is avoided. Simply rough-shape the piece in regular modeling clay on the glass surface, isolate it with wax lubricant, and build up directly on the clay, covering the clay completely down to the glass plate (Fig. 6.4b). After you are finished and the wax has set, pick the piece off the plate and remove the clay from the back (Fig. 6.4c).

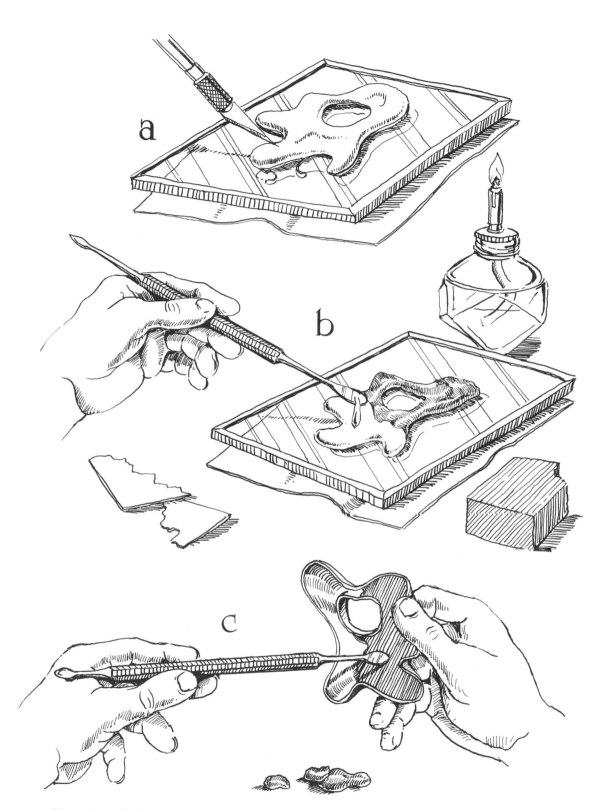

Fig. 6.4 a. Refining the outline to prevent sharp edges. b. Building wax over a clay structure. c. Removing clay from wax model.

FREE-FORM RING

The second project is a variant on the first: a ring made in the same way that the pin was made. In place of the free-form sketch, you need an exploded drawing of a ring, which should look like an opened cigar band. Cut out a strip of tracing paper, and wrap it around your finger, leaving approximately ⅛ inch (3mm) overlap. Flatten it out, put a piece of tracing paper on top of it and, using it as a guide, create a free-form pattern which, when bent around the finger, can be worn as a ring. Once this pattern has been obtained, proceed as you did with the pin, removing the wax from the glass when finished.

Immerse the wax piece in fairly hot water for a moment. You must find the exact temperature of the water by experimentation; if the water is too cold, the wax will not bend, and if it is too hot, the wax will actually melt. A good guideline is to get the water so hot that one degree hotter will burn your finger. The piece must then be bent slowly around your finger—it should take several immersions—until the ends touch. A bit of heat on the overlap will bond the ends; and the ring is ready for casting.

OPEN-WORK RING

For this project, you will use sheet wax. As you know, from Chapter 3, sheet wax comes in various thicknesses and degrees of hardness. Most were originally designed for use in dentistry, but model-makers have

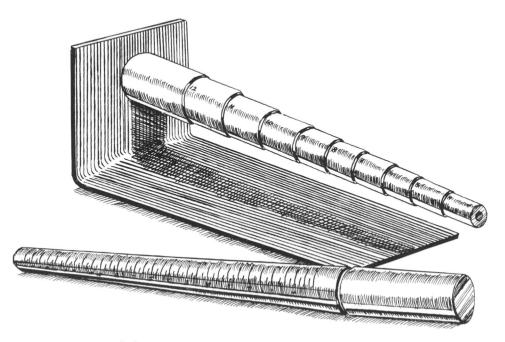

Fig. 6.5   Ring mandrels.

154

become increasingly more dependent upon sheet wax for saving time and for insuring uniform thickness in their pieces. The use of this expedient will be discussed more extensively in the next chapter, when you will use sheet wax by itself and with wax rods. For this ring, however, the sheet wax is a purely structural component, upon which you will build the piece.

If you are wondering why I have so frequently chosen rings for projects, the reason is simple; a ring is a very difficult piece of jewelry to make well and if you succeed with it, the process can always be reapplied easily to other pieces.

Tools and Materials

Spoon-shaped spatula
Alcohol lamp
X-Acto knife, number-11
Few sheets of regular pink sheet wax, gauge 22
Casting wax or Carving wax
Glycerine (or Microfilm, or Waxlube)
Saucer
Stepped ring mandrel

This last piece of equipment is a mainstay of any wax model-maker. Ring mandrels come in many price ranges but in only two distinct styles: tapered and stepped, and each has its particular function in the jewelry business (Fig. 6.5). The tapered mandrel, which is graduated through all ring sizes, is generally a solid piece of steel, around which a metal ring is sized. Because of the mandrel's solidity, a ring can be beaten a size or so larger directly on it. However, the tapering makes uniform sizing in the wax extremely difficult. The stepped mandrel is light, generally being made of aluminum (remember that wax does not stick to aluminum), and comes with a stand that makes working a ring on it an easy matter. Primarily, this mandrel is preferred because its stepped profile provides a uniform working surface at each plateau. There is also a minor graduation at each step which allows for half sizes, although, in general, extremely precise sizing is not required of the model-maker.

Cutting Pattern

First decide how wide the band is to be and whether it is to be uniform or tapered in width, Then, make a tracing of the pattern on a piece of paper. Prepare the mandrel by dabbing it with wax lubricant at the narrower side of the desired size step. Filling a shallow dish with warm water, immerse about one-third of a sheet, and when it begins to bend slightly, cut it off. Never attempt to work sheet wax cold; it will shatter or fracture where you least expect it. Place the warm sheet wax on top of your tracing—the wax is transparent at 22-gauge—and cut out

155

the pattern (Fig. 6.6a). If you sense the wax becoming brittle, reimmerse it in the water, or else exhale on it—the heat will be sufficient to allow you to continue working on it. Once the pattern has been cut out, still keeping your wax warm, bend it very gradually around the stepped ring mandrel until the ends overlap (Fig. 6.6b). Cut off the overlap so that the ends just touch, and tack them together with a hot spatula. This sheet wax pattern is the structure upon which the ring will be built; after the work has been completed, it will be removed and discarded.

Build-Up Waxes

The wax used for this project will be a good deal harder than the pink set-up wax. It will not flow as readily, and the melting temperature will be considerably higher. Therefore, it may be controlled with much

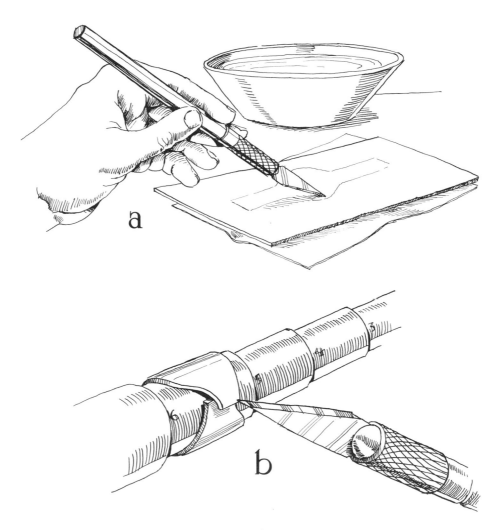

Fig. 6.6 a. Cutting pattern from sheet wax. b. Sheet wax bent around ring mandrel.
156

more precision. The rounded, rather amorphous surface obtained with the set-up wax will now give way to a variety of textures ranging from sharp peaks, to a nugget-like texture, to complete smoothness. Also, the edges of the piece will be sharper; there will be very little of the spreading encountered in the earlier wax build-up.

Take a little time out to experiment with the wax. Melt it with the spatula as hot as you can get it. Melt it at lower heats. See how thin a line you can create with it, how thick a line, how high a peak, how smooth a curve. Much of this is, of course, determined by the intrinsic properties of the wax you have chosen. Casting wax will melt at temperatures considerably lower than carving wax; it will be more difficult to control, but will contract less upon setting. Casting wax, like carving wax, usually comes in three grades; hard, medium and soft. All of them flow readily, a property which is essential in order for wax to be injected into the rubber mold, and all of them retain their fluidity much longer than carving wax does. The difference among them occurs only after the wax has set. The harder the wax, the more detail it will hold but the less flexible will it be. Therefore, even if the amount of detail on a highly convoluted piece would seem to require the hardest grade wax, the caster may be forced to make a trade-off to the more flexible medium grade in order to pull an unbroken wax from the mold. Casting wax generally comes in very large pieces which, though not nearly as expensive as carving wax per pound, would be quite an investment even for a minimum quantity. The best bet is to petition your friendly nighborhood caster who, most likely, will sell you smaller quantities.

As for the carving waxes, the Ferris blue is the only major one acceptable for build-up; however, many of the cheaper brands of carving wax, while unsuitable for carving, are ideal for this process. They will remain flexible after setting; they can be carved with a knife; and they will be roughly half the price of Ferris or Kerr products. Keep in mind, though, when purchasing a wax that is unfamiliar to you, to test it first with your fingernail. Simply scratch a line into it. Two ridges of displaced wax should stand up on either side of the line, no matter how faint the line. If, instead of these two ridges, the displaced wax falls into a powder, the wax probably cannot be carved.

Forming Open-Work

In order to build up an open-work ring, you apply the melted wax directly onto the pink sheet wax pattern. You will notice that unless you accidently touch the sheet wax directly with the hot spatula, the molten wax will not really bond to the pattern; rather, the wax will sit on top of the sheet wax (Fig. 6.7a). The object is to create sharp contours and planes, so the wax should be applied stiffly, without much flow.

Working gradually from the center of the ring outward to the thinnest point at the back of the shank, define the borders of the ring with as thin

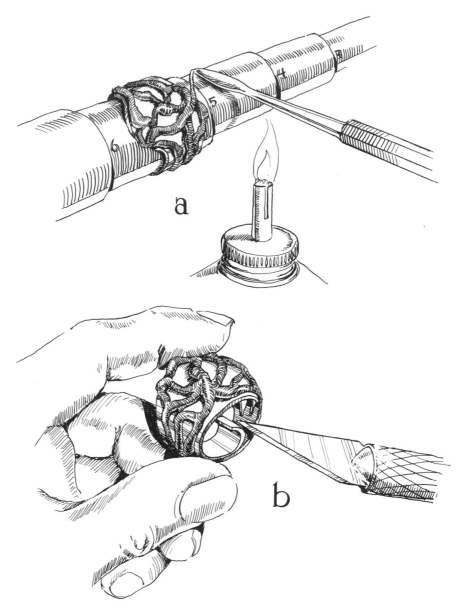

Fig. 6.7   a. Building up open-work. b. Peeling away sheet wax.

a strand as possible. Then, looping thin strands back and forth across
the pink sheet wax pattern, build-up a pleasing arrangement. The shape
of the holes created by the lines is every bit as important as the tilt and
flow of the lines themselves. No matter how interesting the arrangement
of the lines might be, a uniformity of the negative areas will render the
entire design dull. You should aim instead for a harmonious arrangement
of both positive form and negative space.

Build up the open-work slowly and carefully, always forming your design from the center outwards in order to insure balance. Add a few lines, then rotate your ring mandrel slowly to observe the result. Mistakes can be popped off with an X-Acto knife without too much disturbance to the sheet wax. Vary the thicks and the thins, but do not leave any of the lines less than 0.5 millimeter wide by 0.5 millimeter high. Such lines will not cast.

When you have woven a pattern to your satisfaction, gently ease the ring off the ring mandrel. If you encounter any resistence, dip a cotton swab in the wax lubricant and try to run the liquid between the mandrel and the sheet wax. If should come off easily.

Now, dip the ring into very warm water. Then, slipping an X-Acto knife into the juncture of the two ends of the sheet wax on the inside of the ring, pry up one end and gradually begin to peel the wax away. If necessary, use tweezers, but do not be afraid. The sheet wax is much softer and more pliable than the carving or casting wax on the outside; it should peel away in one piece (Fig. 6.7b). If pieces cling to the casting or carving wax, carefully scrape them away with the knife, working from both the inside and from the outside of the ring, through the holes.

When you have cleaned the piece thoroughly, replace it on the mandrel (which you have lubricated again) to check the size and shape. In the event of distortion, simply dip the wax in hot water and force it onto the ring mandrel, holding it tightly in place, until the wax is hardened.

Sizing a Model

The ring must now be sized. The sheet wax band has added thickness to the model. When it is removed from the inside of the ring, you will find that the ring will slide up the ring mandrel about one full size. This should present no problems if you take this size increase into account when beginning the project. If the ring is too small, you can probably correct this by filing out the cast piece. If, on the other hand, the ring is still too big, you must make your modifications right now, in the wax itself. In order to size a ring made of Ferris blue wax or the more flexible grades of casting wax, first slit the piece in the back (Fig. 6.8a). Work at this slowly and carefully with an X-Acto knife, holding the ring securely on the mandrel. If you observe shattering, immediately change to the wax saw—or you can stretch a thin steel wire onto your saw frame, heat it, and just touch the hot metal to the back of the ring. Once the ring has been slit, fit it to the correct size on the ring mandrel, squeezing the sides together until they overlap. Holding the ring together, apply a hot spatula to the top edge of the overlap. Once this top edge has melted, the side of the shank on top will move downward to butt ends with the other side, while the melted wax will form the bond between the two (Fig. 6.8c). Do not attempt to remove the ridge of wax created; wait until the piece has been cast to file it. After the wax has set, remove the ring from

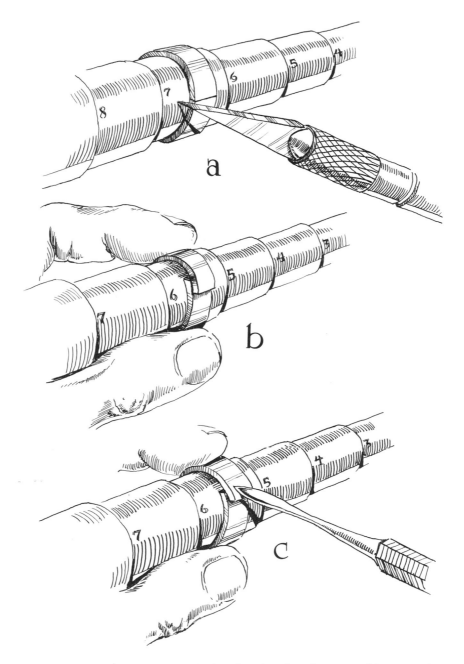

Fig. 6.8 a. Slitting back of ring. b. Overlapping the edges. c. Holding spatula to top of overlap to create bond.

the mandrel and inspect the inside of the shank where you have bonded it. Make certain that the bond has gone completely through the shank to the inside. If the slit line is still visible, add wax to the inside and wait until the piece is cast in order to file it out. Any repair work done on the wax model must be of the simplest order; otherwise you run the risk of deforming or even of shattering the piece.

OPEN-WORK STONE SETTING

The last project in wax build-up is an open-work ring set with a large stone. You need all the materials previously required, plus a stone and a bar of Kerr Perfect wax.

In selecting a stone, consider several factors: size, shape, cut, color, pattern (if any), hardness, and cost. For this ring, you should select a rather large stone, about 18 by 14 millimeters or 16 by 12 millimeters. The larger the stone, the easier it will be to make a setting for it. The stone should be opaque rather than transparent or transluscent, because the setting will be flush against the finger with no light source to highlight the stone. Select a stone with a flat back and a fairly low profile—either a low cabochon or a totally flat cut about 3 millimeters thick. These latter stones have become increasingly popular among craftspeople because they show big, are pretty, are relatively inexpensive, and are easy to work into both bezel and prong settings. They are available in an assortment of agates, which range from brown and white stripes on concentric circles to green foliage, and jaspers, some of which look like sunsets over the Rocky Mountains, as well as lesser known minerals, such as rhodonite, sodalite, and labradorite. Most of these are widely available in gem shops and in shops devoted to rock and mineral specimens.

The stone you select should be harder than metal, so that it is not scratched when you set it; and it should be of a color that will look good with the metal into which the ring will be cast. For example, if you select a very pale jasper, known as Mauseleum Jasper which looks like the ruins of Pompeii, it might look lovely against gold but be lost if set in silver. Similarly, hematite, a metallic gray stone, will look smart when set in silver and like a cheap imitation black onyx when set in gold. Always consider the design as you work.

Forming Bezel

Begin by immersing a piece of 22-gauge pink sheet wax in water that is quite warm; when it becomes flexible, press it against the back of the stone (which you have first dabbed with wax lubricant), shaping it to all the contours; then, before it sets, cut out the shape of the stone's outline in the wax (Fig. 6.9a). This piece of sheet wax—unlike the sheet wax band used for the last ring—will ultimately be cast with the built-up sections; therefore, care must be taken to smooth off the edges by scraping

161

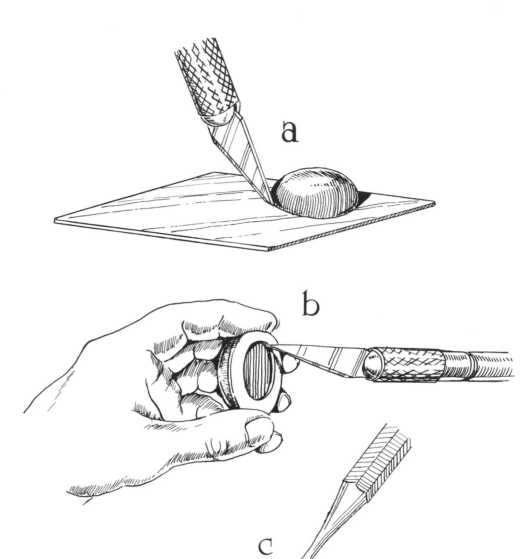

Fig. 6.9 a. Trimming wax around stone. b. Removing most of wax on back of stone. c. Building up the bezel.

the knife over the wax while it still adheres to the stone. Also, it is always best to leave a hole in the bottom of all settings, whether bezel or prong, for several reasons: in the case of a transparent stone, light may pass through; in casting in gold, the expense can be reduced considerably; and if the stone requires adjustment in the setting, it may be maneuvered into position from the back. It also looks better. So, with the wax still attached to the stone, score out a hole, leaving at least a 2 millimeter border on all sides. After having dipped the whole business in warm water, cut out the hole with an X-Acto knife and peel away the inner piece, leaving the border in place on the stone (Fig. 6.9b)

You must now build up a bezel around the stone, which will be permanently bonded to the sheet wax plate behind it. This operation requires some skill since the sheet wax melts at a much lower temperature than the carving wax, or even the casting wax. Therefore, you must be careful not to touch the sheet wax with the spatula but must, instead, allow the heat of the molten build-up wax to melt the sheet wax enough for bonding to occur. Place the stone, sheet wax-side down, on the plate glass. Then, beginning with one small section of the edge of the stone, melt a thin strand of casting or carving wax around the border of the stone, from the sheet wax plate in back right up to—but not beyond—the top edge (Fig. 6.9c). When you have finished this step, sheet wax and build-up wax should form a continuous and unbroken covering over the back and sides of the stone, while the top surface of the stone should remain untouched—for the present.

Next, you must form your sheet wax band around the ring mandrel exactly as you did in the previous project, having first, of course, designed the contours of the shank according to the size and shape of the stone. Dab a little wax lubricant onto the front of the band, and set the stone unit, wax side down, onto the shank so that it balances there.

Tack the stone setting onto the sheet wax shank by running a few thin strands of melted carving or casting wax from the built-up bezel down to the sheet wax shank (Fig. 6.10a). Be careful not to melt the sheet wax plate itself onto the shank. The one is to be a permanent part of the ring and the other is to be discarded. Check the angle of the stone to make certain that it is true. At this stage, imperfections can be corrected easily; later they will require major surgery.

Building Up the Shank

Once you have assured yourself that the stone is positioned correctly, you may begin the final stage of the ring: the wax build-up. This is accomplished, basically, with the same techniques that you have already become accustomed to using, only here you must be concerned with gracefully integrating the stone unit into the shank. Therefore, begin with the outside borders of the ring and define them with strands of wax (Fig. 6.10b), then, gradually, run other strands of wax from different

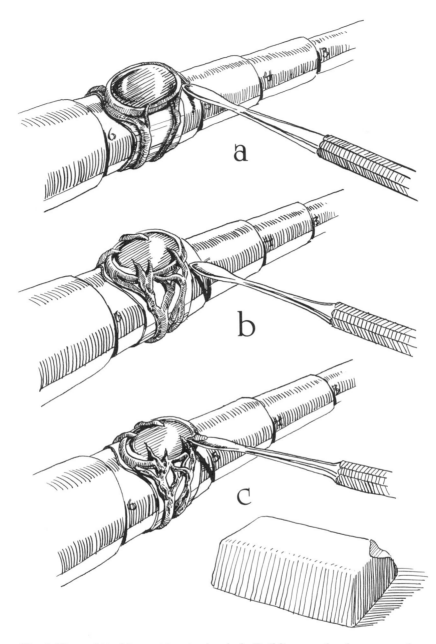

Fig. 6.10   a. Attaching setting to shank. b. Building up shank open-work.
c. Adding Kerr Perfect wax to prongs.

places along the bezel right down to the sheet wax structure, taking care
to carry the major movements of the pattern all the way around the
shank. Once the major design begins to form, you must approach the
most difficult part of the job: extending the strands of wax inward from
the bezel, creating prongs.

164

Building Prongs

The size, thickness, and number of prongs is dependent upon several factors: the size of the stone, the intricacy of the design, and the material into which the piece will be cast. Gold is much stronger than silver; therefore, the prongs can be much thinner and shorter than if you anticipate casting in silver. These prongs are meant to hold the stone in place, but they should not obscure it or detract from it. If your stone has a pattern on it, position your prongs accordingly. Also, someone (either you or a professional stone-setter) is going to have to bend those prongs over the stone; if you make them too thin, the prongs will not hold; too thick and it will require the strength of a Hercules to move them.

The prongs are no different from any of the other strands you have built-up; they should carry through the pattern of the shank in size and in texture—and in placement, if that is at all possible. The only real concern is to make certain that most of the bottom surface of each strand touches the top surface of the stone. Usually, for this size stone, six prongs are sufficient; however, if the pattern dictates otherwise, let the aesthetic considerations predominate, but within reason. When you have finished, the entire ring—stone, prongs, bezel, shank—should be a fully integrated unit. No single part of it should overwhelm the others.

Kerr Perfect Wax

There is just one thing left to do: remove the stone. In order to do this, you have to bend back the prongs and pop the stone out of the bezel. Unfortunately, the prongs are not strong enough to sustain such abuse; they will break off. Before even attempting to move them, you must first see that they are reinforced with Kerr Perfect wax.

Kerr Perfect wax comes in a little bar and, for its weight, is quite expensive. The price is well worth it. A bar should last for years, its function is so specialized. It is used for strengthening weak sections which require further work, or for building up the finest of details. It is a wax which flows easily and sets fairly flexible, but which may be carved and, miraculously, is able to hold the tiniest of details beautifully. For example, if you are carving a bouquet of flowers out of Ferris green wax and a few of the delicate branches snap off and are lost, you should not attempt to build them up with the green wax; they would not be strong enough. Instead, you would use the Kerr Perfect wax, which was designed for just such a job. The final built-up branches will be stronger than the original green wax branches had been. However, do not attempt to carve pieces out of the Perfect wax directly; the wax was intended to be melted onto small areas and then carved. If you work too large a piece, the wax will chip away under the pressure of the knife.

Finishing Touches

For the final touches on the ring, melt the Perfect wax onto the prongs (Fig. 6.10c). Try to cover the entire prong with Perfect wax, taking care that true bonding between the two types of wax has actually occurred. Then, carefully slip an X-Acto knife under the prongs and pry them up one at a time. When all are roughly perpendicular to the stone, remove the ring from the mandrel. Then, pushing with a pencil's eraser from the back of the stone and working an X-Acto blade between the stone and its wax bezel, gently pry out the stone. If you have properly covered it with wax lubricant, it should pop out. However, if you see that you are having undue difficulty, do not force it; instead, slice the bezel at its top edge and gently open it slightly. The stone may then be pried out with ease, and a touch of the spatula will repair the damage.

Once the stone is removed, the wax bezel will have contracted so that, in all likelihood, you can not reinsert the stone into it. Whichever wax you have used, such contraction will occur—only the phenomenon will be much more pronounced if you have used carving wax. Use your X-Acto knife as a scraper (taking care not to slice the prongs) and work around the inner walls of the bezel. Do not scrape away too much—you can always grind away the casting—but from time to time try to replace the stone in its setting; when it seems that just one more turn with the X-Acto knife will make the fit perfect, quit right there before giving it that final scraping. Your ring is finished.

Wax build-up is a technique which allows the craftsman an opportunity to experiment with many varieties of form and texture. It lets him utilize many types of wax, often combining waxes freely. The ultimate effect is almost always one of spontaneity and movement. The results can be very beautiful.

Chapter 7

Sheet Wax and Wax Rods

IN the preceding chapters, I have presented several uses for sheet wax. At this point, the properties of this extremely versatile and useful material have become at least somewhat familiar. However, up until now, you have always used sheet wax as either a substitute technique or else in conjunction with other types of waxes. In short, you have barely touched upon the uses of this wax.

Apart from its uses in forming "accidental" jewelry, which will be fully discussed in the next chapter, it is an ideal material for making mock-ups, three-dimensional "sketches" which will later be converted into carved models. Many problems, unforeseen in a drawing, can be avoided when working with a rough three-dimensional model. It can take you an hour to make a tentative model in green wax, an hour which will be absolutely wasted if the design turns out unpleasant; a few minutes is all you will have to invest before the ultimate form of any design becomes apparent in sheet wax.

Nor is sheet wax confined only to a preliminary or auxiliary role in the model-making process. Wax in this special form has an intrinsic quality which can be duplicated in no other material, a quality which has long made it a favorite of model-makers who specialize in silver work and which, more recently, has been found admirably suited for castings of 18-karat or 22-karat gold. Indeed, in using sheet wax directly for a final model, there are two distinct approaches; the first is to use it as a substitute for sheet metal, and the second is to capitalize upon its own unique properties. This chapter will explore both approaches.

ROSE PIN

For this first project, you will make a fairly typical ornament: a rose pin with a number of petals, a stem with thorns, and two leaves (Fig. 7.1a).

167

Fig. 7.1   a. Design for rose pin. b. The nesting structure of the pin. c. Pattern for rose pin.

Tools and Materials

Three sheets of pink sheet wax, 18-gauge or 20-gauge
Several feet of wax rod, assorted thicknesses
One small piece of green carving wax
Electric spatula (preferred) or your most finely pointed spatula
    with alcohol lamp
X-Acto knife, number 11
X-Acto swivel blade set in mechanical pencil holder
Bowl for water with hot plate or heating coil
Glass plate
Blotter
Bond paper
Scissors
Cellophane tape
Tracing paper
Pencil, 4H

Unlike the previous materials with which you have worked, sheet wax will admit of no mistakes; it must be handled deftly, quickly, and set into position with a minimum amount of shifting. In order to accomplish this, you must know *exactly* what you are going to do. For each piece, you must make an exact drawing, even a rough model in sheet wax before cutting and bending it into position. In fact, even though the forming of the finished model takes comparatively little time, the preparation must be carefully considered and a good deal of time must be spent experimenting. It probably takes at least twice as long to prepare for the finished piece as it does to make it.

Creating a Pattern

Obviously, a rose, with all its recesses and inaccessible places can never be polished in a single piece; it must be cast in sections. Each section can then be cleaned and polished and soldered into place. It is the job of the model-maker to consider the steps in production. In this case, the stem and leaves will present no problem; they can be made and cast as a single piece. It is the rose itself which must be taken apart and reconstructed. The simplest way to accomplish this is to think of the flower as three irregularly shaped cups, each one nesting inside another (Fig. 7.1b). These cups will fit into a specially formed base attached to the stem. When they are finished, each cup should require only a touch of solder to hold it in place, giving the illusion of a full-blown rose.

A pattern must be created for each section; not an easy matter, since a curved piece is being fashioned from a flat sheet. There will be distortion; quite frequently, it is impossible to determine what accommodations must be made in the flat pattern in order to arrive at the desired form in the round. Experimentation is the only solution: with scrap paper and scissors, or with the sheet wax itself, bending a strip of it into roughly the desired shape, refining it with a knife and then, after reimmersing the piece in warm water, flattening it out again. In either case, the procedure is tedious and less than precise. You will find, after the first few pieces, that your eye will begin to compensate for the unavoidable distortion, and you will be able to cut your stencils with much more certainty of success. Once you have defined the inner cup of the rose and have established a flat pattern for it, it is a much simpler matter to arrive at the patterns for the two outer cups.

Once all these patterns have been finalized, it is generally good practice—especially if you intend to specialize in working sheet wax—to make a clear pen-and-ink drawing on stiff white paper so that the pattern (or variants of it) can be used over again (Fig. 7.1c). Indeed, once the pattern has been created, many craftspeople actually eliminate the need for rubber molds, preferring to shape each piece directly from the sheet wax. In this way, not only is each final piece unique; it is also significantly lighter in weight than anything originating in a rubber mold could possibly be.

Cutting Wax Pieces

To begin, place the plate glass directly on top of the pen-and-ink pattern. The sheet wax, having been immersed in warm water, should be quickly blotted dry and placed on top of the glass. If you have made your drawing dark enough, it should be visible through the sheet wax. If you have difficulty seeing it, place an acetate sheet on top of the drawing—so that the moisture from the recently immersed sheet will not run into the paper, causing it to wrinkle—and, with your scribe, lightly outline the pattern in the wax. Then remove the wax from your drawing and place it back on the glass plate for cutting. Be sure, before you begin to cut, that your blade is a new one (working on the glass will, unavoidably, both dull your blade quickly and incise a network of scratches into the glass) and that a bowl of hot water is nearby for constant reimmersion. A good means of keeping the water at a fairly constant temperature is to set it on an electric hot plate or, failing that, to use an electric coil. Use only as much water as you need to cover the entire piece of wax, and do not let the wax soak unduly long; ideally, it should just be dipped in, removed, blotted, and cut.

The cutting operation should present no real difficulties. If the wax is the proper temperature and flexibility, it will yield readily to a knife—like a thin slice of cheese.

Forming the Leaves

The leaves—with their saw-toothed edging—will be the most difficult to reproduce in the wax. To cut them, you need a very sharp small blade, such as a swivel blade or even a surgical blade in its special holder.

First cut the general outline of the leaf from the sheet. In the cutting operation, a burr will be raised along the edge. Ordinarily, you would not attempt to reduce this irregularity in the wax, waiting instead to grind it away in the metal casting; however, since very precise detail is going to be worked into the edge, you must prepare the surface to sustain it. If you simply wish to remove the burr roughly in the wax, you would run a piece of sandpaper lightly across the raised burr on the *cold wax*. This method applied here, however, would be entirely too rough; very delicate work is to come. Therefore, you must warm the wax and slice the burr away with your sharpest blade, applying the blade parallel to the surface of the wax, and slicing the burr off in a single shaving (Fig. 7.2a). You can also burnish the wax by scraping the blade backwards, compressing the wax so that the burr—rather than rising up from the surface—now extends over the edge (Fig. 7.2b). At this point, the burr is sliced off with a sharp blade held vertically (Fig. 7.2c).

Cutting in the saw-tooth pattern is fairly simple to accomplish—if you take sufficient time and care. Do not attempt to cut it free-hand, if you expect it to be uniform; instead, you should *lightly* scribe in the pattern—or even make an exact tracing of the pattern which could then be glued directly onto the wax with rubber cement, where it would remain in place while you cut the pattern through it. (After the job is complete, you can peel off the tracing paper and remove the residue of rubber cement by rubbing it with your finger.

While cutting, make certain that the wax is flexible at all times; the tiny detail is very liable to snap. Simply immerse the edge upon which you intend to work; remove the piece when it becomes flexible and, using a knife blade held at 90 degrees to insure an even edge, cut away

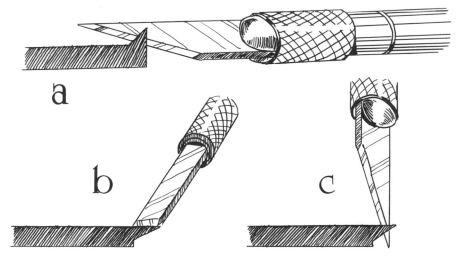

Fig. 7.2   a. Slicing off burr (method one). b. Burnishing the wax. c. Slicing off burr (method two).

171

each tiny triangle to create the proper effect. When working with sheet wax in this way, always make your cut toward the edge. Begin by carefully placing the point of the knife at the apex of the triangle, and cut the two lines away from it (Fig. 7.3a). Do not try to cut completely through on the first try; several light passes are more easily controlled than one heavy cut. It is virtually impossible to repair tiny mistakes on sheet wax. When molten wax is applied to the edge, more often than not, the edge will melt away completely. In order to repair an edge, you must melt a blob of wax onto the affected area large enough to be cut down to the original contour—and, even then, the consistency will never be the same. Often, it is much less time-consuming simply to throw away the broken piece and start again. However, if you are careful to keep your wax flexible and your blade sharp, no such calamity should occur.

Shaping the sheet wax must be done quickly; too much handling will impress a texture of fingerprints into the material, and will make the shapes themselves uncertain. Therefore, before any shaping is to be done, the final form must be fairly certain in your mind. The leaves will be divided into two slightly domed halves separated by a fairly sharp depression down the middle, into which a length of thin wax rod is to be placed. In order to form the wax, it is actually best to work under water—warm, not hot, water—no matter how wrinkled your fingertips may become in the process.

First score the leaf lightly with a wooden tool and then simply bend it along the score mark so that a gentle V is created. With the leaf still immersed in the water, dome each half by pressing your thumb up into the flat sheet from underneath while shaping the contour from above with the other fingers. When both sides have been sufficiently domed, remove the leaf from the water and examine your handiwork (Fig. 7.3b). Decide if the leaf is graceful enough; perhaps it needs more refining. Reimmerse it in the water. Perhaps you might bend the point downward, tilt up a section of the edge, give it a slight twist so that it no longer seems stiff and rigid. You might even want to suggest a pattern of veins with a wooden tool, or else set in additional channels to accomodate additional fine wax rods.

Wax rods are just that: wax which comes in thin spaghetti-like sticks. There are many profiles from which to choose: round, half-round, square, triangular, and flat. There are also shapes specifically intended for use in making settings: wax which comes in bezel form, wax that may be split into three-prong, four-prong, and six-prong settings. Most professionals buy their wax rods either in tubes which contain a quantity of sticks of whatever size and shape they require, or else in spools. There are also various assortments on the market, which offer a selection of many sizes and shapes: an excellent choice if you are just beginning or wish to experiment.

172

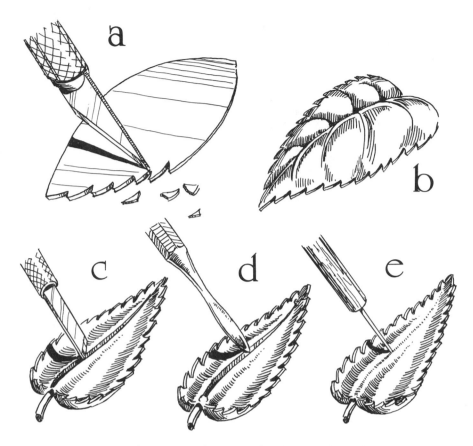

Fig. 7.3   a. Cutting the saw-tooth pattern. b. Shaping the leaf. c. Cutting the channel. d. Depositing wax on one side of the channel. e. Tacking from the back of a piece.

This material, like sheet wax, is also very fragile. Everything must be worked gingerly; the touch must be light and deft; the temperature used to melt or bond must be low; the instruments used to shape it must be small and sharp. It is wax model-making at its most delicate. Wax rods are, in most cases, always flexible; they melt at a very low temperature and turn fluid almost immediately, making them fairly impossible to approach with direct heat. Instead, you must try to heat the wax indirectly, by heating the sheet wax and allowing the fluid pink wax to melt the blue rod. Remember, though, that the pink wax is very delicate in its own right. Excessive heat will open a hole that will be impossible to fill. Therefore, the very lowest heat which will do the job should be used. The electric spatula with its precise heat control is almost indispensible; with it, you can be assured of a constant low temperature, allowing you to devote complete attention to the joining operation without worrying about a spatula which is too hot.

In order to join the rod to the wax leaf, first cut the rod to the correct size, leaving ample room on either side for trimming. After lightly pressing the rod into the central channel on the front of the leaf, turn the wax to the back to bond the two units. This bonding requires a very steady hand.

Reimmerse the wax leaf one last time in the warm water; remove it and, with the point of the knife blade held backward to the normal slitting position (Fig. 7.3c), cut a small V-shaped channel down the center of the back, following the rod. The thickness of the sheet is only 1 millimeter, so the cut should not exceed 0.5 millimeter in depth. The piece is now about as fragile as it will ever be; the slightest knock or mishandling will split it right down the score mark.

Take a little wax on the point of the spatula and, taking care not to touch the metal to the leaf directly—only touching molten wax to the sheet wax—deposit a bead of wax at either end of the channel to tack the rod in place. If the temperature of the wax is the correct one (test it *before* you begin), the thinner section of the sheet wax, being able to sustain less heat than the surrounding areas, should melt, leaving the rest relatively unaffected. Then slowly work down the channel, one side at a time, with molten wax (Fig. 7.3d). If molten wax were deposited into the center of the channel, the leaf would fall into two halves. By making certain that at least one part is stable, you run little risk of ruining the piece. Notice, too, that your wax rod is twice removed from the source of heat: the spatula. The liquid wax on the tip of the spatula melts the sheet wax which, in turn, melts just enough of the wax rod to bond it neatly and permanently to the leaf. After the operation has been completed, touch up any irregularities in the back: depressions and gaps by adding wax, knobs and peaks by scraping lightly with a knife. Sharp nicks may be smoothed out with the fiberglass brush; however, do not expect to return the surface to anything remotely resembling its original condition. Final polishing will have to wait until after the model has been cast into metal.

This method of joining layers from the back can be applied to waxes other than sheet wax. It is a very useful concept to remember, especially when the units would be ruined by the application of heat from the front. Often, if the pieces to be joined are perfectly flat, and the points of contact perfectly level, bonding can be effected by simply inserting a heated pin, at several points, through the back layer until it reaches the front (Fig. 7.3e). This method can be used as a substitute for the one just described; it will not be as thorough, but it will be a good deal neater.

Make a second leaf in exactly the same way, taking care to leave enough rod extended to allow the leaves to be joined to the main stem in a graceful manner. Then put the leaves aside until it is time for the final joining.

174

Forming the Flower

Here it is good to remember the comparison to three cups nesting one inside another. In order to make them fit properly, you must first fashion the innermost cup, and then work the outer two around it. Transfer the pattern onto the sheet wax, and cut out the shape of the central unit. The beauty of a rose resides, in large measure, in the asymmetry of its petals. The inner cup is basically a circle divided into three, four, or five units, somewhat resembling clover leaves, and separated by slits emanating near—but not from—the hub. In order to achieve the cup-like effect, this flat circle must be immersed in hot water and each of the sections bent up slowly so that they overlap at the "rim" of the cup (Fig. 7.4a). Do not strive for a particularly even distribution in the overlapping: one over, one under, one bigger, one smaller is to be preferred.

Refining consists of shaping the upper section of each petal. Reimmerse the top half of the cup in hot water and, by grasping each petal individually between thumb and forefinger, bend the top edge backward until the familiar shape has been achieved (Fig. 7.4b). Several small nicks can be cut into the edges of one or two petals in order to render the total effect more realistic.

Next, attach a short piece of wax rod, about 12 millimeters in length, to the very base of the central unit. In order to attach wax rod, you must allow ample rod to hold the piece in place while applying heat. Touch one end of a 7.5-centimeter length to the desired spot on the sheet wax cup and, with the lowest possible usable heat, melt the rod directly onto the sheet. Do not release the rod until the wax has set. Both wax rod and sheet wax melt much more quickly than carving wax and take much longer to set permanently. After you are certain that the wax has hardened, take a sharp scissors and snip off the rod at the desired length.

This rod is purely a structural element; its sole function is to lock all the units together. It will be threaded through the two outer shells of the rose until, ultimately, it will engage into an opening at the top of the stem, securing the entire rose in place. The next two sections will be fashioned so that this rod passes through a hole in the center of the cup (Fig. 7.4c).

Fashion a second petal cup in the same way as the first. Make sure that the two pieces nest nicely, that the base of the inner section fits as flush as possible into the cup of the outer section, that the rod easily finds its way through the hole. After these mechanics have been attended to, the rest is aesthetics, bending the petals to achieve the desired effect in conjunction with the bud at the center. Try, also, when bending the petals, to engage one unit into the other so that, when the two are in place, there will be a minimum of slipping and rotation of the outer cup around the rod. Then simply repeat the process for the outer shell.

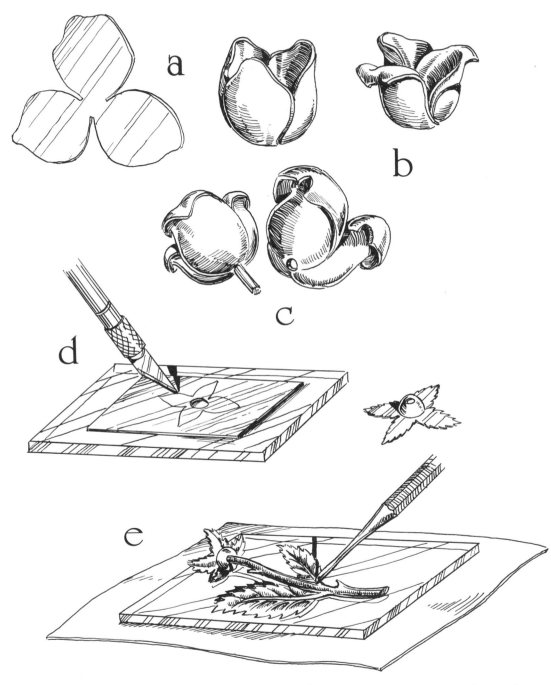

Fig. 7.4   a. Pattern formed into cup shape. b. Refining shape of petals. c. A locking rod holds the petals together. d. Forming the socket. e. Joining the stem units.

Forming the Socket

The last piece to make is the socket into which the locking rod will fit. It is unnecessary to conceive of it as a totally functional element; in a real rose, the flower is separated from the stem by a tiny cup of little leaves; the leaves which had originally protected the unopened bud. These little leaves will become the functional socket. For this unit, it is easier and more precise if the socket itself is fashioned of carving wax instead of sheet. Drill a hole, the size of the rod to be inserted, directly through a small slab of green carving wax, ¼ inch (6 mm) thick. File the wax until it takes on the familiar shape of a rose cup. Polish it and set it aside; later it will be joined permanently to the stem. Next cut out from sheet wax the tiny leaves that will hold the flower in place (Fig. 7.4d). While this unit is still perfectly flat, place the green wax cup in the center. Using the cup as a stencil, mark a line around it; then cut well inside that line. Heat the sheet and cut out the hole. While the sheet wax is still soft, press the green wax socket through the hole, pushing up a ridge of sheet wax around it. Then, touching your spatula to the *green wax* so that it just begins to flow, melt the two units together. Carving wax melts at almost 100°F higher than the surrounding sheet wax. The heat of completely fluid green wax will melt a huge irreparable gap in the sheet wax. Therefore, the green wax should be melted only up to the point where the pink sheet wax begins to meld with it. Then remove the heat and let the unit cool completely before you reimmerse it in warm water and shape it to fit the form of the flower.

Joining the Stem Units

Lay out the various elements on the glass plate: leaves, socket-unit, and a length of fairly thick wax rod which will serve as a stem. If it is necessary, place a tracing of the design under the glass plate to use as a guide. Melt a bit of wax rod onto the tip of the spatula and deposit it at the joints where the leaves connect to the stem (Fig. 7.4e). When the wax has set, you can bend the leaves into whatever position you deem graceful. Add a few short, tapered bits of rod to the stem: the thorns. To finish, insert the stem rod halfway into the socket from below and fasten it with a drop of wax. If you wish to refine the piece further, you can cut away some of the excess wax at the joints to facilitate final polishing in the metal. When you gain further experience in the medium, you might want to pass an electric spatula, turned up quite high, near these irregularities; the heat will make the surface flow while leaving the basic structure unaffected. The result, when the spatula is placed in expert hands, is a flawlessly bright and even surface; the result, when the spatula is placed in the hands of anyone less than an expert, is disaster.

ORNATE BROOCH

The rose pin used the sheet wax fairly much as if it had been metal: a highly traditional approach to wax working altogether. Working sheet metal would have taken ten times as long, and the results would have taken on that unmistakable stiffness of a model fashioned from metal plate. But it could have been done. Similarly, many of the pieces you have made from carving wax could have been fashioned from metal—and would have been a generation ago. Very infrequently have the intrinsic properties of wax itself been exploited. For the next project, as well as in the entire next chapter, you will use wax, not as a substitute for metal, but in its own right.

You will need the same list of materials as for the rose. In addition, you will be using some cabochon stones, some full baroque pearl drops, and a length of uncut bezel wax rod. You should also feel free to experiment with different types of sheet wax. Thus far you have been restricted to the most rigid form of the material: sheets which are brittle at room temperature and require heat to become workable. However, even within the brittle species of sheet wax, there are variations. There is the regular, which is the all-purpose wax with which you have been working throughout; there are also hard and soft grades that are either more or less pliable to the touch, more or less apt to scratch. There is also a completely different kind of sheet wax, one that requires no heating in order to be flexible. This sheet wax is generally dyed green, as opposed to the three shades of pink used to denote the standard material. This green should, by no means, be confused with green carving wax; it is probably the softest wax you can use. All you have to do is to bend it into position, and it will stay.

I have found green sheet wax a bit too pliable to be valuable in its own right; however, when used in conjunction with a sturdier substance, it may be fashioned in ways impossible for any other medium. For example, it is so pliable that it may actually be cut into strips and woven across a wax-wire "loom." It may be crumpled into rosettes or cut up into pom-poms to be applied to the surface of a more substantial wax. It also has one totally utilitarian function which may be of use to you in the future: it is a perfect material with which to take impressions. If plaster is impractical, you have but to press a sheet of green sheet wax into all the features of any object, cast the sheet wax into a base metal and you have a mold, ready to accept either melted wax or another section of sheet wax. The detail which you are capable of achieving in this way is very fine; a piece of thin sheet wax pressed onto a coin is able to receive almost every detail contained in the original.

However, for this project—in which pieces will be added onto the basic structure, the regular brittle variety is to be preferred. Here, instead of making a series of very deliberate sketches, rely primarily upon a more

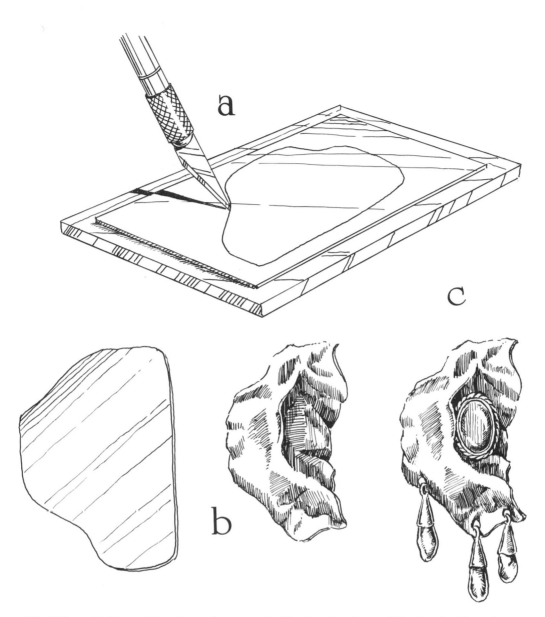

Fig. 7.5 a. Cutting pattern from sheet wax. b. Shaping the piece. c. The finished brooch.

spontaneous mode of creativity. The only predetermined qualities will be the approximate size of the piece, and the stones to be used on it.

To begin, cut from a piece of 18-gauge pink sheet wax whatever shape might be pleasing to you (Fig. 7.5a). Immerse it in warm water and shape it between your fingers, pinching sections, doming out sections, crumbling and straightening, folding until you have arrived at a shape and form which seems attractive (Fig. 7.5b). Remove it from the water and appraise it critically. See if it requires more work, perhaps a

179

reshaping of the silhouette with the knife or a reworking of some section which is less interesting than the rest. Place the stones on it, to see if the sheet must be reworked to accommodate them, either physically or aesthetically. Make sure the edges form a fairly level border so that it will lie correctly when worn. Once you have arrived at a happy distribution of surface forms, you can see that what you have produced is unique, able to be fashioned from no other substance. It will have the grace of draped cloth, the crispness of creased paper and, when it is cast into precious metal, the hand-wrought quality of beaten metal.

The rest of the task is purely technical: attaching the bezel wire to the surface of the sheet wax, perhaps adding a border of twisted wax wire around each bezel, making caps for the pearls, making wax wire loops from which to suspend them.

Bezel Wire

Bezel wire is one of the many different shaped rods available to the wax model-maker. While not a perfect substitute for the metal bezel, it can readily be shaped to fit a stone and, with proper filing in the metal casting, it will do the job nicely. Keep in mind, if you are not successful in forming the bezel the first time, you must discard it and begin all over again; any reworking of this material will cause ripples which no amount of filing can obliterate. There are two methods of applying the bezel wire to the surface of the sheet wax. You can apply it directly onto the wax, inserting a hot pin through the back to secure it, and later, with a warmed knife, cut out a hole within the bezel to maneuver the stone. Or, you can cut out a hole first, one which is exactly the exterior size of the bezel, set the preformed bezel into it, and join the wire and the sheet together from the back. Either way is acceptable; the real trick in making bezels of wax comes not in bonding the wire to the sheet wax but in joining the ends of the bezel wire together to create a circlet.

Thus far, you have bonded materials with different melting points, using one to melt the other. With units of the same material, you must melt both pieces with direct heat. It is a very easy matter to melt the entire joint away. In order to accomplish this type of bonding successfully, you cannot simply butt edge to edge, as you would ordinarily do with carving wax. The heat would melt away too much material for the joint to hold. Instead, you must overlap the edge. Wrap the wire around the girth of the stone and, after it is fitted, snip the wire so that a 1/16-inch (1.5 mm) overlap remains (Fig. 7.6a). With the stone still in place, lending a rigidity to the unit which it would not ordinarily have, touch the hot spatula to the overlap *only*, while using one forefinger to press the top edge down flush to the stone. The melted wax from the overlap should melt the wax below it, so that the desired bond will be effected.

It is important to maintain finger pressure on the joint until the heated wax solidifies: often a surprisingly long operation—and an ex-
180

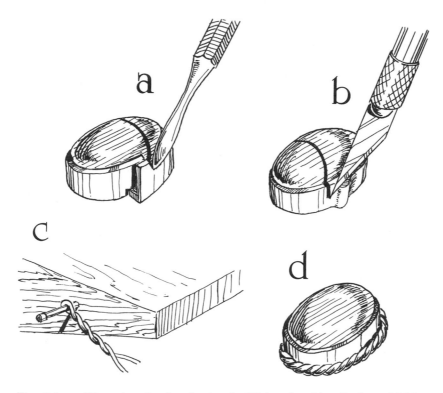

Fig. 7.6   a. Wrapping the bezel wire. b. Slicing the ridge flush. c. Making twisted wire. d. The completed bezel.

ercise in patience, since wax which melts readily takes quite a long while to set again. Do not release pressure until you are absolutely certain that the joint has set. The resulting ridge must be removed before you can apply the bezel to the sheet wax brooch—especially if you have selected the second method of application: cutting the hole and setting the bezel flush into the sheet. Cutting this ridge is perhaps the most difficult job of all. The wax is very soft and the slightest pressure will distort it, even with the stone still set inside it. The only answer is an absolutely new blade dipped in wax lubricant so that the slice will be as free from resistence as possible (Fig. 7.6b). Do not expect perfection, and do not attempt to smooth out irregularities in the wax; all of that must wait for the metal casting. Just set the bezel in place—still leaving the stone in—and bond it to the sheet wax. Only when the bezel is permanently fixed, should the stone be popped out and set aside.

Twisted Wire

Often, however, a bezel applied in this way seems bare, and a bit of ornamentation will spruce things up. One traditionally favored type of ornamentation is the application of a thin strand of twisted wire around the base of the bezel. Generally this operation—as well as the creation

181

of the bezel itself for that matter—is done in metal; however, using very thin strands of wax wire, even this very delicate task can be accomplished by the wax model-maker.

Hammer a small headless wire brad a little way into the side of your bench pin. Cut off a length, about 2 feet, of your finest wax wire, 22-gauge or finer. Gently bend it in half, and slip the loop over the nail. Remember, this is not real wire; it is a very delicate material which must be handled with the lightest of touches. Twist the two strands around each other, starting as near the nail as possible and making the twists as tight as possible without snapping the strands (Fig. 7.6c). When the entire length of wire has been twisted to the desired tightness, cut—do not pull—the wire from the nail. Cut the proper length and save the remainder for another time. (Incidentally, the storage of sheet wax and wax rods requires much more care than the storage of carving wax, which may be set aside just about anywhere. These lower-melting types of waxes should always be stored in closed boxes, away from sunlight and especially heat. Any kind of extreme heat will melt them just enough so that they will all stick together and be totally unusable.)

Wind the twisted wire around the base of the bezel, leaving a small overlap where the two ends meet. With the lowest heat that will do the job, melt the ends together and let the bond set. The result will be a neat band of twisted wire with a bump on one side; the elimination of this bump requires carving the wax wire: not an easy job. The best you can hope for is a rather rough-hewn suggestion of the pattern. Work with your finest blade, first slicing, then smoothing the wax so that the illusion of twisted wire is created. Once again, you will have to wait until the wax is cast into metal before the necessary refinements are possible. Do not worry your model at this time; the chances of distorting the bezel beyond repair are great and not worth the risk. Join it to the surface of the sheet wax by tacking it from behind with a heated pin. After you have placed bezels for all the stones in this way, you are finished with the main section of the brooch; next you must prepare settings for the baroque pearls that will dangle from it.

Making Pearl Caps

Making caps—functional elements into which variously shaped objects are glued or rivited so that they can be suspended from chains or hooks—is one of the prime uses of sheet wax. I have made caps not only for pearls, but for lions' claws, elks' teeth, pipe stems, fossils and minerals. Each piece demands its own specially fitted cap, and no material is so admirably suited for assuming the contours of any given piece as sheet wax.

For a baroque pearl, cut out a triangle of sheet wax, roughly two-thirds the size of the pearl itself (Fig. 7.7a). Immerse the sheet wax in

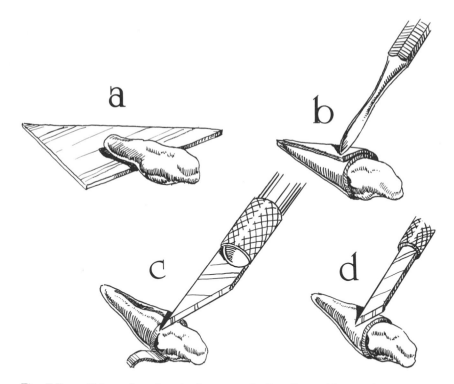

Fig. 7.7   a. Triangular piece to form cap. b. Bonding with spatula. c. Trimming wax evenly around pearl. d. Trimming the ridge formed by the overlap.

warm water and bend the wax around the top third of the pearl until one side overlaps the other (Fig. 7.7b). Make sure that you lubricate the pearl lightly, so that the pearl may later be removed easily. Do not remove it yet, however; melt the wax overlap, joining the edges of the cap, and then *lightly* cut the base line so that it becomes neat and uniform (Fig. 7.7c). Try not to cut completely through the wax because the blade will scratch the pearl (for harder materials there is no danger); just go deep enough so that you can strip the excess away without ripping or distorting the wax. Shave the overlap ridge away with your knife (Fig. 7.7d), and the cap needs only the application of a small wire loop on top to be finished. The irregularity of the pearl will be reflected in the form of the cap.

There are several ways to hang the pearls. First, simply join wax loops to either the back of the piece or along the bottom edge; or else, pierce several holes through the bottom of the sheet wax piece. You may make these holes as unobtrusive as possible, or you may conceive of them as part of the design, carrying over the shape of the pearls into them or surrounding them with twisted wire, or even shaping them to grow naturally from the basic form of the brooch. Whichever way you decide to incorporate them, remember, even though they are purely functional units—just as the caps for the pearls are—they are seen and, therefore, must be carefully considered. The entire piece, spontaneously formed though it might have been initially, must not be allowed to appear sloppy or haphazard in the execution. The beauty of pieces which are spontaneously formed is realized only if the raw surge of creativity is tempered by a deliberate, even painstaking, technique. You can make a lovely start by pure inspiration; the finished product depends upon hard work and careful thought.

Chapter 8

Accidental Effects

MOST of the preceding projects have involved careful thought, with tight preliminary sketches or completely finished renderings. In order to produce most of your wax models, you have used various kinds of tools—knives, files, the flexible shaft machine—and have invested hours in painstakingly precise work. This is, in general, the correct approach to model-making, the professional approach, in fact the only approach a model-maker may employ unless he is working from his own designs or concepts. However, spontaneously formed objects may be just as beautiful as those objects which have been carefully wrought. The danger in relying upon spontaneity alone is that very little is demanded of the artist technically; he is, in effect, relying upon fate and an innate sensibility to produce his pieces. That is the reason why this chapter on "accidental" jewelry techniques was left until you were thoroughly exposed to the more demanding—technically demanding—approaches to wax model-making. The use of accidental techniques is a wonderful addition to a model-maker's arsenal; if properly utilized, it can provide effects impossible for even the most practiced hand to achieve deliberately; if used to the exclusion of all other approaches, it becomes repetitious and dull.

Accidentally created jewelry models are fun to make. They are a constant test of ingenuity in finding new techniques, and a real source of excitement when they are realized. Basically, accidental effects are created in one of two ways: either by the molten wax being poured onto or into various objects or materials, or else by heat-softened wax being manipulated to produce the desired effects. In the first case, obviously, the accident dictates the form of the entire piece; in the second case, the form has generally been established already and the accidental effect is confined to the texture of the piece alone. In the following projects, we shall explore the possibilities of each approach, trying to temper our results with professional methods of converting accidents into fine, finished jewelry.

POURED WAX BROOCH

The design of this brooch will be totally determined by the way in which poured wax forms as it takes on the shape of whatever material or substance you choose to experiment with. You will need the following:

> Several sheets of pink set-up wax
>> or
> A piece of soft casting wax
> Aluminum pot and pouring ladle
> Hot plate or stove burner
> Wax lubricant or glycerine
> Any object or surface which may produce an interesting impression on the wax

The process here is a very simple one; in fact, you have done it before, when you created a mold and poured the wax into it. The principle here is exactly the same; molten wax will take on an impression. The difference is that, in the first instance, the mold was carefully conceived and prepared, and the wax was contained within fixed boundaries; here, the "mold" is only responsible for the texture of the piece and the wax is allowed to run freely along its surface. Of course, if you wish to contain the shape of the piece to some preconceived form, you can build a ridge of wax directly onto whatever material you are using (a piece of tree bark for example) and pour the wax into the shallow reservoir designed to contain it. However, in most cases, you would allow the wax to form as it will, refining your shape afterwards with a sharp knife.

There are just two variables which you must control: the material you will use to form the mold, and the type and temperature of the wax which you will use—as well as the actual method that you employ to deposit it. You should first familiarize yourself with the different waxes. In order best to do this, use the simplest surface possible for the experiments: an aluminum cookie sheet, first lying flat on the table, then inclined to increasingly steep angles.

Testing Wax Properties

Of the carving waxes, you may recall, Ferris green wax runs most freely, while the blue is yet more viscous than the purple. Casting waxes also come in grades, but all casting wax melts at temperatures significantly less than the carving waxes. Set-up wax and sheet wax melt at still lower temperatures and take much longer to set. Each one will form its own distinctive pattern as it is ladled onto the cookie sheet.

186

Begin by melting a tablespoon of each wax and pouring it onto the aluminum sheet. First, just tilt the spoon and allow the wax to run gently into a puddle. Each wax will form its own distinctive setting pattern. Depending upon the wax used, each deposit will vary in surface size, the thickness of each being contingent upon the ability of the wax to flow freely, once having been removed from the heat. Obviously, the longer the setting time, the greater will be the flow. Experiment. Deposit another spoonful of each wax—only do not wait for the wax to melt completely. Observe what kinds of patterns the more viscous material will make. Chop the wax into bits and allow some of it to remain unmelted in the spoon. See what kind of texture can be achieved this way. Pour half the amount onto a piece which is already set. Observe the pattern that the two individual deposits make when fused. Melt some more wax and try to discover any build-up potential.

Vary the height from which you are pouring the wax, first pouring from several inches above the aluminum sheet, then raising the spoon to heights of a foot or more. You will find that the pattern, as well as the outline shape, will become more and more unique the greater the velocity with which the fluid wax strikes the surface of the sheet. In the case of the set-up wax, you will almost be able to sustain the illusion of water splattering against a flat surface. Do not be afraid to play; the whole beauty of creating accidental pieces of jewelry lies in the fact that one experiment leads to another one, and nothing becomes stagnant.

Once you have determined the nature of each wax and the way in which each will react in various situations, prop up one side of the cookie sheet, so that an inclined plane of 30 to 45 degrees is created, and repeat the experiment. Here, you can gauge the amount of flow, perhaps, more accurately, as well as obtain a completely different pattern from each wax. In fact, Ferris has capitalized on this phenomenon by putting on the market a wax specifically designed for the creation of accidental models: Pour-a-Tex, a hard green wax which, when poured onto an inclined surface, will set into patterns resembling the flow of lava. With bright polishing, the effects can be quite attractive and if you do not like the pattern which has formed, you simply remelt the wax and repour it.

Molds

However, the real pleasure of creating pieces of accidental jewelry comes in the selection of surfaces upon which to pour the wax. There is one thing to remember when selecting a surface; it must either be non-porous, so that the wax does not stick to it so tenaciously that removal of the set piece becomes impossible, or else it must be prepared with a wax lubricant (Microfilm, Mold Release, glycerine) before you attempt to pour wax onto it. The application of a wax lubricant makes practically every surface a fit subject.

Finding suitable molds should present no problem. Of the non-porous materials, try any kind of rock, gravel, or mineral with a crystalline formation, shattered glass, crumpled aluminum foil, old etching plates, window screen—anything, even ice and, oddly enough, water. Of the materials which may be used in conjunction with a coating of wax lubricant, try tree bark, open-grain woods, fish scales, coarse cloth, sponge, or old bicycle tires.

Forming the Piece

For a beginning, use a sheet of crumpled aluminum foil. Use a thick gauge foil so that it will be easier to handle. Perhaps, to make it more stable, you could fasten the foil onto a board with thumbtacks so that no shifting will occur when the wax is poured onto the surface (Fig. 8.1a). Study the patterns carefully, perhaps even cutting a 5-centimeter square mask and moving it across the various sections of the foil until you have selected the area you deem most fit to lend its particular contours to the wax (Fig. 8.1b). Then, heat your wax to prepare it for pouring. Pouring wax onto a highly textured surface is not the same as pouring it onto a perfectly flat cookie sheet. Here, very fluid wax will run down the peaks and settle in the valleys, leaving a deposit of uneven thickness (the only textured surface onto which very fluid wax can be poured without fear of unevenness is ice; the wax cools too quickly to really run). Therefore, the wax must be handled somewhat differently. It cannot really be too fluid, obviously, and it must be deposited in small areas instead of being dropped onto the surface. Nor is it necessary for the surface itself to remain stationary; it may be tilted to reverse the flow of the wax in order to create a more uniform application. These procedures, however, will not spoil the effect of spontaneity since it is the *under* surface of the wax—not the top—which will be exposed.

Deposit the wax (set-up wax is best) little by little onto the high points of the area you have selected (Fig. 8.1c). Since the wax takes a fairly long time to set, you can readily blend one deposit into another while tilting the surface to modify the direction of the flow. Gravity will aid you in applying the wax to the depressions in the pattern. When a uniform coat has been obtained, ascertain the thickness of the deposit by making several small sample patches of wax on the aluminum surface. After these have set, simply pick them off the surface and gauge them. Using this as a standard, you should have no difficulty in noting the relative translucence of the model as compared to the sample wax. Any spots which seem thin should be reinforced now, before the wax is removed from the aluminum surface; it will sag if any attempt is made to repair it later. Once you are certain that sufficient wax has been deposited, scrape down any areas which seem unnecessarily thick, in order to avoid work later, in the metal clean-up. Remove the foil from the board and immerse the entire business in a pan of cold water. Peel the

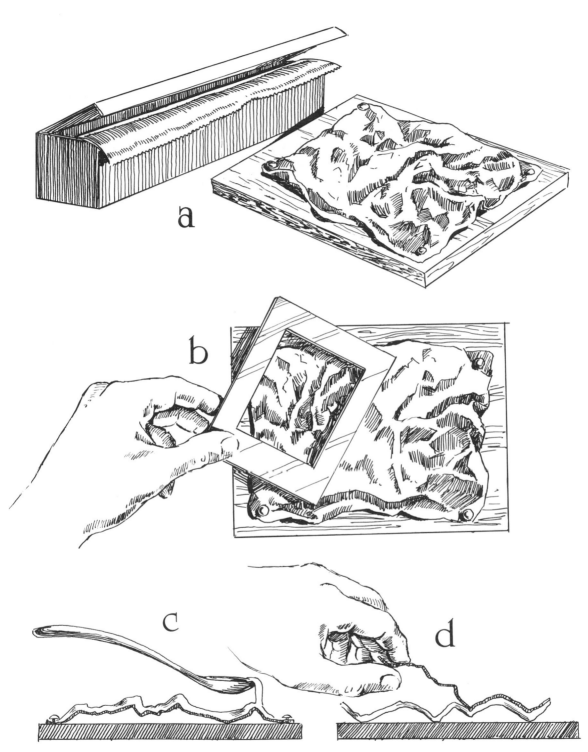

Fig. 8.1 a. Aluminum foil fastened to board. b. Using mask to select pattern. c. Depositing wax onto aluminum foil. d. Peeling away the foil.

189

aluminum foil away (do not peel away the wax; it will crack) and the model—at least the front surface of it—will be complete.

Now you must refine the silhouette of your piece. Ordinarily, the wax will form an interesting shape more or less naturally and will only require definition of the edge in order to remove any thin sections which might have been overlooked. However, you might possibly want to alter the form of the piece altogether, cut out a geometric form, a square or oval, or else pick up a prevalent pattern from the textured surface itself and carve the silhouette to reflect that pattern. Or you can alter the basically flat orientation of the piece; immerse it in warm water and roll it half-way around your finger or a mandrel so that it forms a half-tube, or else dome it up by pressing from underneath with your thumb. After all, it *is* sheet wax and can be handled just as you have always handled ordinary sheet wax—only this material has a texture. It can be cut into strips, twisted into spirals for earring drops, wrapped around a ring mandrel and made into an unusual band or—as here—it can be fashioned into a highly unusual brooch.

There is, however, a two-fold danger in making a brooch from a piece of textured sheet wax. The first is that the accidental mode of creation may be apparent, that it will look like exactly what it is: a metal casting of wax dribbled onto some kind of textured surface. This is how many "craft" pieces look. The other danger, conversely, is that the piece will, if anything, look too "professional," that it will look like a stamping. Stampings represent the cheapest form of jewelry; literally hundreds of thousands of pieces may be stamped out of flat metal sheet, slightly domed to create the most superficial illusion of three-dimensionality. This is always a danger when working with sheet wax. The surest way to cheapen your work, to make it look like either a "craft" piece or a stamping, is to imagine that, once the textured surface has been properly refined and silhouetted, it simply has but to be cast and buffed and it is ready to have a pin-back soldered to the undersurface. The effect would be the same were you to solder a pin-back to the slightly crumpled lid of an old tin can. Only in very special cases would such a flimsy display pass as a piece of finished jewelry. You must invest further time in order to render it acceptable.

There are actually two basic ways of finishing the piece, with one variation. In order to accomplish the desired illusion of solidity, you will require all the materials used on the sheet wax projects. Begin, then, with the simpler of the two methods.

Simple Gallery

Set the flat model directly onto a piece of sheet wax, trace around its border lightly with a scribe, immerse the sheet in warm water, and cut out a piece which is exactly the size and dimensions of the top (Fig. 8.2a). Then, cut out the center of the sheet so that a narrow border,

190

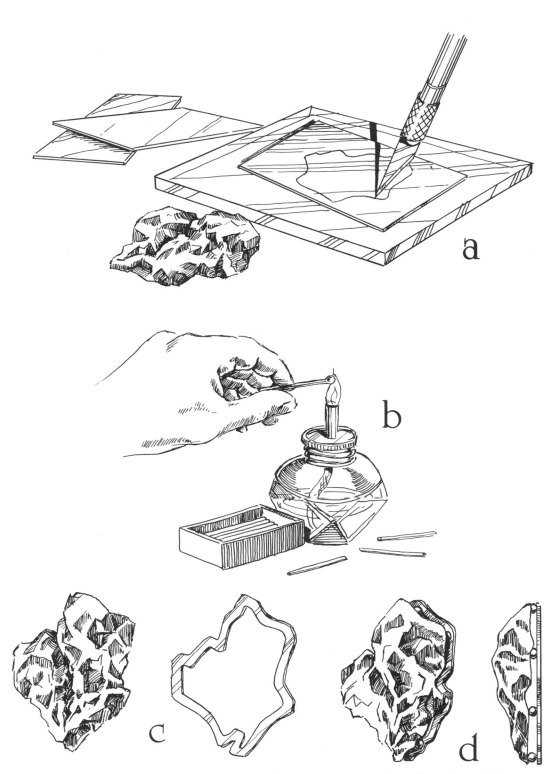

Fig. 8.2   a. Cutting the pattern. b. Making a small wax bead. c. The gallery plate. d. The completed unit.

perhaps 5 millimeters, remains; this will form the bottom section of what is called a "gallery": an openwork edge which is soldered onto more or less flat ornaments in order to impart an illusion of three-dimensionality without adding very much actual weight to the piece. Traditionally these galleries are attached by means of six or more small round beads. Simply take a fairly substantial wax rod and hold one end over a flame for a moment; the wax will melt into a globule at the end (Fig. 8.2b). After it has set, snip off the end section and apply a hot spatula to the freshly cut part until a ball forms. Make up six such balls and, spacing them out carefully, attach them to the sheet wax border by piercing the sheet from behind with a heated pin. Make sure that the edge of the ball does not exceed the edge of the border; the entire mechanism should be obscured when the front piece has been set in place (Fig. 8.2d). The two pieces should be cast separately to insure ease in polishing and, only then, should they be soldered together. If this is unfeasible, join them in the wax by touching the point of a fine spatula to the inside of each ball, fixing the top section in place.

Complex Gallery

The structure you have just created is rather a slap-dash affair, useful for more inexpensive pieces or pieces which demand a very light weight, but inappropriate for really fine work. A much better type of gallery is created by cutting a long thin strip from sheet wax, at least 6 millimeters wide; this strip, after the usual immersion in warm water, is fitted around the perimeter of the initial wax (Fig. 8.3a). This job requires fitting the two units together, for the bond here will be a permanent one. If the piece is level, it should present no problem; however, if you removed the wax from an irregular surface, most likely it will not be at all level. Try, by bending it slightly, to minimize as much of this irregularity as possible; the rest of the unevenness will have to be taken up by the gallery. Working gradually with your sharpest knife, cut out from the strip of sheet wax, a negative impression of the model's contour. Keep bending the wax as you shape it so that, when the entire edge has been accounted for, no gaps will show between strip and model—and the base line will be perfectly level (Fig. 8.3b).

You can attach the two units as is, creating an illusion of great thickness and weight, or you can convert this band into an open-work gallery.

The latter is a very ticklish task. The strip must be softened and flattened out again. Two very light lines should be traced onto the surface, no more than 1.5 millimeters from each edge and following the contour of each edge. Evenly spaced vertical lines are then inscribed into the wax, creating the effect of a row of long low windows. Each of these windows must then be cut out of the wax, leaving behind a very delicate open-work pattern (Fig. 8.3c). This band should be softened and reshaped to

192

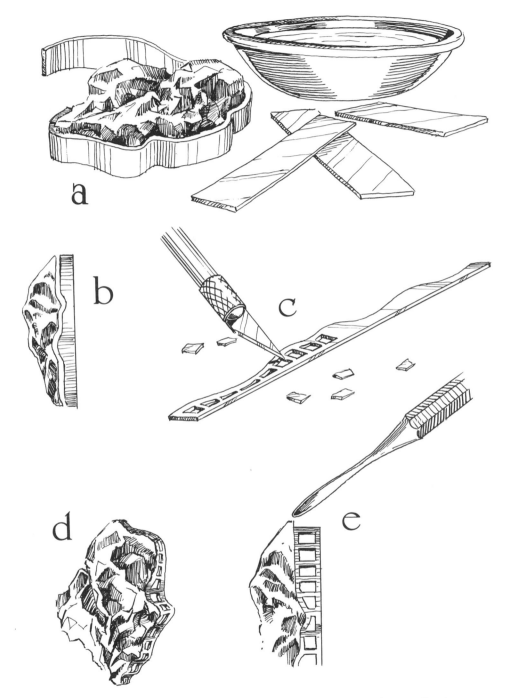

Fig. 8.3   a. Fitting the perimeter. b. Fitting gallery to uneven edge. c. Cutting open-work. d. The complete piece. e. Bonding technique.

fit the contour of the model; then it should be permanently bonded onto the front piece.

Remember, you have only 1.5 millimeters to work with on the gallery; the slightest excess heat will melt it all away. Therefore, the spatula should touch only the front surface. Place the gallery edge *behind*—not around—the border to your model (Fig. 8.3e), and leave a small lip as overhang. With a little melted wax on the spatula, touch only the lip, allowing the melted wax to fill up the crease where the two units meet. If possible, leave just a bit of the overhang so that, when the cast piece is filed and cleaned, the edge will be sharp and crisp. If however, the unforeseen occurs and you do melt away a section of this delicate gallery, do not attempt to add a blob of wax to the ruined section. Nor is it quite necessary to start over from scratch. Simply remove the afflicted section with a sharp blade and fit a fresh piece of unworked wax into the gap. Join the new piece to the existing gallery, allow ample time for the bond to set, cut the surface back to its original level, and cut out your windows. Do not worry about any roughness; wait until the casting for finishing touches.

An adequate substitute for poured wax in "accidental" jewelry is softened sheet wax. In fact, quite often the sheet wax is preferred. This becomes especially true when working with highly porous but fairly rigid materials, such as tree bark and pumice, or when working with material that might adhere permanently to the poured wax, such as sand or dirt. In these cases, it is simply a matter of immersing the sheet wax in fairly hot water until it is limp, and then pressing it lightly onto whatever surface you have selected. Remember, the more varied in height the surface, the thicker the wax should be in order for it to stretch down into the more recessed areas. Using sheet wax in this way will provide you with a vast array of textured surfaces which you can store away, ready to be used whenever the need arises.

OPEN-WORK BANGLE BRACELET

Bangle bracelets come, basically, in two styles: complete circlets or cuff bracelets, which are open on one side. The cuff bracelet has several advantages over the more traditional bangle. For one, since it does not have to fit over the hand but is fastened directly on the wrist, it can be smaller in diameter and therefore, will not slide up and down the arm as the circlet is apt to do. Since it has a distinct front and back, it may be more elaborately designed than the bangle which is intended to be viewed from all sides. It is lighter also. However, it has one drawback; it requires some spring in the metal to work properly. Ideally, the opening is to be spread, the bracelet put onto the wrist, and then—once the pressure has been relaxed—the bracelet will return to its original shape, eliminating any danger of it slipping off the wearer. This is impossible with a casting; once the casting has been deformed, it remains that way.

194

Cast metal has no spring to it. Therefore, even though the cuff bangle is a more practical object than the circlet, you must write it off as one of the few things which are strictly in the province of the metalsmith.

The circlet must pass over the hand to be worn. The idea, in creating a true bangle, is to make it as small as possible while still being certain that it will fit over the knuckles. If it is slipped on too easily there is danger of it slipping off too easily. The average diameter of the opening should be about 2½ inches (64 mm); this will cover most cases, unless you receive a special order and have to take your own measurements. As to the width, that is left entirely to your judgement—within limits, since the essential slipping-on operation might be hindered by an excessively wide band.

For this job, select a fairly thick piece of sheet wax, two fairly thick pieces to be exact, 8- or 10-gauge in thickness. Butt and join the narrow ends of the two pieces so that a unit approximately 12 by 3 inches (30 by 7.6 cm) will be formed. Do not worry about smoothing out the surface; that will all be done later. Immerse the piece in warm water and, depending upon your design, cut the piece lengthwise into two or three strips. Place the pieces not intended for immediate use between pieces of cardboard or stiff paper, to prevent warpage while in storage, and put them somewhere away from light and heat.

Take the remaining piece and dome up a central ridge uniformly along the entire length (Fig. 8.4a). Then, using either a bracelet mandrel or your forearm, bend the softened wax until a circlet of the correct size has been created. Snip off the excess wax, sand the surface smooth, and bond the two edges together (Fig. 8.4b); the basic form of the bangle is complete and ready to be made into a delicate open-work band.

This process is quite a simple one. With your finest pointed spatula or with a good thick needle mounted into a wooden dowel, melt a hole directly through the wax. The molten wax will cling to the surrounding area, like a membrane. In order to free it, just blow and the puff of air will open up the hole. To create a pattern, just insert the heated tool into the wax far enough away from the original piercing to insure ample wax between the two holes (Fig. 8.4c). Blow, perhaps this time from the inside to alter the surface texture. Do not attempt to complete one small area to your satisfaction while leaving the rest of the bangle untouched; aside from the dubious artistic merit of such an approach, the wax would simply get too soft and begin to deform. Work all around your bracelet so that no single section is appreciably more delicate than any other and, to prevent deformation, keep a pan of cold water nearby in which to soak the wax should it begin to soften. Experiment with two or three tools of different sizes to give variety to the open-work pattern. Or move the spatula around, while inserting it, to give variety to the shape as well. After you have completed the center row of holes, begin to pierce both above and below the central line, trying to keep the borders which

195

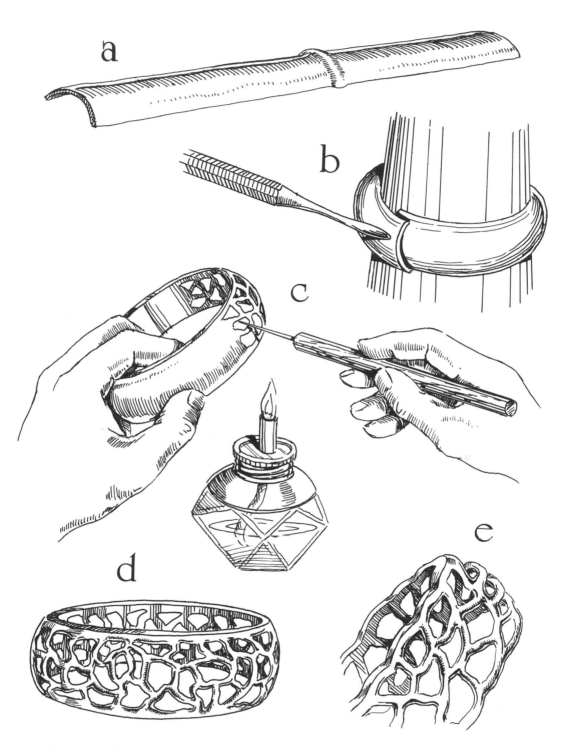

Fig. 8.4   a. The domed strip. b. Forming strip around bracelet mandrel. c. Creating the open-work pattern. d. The illusion of strands. e. Forming the edges.

196

separate the holes of a fairly uniform thickness. The illusion should be one of a network of more or less uneven strands criss-crossing to create an effect of laciness (Fig. 8.4d). You might have to make your holes fairly irregular in shape in order to attain this effect but the design will only be altered for the better.

The only real challenge you will face will be the two edges of the bangle. These should not retain their mechanically straight profile; the illusion of an organically formed entity will be destroyed. Nor can you really follow the pattern of the openings as you had been doing; the border might become entirely too irregular, imparting a haphazard quality to your piece. Try to keep the holes near the edge somewhat flattened, so that a fairly even border is suggested. Then, simply indent the border at the proper places to carry the design through (Fig. 8.4e).

You may now make the wax either lightly textured, by stippling it with a warmed needle, or you can create a glass smooth surface on your wax. This is easily accomplished by passing a red hot spatula near the wax so that the surface melts slightly. A less precise, but quicker method—for those who are inclined to be daring—is to hold the piece over the open flame of your alcohol lamp until the entire surface of the wax becomes glossy. If your piece is still intact, it is finished.

An alternate method of creating the same bracelet would be to use two ³⁄₃₂-inch (2.5 mm) pieces of blue carving wax instead of the sheet wax. Instead of first shaping the bracelet and then piercing it, you would pierce the flat slab until you were satisfied with the pattern. Then you would immerse the flat pieces in boiling water until they soften. Blue wax can sustain a bend of 180 degrees and retain the shape after it cools. Bend both pieces into semicircular shapes and join them (Fig. 8.5a). All you have to do to finish the bracelet is to align the pattern at the places of juncture by either adding or removing the wax where it might be necessary. Here, too, you might expose the wax to an open flame in order to restore the surface finish—with somewhat less risk than with the sheet wax.

On delicate pieces of this nature, it is imperative that the model-maker do his own spruing. Because of the many open spaces in the model, the sprue network must be fairly elaborate. In this case, an actual wheel with spokes should be created to insure even flow into the model (Fig. 8.5b).

Thus far, we have concentrated primarily on the low-melting waxes for accidental jewelry. However, as we have just seen, blue carving wax may be used to good advantage in making this sort of jewelry as well. Indeed, many waxes may be put to use in the creation of accidental jewelry. What is more, one may feel quite safe combining different types of waxes in order to produce the desired results. For example, if you

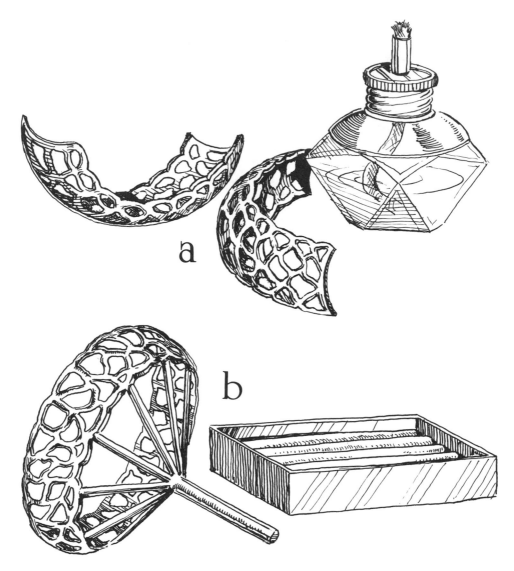

Fig. 8.5   a. Blue wax units ready to be joined. b. The sprue network.

wish to make your blue wax somewhat more fluid while still being able to retain its elasticity, add some green wax to the melt. You might wish simply to experiment by combining totally different types of wax, say carving wax and casting wax, in a ladle in order to see what effects might be achieved. Nor must you confine your experimentation solely to wax; use the wax as an adhesive and introduce various other substances into the pot—anything, just so long as it is organic in origin so that it can burn out in the investment flask. And here all sorts of novel effects are possible.

198

A very good source of organic material, for example, is the kitchen. The spice rack alone will yield a wide assortment of textures, from the subtly granular surface provided by sugar to the cross-hatch effect of oregano to the knobby effect provided by mustard seeds or pepper corns. Rice, spaghetti broken into bits, crumbled bread crumbs, corn flakes, all will impart a distinctive and often highly appealing surface texture to your wax. Crumpled newspaper, wood shavings, sawdust, broken-up almond shells—anything that will burn out in the casting process is admissable. Two things to remember, though: the wax which you use should be thin in consistency so that the unique features of whatever you might have added to it will not be blurred over by too thick a coating of wax; and second, make certain that your caster is aware that something other than pure wax is contained in your model. Indeed, many casters, not wishing to run even the remotest risk of fouling an entire flask, will refuse any mixed-media models. Others, however, will set aside a special flask just for you and await, with a mild curiosity, the results of each experiment.

Leaf Necklace

For your last project, you will make a necklace of leaves or flower petals or, even, of feathers. You will need the following materials:

> Aluminum pot
> Hot plate or gas burner
> Several sheets of set-up wax
> Inexpensive bristle brush, ¼-inch (jeweler's acid brush)
> Glass plate
> Thin wax rods
> Distinctively veined and shaped leaves or petals

This is truly a simple operation; the only real challange lies in being able to find and select leaves of the appropriate size and shape. Autumn, of course, is the ideal season for beginning such a project. If, however, nature is unwilling to cooperate with you, then a trip to the florist should yield enough material for half a dozen rather nice necklaces.

Begin with an assortment of ginkgo leaves: simple, distinctive, light, and well-veined. Select the leaves so that some sort of order is evident in the placement of them. A haphazard arrangement of natural forms might be fine in nature; when worn around a lady's neck, it just looks sloppy. The beauty of natural objects, when they are converted into ornamental pieces, is best displayed if the hand and eye of the designer are evident. If you wish to display five leaves in the necklace, choose three different sizes: a large one to be placed in the center, two slightly smaller ones to be placed on either side of it, and two considerably smaller ones to be used as end pieces.

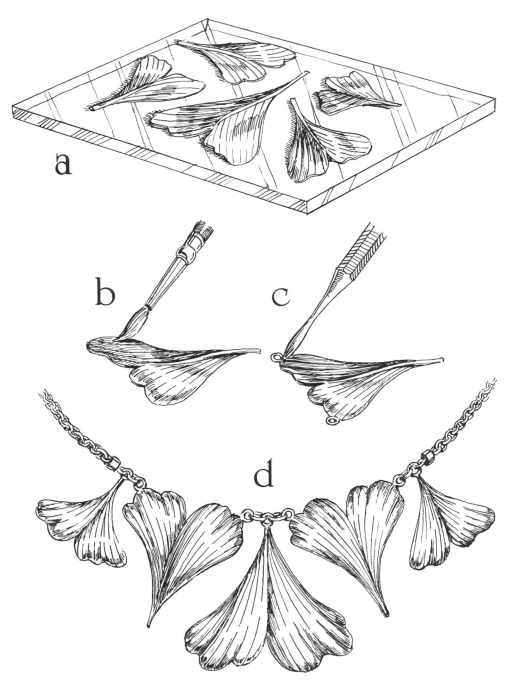

Fig. 8.6　a. Leaves placed on glass plate. b. Brushing leaf with wax. c. Adding wire loops to the leaf. d. The completed necklace.

Once this sorting has been completed, take the leaves and turn them face down on the glass plate. Make sure that they are lying as flat as possible, even if you have to secure them in place with a bit of rubber cement, or masking tape (Fig. 8.6a). When the wax is as fluid as it can be without boiling, dip a stiff bristle brush—to be bought in an art or jewelry supply store rather than in a hardware store—into the solution and take a small amount of wax onto the tip of the brush. Try not to dip the brush into the wax up to the ferrule; when the wax sets, there will be no way to unclog it. Immediately apply as thin a coat of wax as possible to the exposed side of the leaf. Work quickly, but deliberately, trying to leave a uniform deposit on the leaf (Fig. 8.6b). Work from the center out to the edges, being careful not to brush when the wax is beginning to set; it will leave lines in the surface. Be careful also not to flood the wax onto the leaf so that wax runs underneath it, obscuring details on the front. The front should not be touched; all the veins and distinctive features of the leaf should be left intact. The coat of wax which you have deposited on the back will lend sufficient strength to the fragile leaf so that it will be able to withstand the casting process unimpaired. Attach wax wire loops to the appropriate spots (Fig. 8.6c).

FINDINGS

At this point, it would be well to mention one aspect of the jewelry business which is absolutely essential, not only to the production houses but to the model-maker as well. It comes under the general heading of "findings."

"Findings" is a term which loosely covers all of the purely functional elements of the various types of jewelry: pin-backs, earring backs, bales from which to hang pendants, spring-rings, jump rings, plunger snaps, settings—all the things taken for granted when buying a piece of jewelry. Almost no piece of jewelry—with the notable exception of rings—is produced without at least one finding being included in the package. It is *essential* for the model-maker to become familiar with those findings that are available. Often an ornament can be lovely, but totally unusable as a piece of jewelry, simply because the model-maker has failed to consider the lowly finding while creating it. Instead of running this risk, obtain a catalogue from a finding house and study it. Then design your piece—no matter how spontaneously you wish to form it—to accommodate the purely functional element that will make it wearable.

Even the ginkgo leaf necklace would only be five interesting objects without the finding house. Jump rings connect the sections; chains hold the ornament around the neck; caps connect the chains to the leaf sections; and a spring ring fastens the whole thing in place (Fig. 8.6d). No matter that the initial model has been created accidentally, by brushing wax on a leaf, the final product must reflect the quality and the professional touch which is traditionally expected of fine jewelry.

Chapter 9

Specialized Wax
Techniques

THE wax model-maker is basically a sculptor, using various implements to shape objects from solid blocks of wax or from sheets. The quality of his work is gauged by his skill in executing certain basic procedures to produce a flawless model. Innate ability coupled with experience and common sense are generally the prime assets of any model-maker. Over the years, however, the professional will acquire various techniques, or shortcuts, that will enable him to attend to certain aspects of the work in a way that will assure both success and a vast saving of time. These aspects, in general, will not be creative ones; they will be those tedious and time-consuming jobs which are purely functional and only noticed if they are *not* executed correctly.

These tricks are generally the result of a reapplication of some basic wax-working principles to a very specific context. The model-maker must be alert to all the possibilities implicit in each technique he masters; the outcome will be an assortment of truly ingenious time-savers. Quite often, it is one of these shortcuts that will keep your estimate low enough to win an important job or secure an important client. Even though an assortment of tricks is hardly enough for a model-maker to survive on, it often represents the only distinction between the established professional and the talented beginner.

OPEN-WORK BEAD

Were you to approach this particular job equipped only with the basic tools—the wax file, a few needle files and knives, a hollow scraper perhaps, sandpaper—the possibilities of producing a perfect sphere would be slim indeed; perfect geometric forms are the most difficult for the human hand to create unaided. The best you could hope to achieve,

202

after hours and hours of painstaking work, would be an imperfect globe, a little lopsided perhaps, a little flat on one side.

However, anyone familiar with wood-working knows the precision attainable by turning the wood on a lathe. A cylindrical piece of wood is made to rotate while the carpenter holds sharp knives of various shapes against the spinning surface. The result is a row of absolutely symmetrical shapes; the carpenter can simply saw off the individual forms or leave the entire unit intact. Spindles and spools are made in this way, table-legs and bed-posts as well. This method is also employed for making wooden beads, and it is here that you can adapt it for your own purposes.

Turning Wax

In order to "turn" wax, you need a flexible shaft unit, the rough wax file, a rigid knife or hollow scraper, different grades of sandpaper, and a felt wheel buff. You also have to manfacture your own special mandrel to hold the wax. This piece of equipment can easily be fabricated from a worn-out or broken burr with the correct size shaft, or even from any nail that will fit the opening of the handpiece. However, you can make the job easier for yourself by using a shaft which has a cylindrical burr slightly wider than the shaft itself. The mandrel must be flattened, paddle-like, so that it will offer resistance to the rotating wax.

There are several ways to accomplish this flattening. You can bang it on an anvil with a sledge hammer, if you first heat it red-hot and let it cool gradually. You can file it flat on either side. Or, if you have chosen a cylindrical burr shaft, you can grind off two opposite sides of the burr with a stone wheel and file it smooth. The burr will produce a wide paddle on a shank of standard length; and the edges of the paddle will have teeth for additional gripping (Fig. 9.1a).

Before the wax is attached to the mandrel, the block must be roughly shaped: a five-minute job with the coarse file. After this has been done, hold the paddle-ended mandrel over the flame by gripping it firmly with pliers; wait until the end is as hot as it can get, then bury it into the roughly formed piece of wax. Be carefully not to jiggle it around, but insert it in one deft thrust as far as it will go (Fig. 9.1b). The hot metal should melt the wax just enough to allow entry, without much displacement of molten wax at the top of the hole. The idea is to melt just enough so that when the wax sets, the paddle-shaped mandrel will be firmly fixed in place.

Once the wax has set—and the process may be hastened by immersing the entire unit in cold water—snap the mandrel into your handpiece and begin. In order to adapt the use of the flexible shaft for this purpose, you must try to emulate, as much as possible, the basic action of the turning lathe. Only in this case, it is the rotating object which is moved while the cutting edge remains stationary (Fig. 9.1c). It is essential

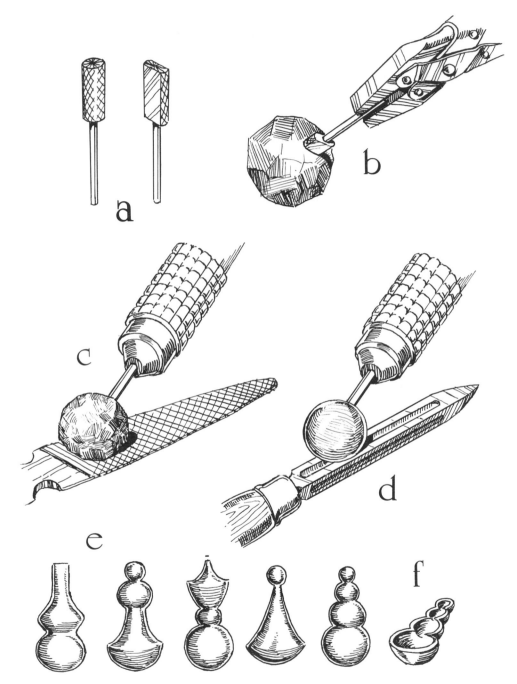

Fig. 9.1   a. Making mandrel from cylindrical burr. b. Attaching roughly shaped wax to mandrel. c. Turning the wax on a file. d. Turning the wax on a hollow scraper. e. Elaborately turned shapes. f. A shape hollowed out.

that the knife or file be as firm as possible so that the wax can be worked against it. If the bench has a hole drilled into the front to accept a ring mandrel, this may be utilized to secure the tool. If not, use the left—as well as the right—armrest to brace your arm while holding the file against the bench pin.

Using the flat side of a coarse wax file as the cutting surface, bring the rotating wax *lightly* into contact with the file. Allow the rough edges to be ground away first; too great a pressure at this point might loosen the wax from the mandrel. Begin lightly at the outer end of the ball and run the tool toward the mandrel side, defining the shape of the bead. At first, the outline will appear fuzzy; the rotating wax will not yet be uniform but will, rather, be a lopsided form that has only the semblance of symmetry lent by the whirling action of the drill. Gradually, however, as the shape becomes more regular, the rotating outline will become sharper until there is practically no blur at all. At this point, exchange the file for either the hollow scraper or a knife. Now you should try to hold the handpiece rigid and move the blade (Fig. 9.1d). If your touch is light enough, you should be able to smooth the surface and render the bead perfectly round in a matter of minutes. A final substitution of a piece of emery paper for the cutting surface should finish the job nicely. Buff it with a felt cloth while it is still rotating. Then remove the mandrel from the chuck, heat the metal shaft only and, when the wax that holds it in place begins to melt, use pliers to extract it. A few drops of wax in the resulting opening will complete the job.

Turning need not be confined to making beads. All sorts of symmetrical shapes are possible. Elaborate finials for neckchains and earring drops of the most fantastic sort are possible. The ingenious model-maker, having learned this very simple technique, should be able to reapply it in any number of ways to produce many objects that would be virtually impossible to make in any other way.

Cutting Open-Work

Your first impulse might be to slice the ball in half, hollow it out to 0.5 millimeter, join the halves, and work the pattern until daylight appears. This is the wrong approach; the bead would be so fragile that you would be in constant danger of breaking it. First, score the ball down the middle (to guide the arrangement of the pattern), then cut the design into the wax with the flexible shaft machine, working the depressions down to a millimeter below the surface plane (Fig. 9.2a). Be as precise and sharp in shaping the pattern as possible; *then*, when you are satisfied, saw the bead carefully in half and hollow it out with the largest round burr you have. The open-work pattern will show up as you approach the correct thickness for the bead. Any ragged or irregular spaces may be refined easily with a knife or a very fine cut file (Fig. 9.2b). For most open-work pieces, this approach will work best. Quite often, the differ-

205

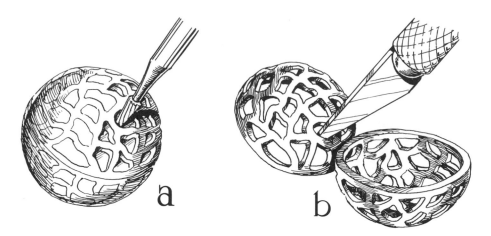

Fig. 9.2 a. Incising pattern into the wax ball. b. Refining the open-work after hollowing.

ence between success and failure in the creation of a model lies merely in the order in which the model-maker arranges the various steps in the process: the sawing, the carving, the polishing, and the hollowing. For example, if you are given the task of carving a great many details into a very small object, you would not adhere to the standard order of things. You would not first saw the exterior shape out of the block and then carve it; the piece would simply be too difficult to hold while you are working it. Contrary, then, to the accepted order, first you would carve the details, as a bas-relief, then you would free the carved object from the block with a saw, or with the flexible shaft, and touch up any raw spots later. A little common sense will make a difficult job simpler.

Water-Soluble Wax

There is a method whereby a hollow open-work bead can be created without the necessity of splitting it and rejoining it—indeed, without the necessity of hollowing it at all. This method employs a remarkable substance called water-soluble wax; it dissolves in water.

Water-soluble wax generally comes in one-pound blocks. It is a brittle substance which has the tendency to flake, and cannot be carved or filed with any grace; however, because of its unique property, it should be known to every model-maker. Used in conjunction with the build-up techniques outlined in Chapter 6, it can serve as a perfect base upon which to build elaborate open-work structures. A bead created in this manner will not be as precise, either in external form or in the inscribed detail, but it will have its own distinctive character quite in keeping with the more spontaneous approach offered by wax build-up.

Using your coarsest saw blade, cut a cube from the block. Rough-shape it with a knife; then, using a coarse wax file approximate, as best you can, the shape of the bead. Be aware, as you are forming the water-
206

soluble wax, that you are going to be building *on top* of this form; it represents the inside dimension of the bead and should, therefore, be a good deal smaller than the size you have determined for the finished product. Finish the job with sandpaper. Unfortunately this special wax cannot be turned as carving wax can; it will split and powder. For ease in handling only, heat up an old burr and bury it into the wax so that it forms a handle. Then begin building the open-work wax pattern on top of the water-soluble wax core.

You are already familiar with several methods of wax build-up. You can use a fine spatula and blue carving wax; you can use Perfect wax; you can even use half-round wax rods, joining them with heat. Or else you can employ a highly specialized piece of equipment intended for building up patterns in wax; the wax pen (Fig. 9.3).

The wax pen, like the electric spatula, consists of a box which controls the heat of the essential apparatus, in this case an airbrush-like device which extrudes a stream of liquified wax from its nozzle. It is a simple mechanism; a pellet of wax, usually blue carving wax, is inserted into an opening on the top of the pen. The pressure of your fingertip on a button set just behind this opening will push the wax pellet against heating coils, melting it and extruding it at the same time. Depending on the temperature setting, the type of wax, and the amount of pressure you employ, the extruded wax will either be runny or viscous; it may be deposited in tiny beads or large dollops, strings, wires, or crests. Anything which can be done with the hot spatula can be executed by the wax pen—and the results will be much more controlled, much more

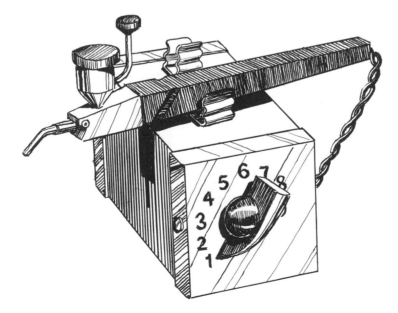

Fig. 9.3 A wax pen.

207

precise, and much more varied. If you intend, in fact, to specialize in built-up models, the wax pen might be a very good investment. It does have a tendency to clog, so you must make certain that all the working parts are clean and that the special wax pellets are kept well covered until you are ready to use them.

Indeed, with the wax pen, any object at all becomes a fit form for an openwork design. Remember, blue wax is flexible in its own right; when it is extruded it becomes yet more flexible. It is a relatively easy matter, then, using a marble or a wooden bead as the core, to build the openwork pattern around that model, slice through just enough of the blue wax to allow the marble to be popped out, and then to repair the bead with a hot spatula.

Here, however, the core has been fashioned out of water-soluble wax. When you feel that the built-up wax has achieved the desired effect, simply place the bead in a pan of warm water. In a very short time, the wax core will begin to dissolve, seeping out through the open-work in the design. When it dissolves completely, you will be left with only the hollow blue wax bead, ready for casting.

Matt Gun

The Matt gun is a rather recent addition to the market. Built along the principles of a glue gun, this device, again like the wax pen, extrudes wax from a nozzle. Unlike the wax pen, however, the Matt gun is able to extrude long unbroken, uniform strands of strong and extremely flexible wax, called weaving wax. Simply insert a wax pellet into the gun and, by applying slow even pressure, you can extrude several yards of fine round wire. The thickness of the wire can be controlled by changing the thumb pressure on the pellet, the temperature setting of the gun, and the size of the nozzle.

Extruding wax is all the Matt gun does, but the possibilities created by this very special wax wire are surprisingly great. The wire itself is completely different from the wax rods you are familiar with. Wax rods are very soft, very fragile, and have a very low melting point; once they have been twisted in one way, it is virtually impossible to reshape them in another direction. The wax extruded from the Matt gun is sturdy and hard, yet highly flexible; the melting point is comparatively high and the wax can even withstand carving. Moreover, the wax rod, when it is extruded, retains a high gloss due to the fact that it has been melted into shape. The rod requires, literally, no cleanup in the metal.

Given these properties, the models made possible through the use of weaving wax can be incredibly intricate. Anything, *anything* at all, possible through the use of metal wire is an easy task for the Matt gun. For example, a ring with a "woven" pattern can be fashioned from gold wire; chances are that only the illusion of actual weaving will be attained, and that a great amount of time will be spent in soldering and filing points. With the weaving wax, actual macramé can be accomplished; any type of knot able to be tied in a rope can be tied in this wax. Simply tie or weave the pattern to the appropriate width, bend it around a ring mandrel for shape and size, and join the ends with a touch of a hot spatula; the final casting will give no hint that this highly detailed knotting was not actually accomplished in metal wire, by a jeweler of superhuman capabilities.

There are two ways to create an open-work bead with this wax. The first is to apply different pieces of the wire, in whatever pattern you choose, to a ball of water-soluble wax, bond them with a hot spatula, and allow the core to dissolve in water. An alternative method would be to use red Mold-a-Wax as the core, pressing the wire into position so that the entire design could be studied and rearranged before the application of the hot tool. Afterwards, the wax wire bead would simply be split, to allow removal of the core, and then rejoined.

There is, however, an approach made possible only by the use of the Matt gun; the bead can actually be made free-form, in the air. This technique relies on the fact that the extruded wax sets very quickly when exposed to a direct draft of air; simply by blowing upon the wax, you can shorten the time it requires for setting. Attach the still hot and highly malleable wax, as it is in the process of being extruded from the gun, to a thin metal rod, which will become the axis for the bead (Fig. 9.4a). As you continue to apply pressure on the pellet, loop the hot wire back so that it touches the metal rod a second time, creating a C shape that you immediately freeze by blowing on it (Fig. 9.4b). A number of these C-shaped loops will form a network of staves, though which other strands of wax may be woven, or upon which a pattern of rods may be applied (Fig. 9.4c). Other types of wax can even be incorporated into the design; blue carving wax, Perfect purple wax, pink build-up wax may be applied onto the basic structure of the bead to create many interesting and unique effects.

DIPPING

Dipping is exactly that: dipping some object into a pot of melted wax in order to create a model. The process is, clearly, connected with the concept of molds described in Chapter 3. For example, assume that you have a finished piece of jewelry, a poodle pin, and you want to produce a number of them in the exact size of the original. You know that you cannot simply make a rubber mold directly from the piece; the shrinkage factor would make the finished pieces noticeably smaller than the original. Therefore, you are confronted with the task of creating a brand-new model—or else dipping.

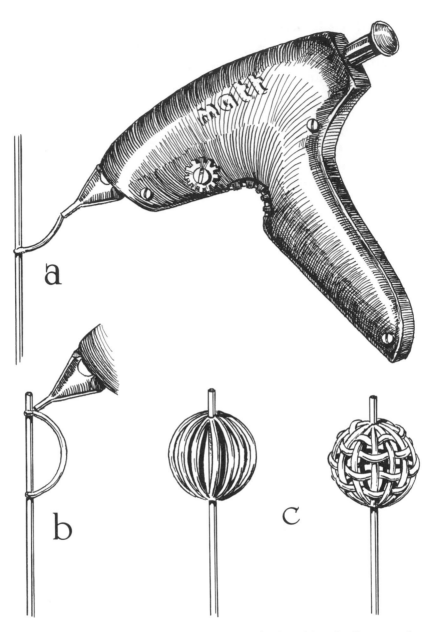

Fig. 9.4   a. Beginning bead with Matt gun. b. Attaching the first strand.
c. Completed structures.

Melting Pots

In order to begin, you need a melting pot: a more sophisticated
means of melting the wax and keeping it molten than your aluminum
saucepan. There is always the danger, when heating wax over the flame
or electrical coil, that it will bubble or burn, making it unusable. When
dealing with production techniques, you cannot involve yourself in wor-

rying about the consistency of the wax. To this end, you need a specially designed wax pot that has a built-in thermostat.

Wax pots come in three basic styles (Fig. 9.5). The most popular model, not only for the model-maker but for the wax injector as well, is a simple unit that will hold up to one quart of melted wax. It is nothing more than an electrified aluminim pot that has a dial whereby you can control the temperature of the melt. After a bit of trial and error, you can be absolutely certain of keeping the wax at whatever degree of viscosity is most efficient for the job at hand—without ever running the risk of bubbling. A second model is basically the same as the first, except that it has a hand-operated injection pump by means of which you can pump carving wax directly into a rubber mold.

The last model is, perhaps, the most useful for your purposes. It is divided into three wells; one well is large and fairly deep while the other two are smaller and shallower. A different wax can be melted in each—provided that the disparity in melting points is not too great, since each compartment is not individually controlled. In this way, you can work with three different waxes if desired.

To begin this job, it would be expedient for you to solder an L-shaped, 3-inch (7.6-centimeter) metal rod onto the side of the pin, to provide a handle and enable you to control the flow of the wax. Coat the piece with a wax lubricant. The wax which you use for the melt should be blue carving wax. It is the most flexible type of carving wax, rendered more flexible by the fact that it has been melted. It is also the most viscous and, therefore, it will build up a thicker coat on the metal piece than a more fluid wax could.

After the wax has then been heated to the proper consistency, simply dip the pin into the pot (Fig. 9.6a). When you have removed the piece from the melt, the wax will tend to run off the high spots and into the depressions, leaving an uneven coating over the metal; you can, in great measure, control the wax layer by twisting and turning the pin so that the wax has little opportunity to settle in the low spots. Once the wax has set—but before it has cooled completely—slice the wax along the outer edges of the piece and pry the wax shell away from the metal (Fig. 9.6c). If you are lucky, the entire piece will pop off; if there are undercuts in the original, you may have to remove the wax in pieces and rejoin it later.

Of course, this is only an approximate method. No matter how well you control the flow of the wax across the metal surface, you will have to resort to adding wax in order to patch up the thin spots. The shape, too, will have to be refined. The exact form of the piece has been reproduced *inside* the wax; the outside—while bearing the basic form of the metal original—has retained only a suggestion of the details; these must be worked with knives, files, or the flexible shaft machine. However, the time consumed is very little when compared to beginning a model from

211

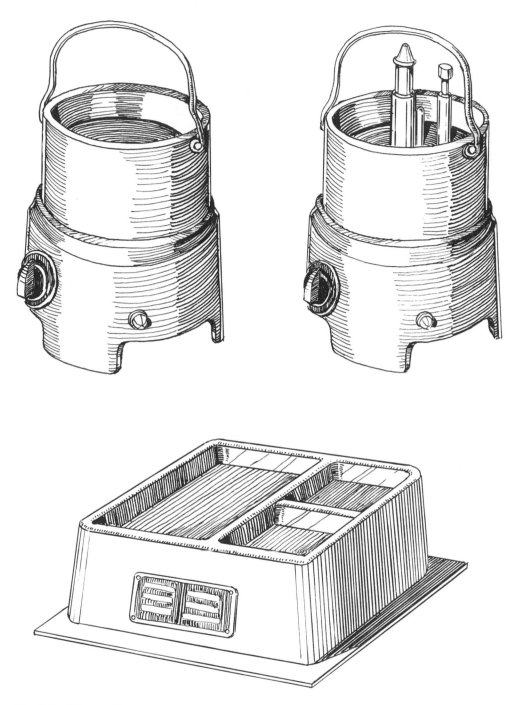

Fig. 9.5   Wax melting pots.

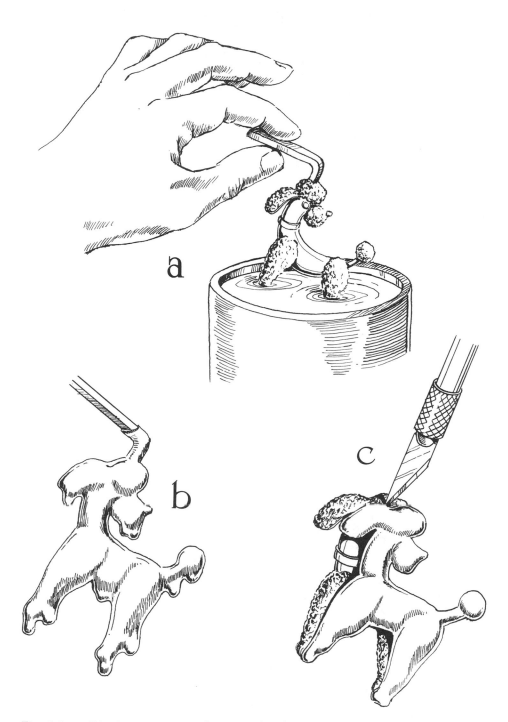

Fig. 9.6 a. Dipping pin into molten wax. b. The wax-coated pin. c. Removing the wax from pin.

scratch. Besides, the model is already hollowed out and the size, due to the fact that the wax has formed a coat over the original, has been increased just enough to compensate for shrinkage and return the finished piece of jewelry to the size of the original.

PRONG SETTINGS

In general, the incorporation of a prong setting into a piece of jewelry is not the concern of the model-maker. The prong setting is either made individually in metal to accommodate a specific stone or else is purchased as a casting made from an original metal model. The setting is then soldered onto each cast piece—never onto the wax model—by a jeweler. There are several reasons for this: polishing the broad surface of a piece of jewelry would be hampered by the placement of settings on the model; also, settings are often of a different metal from the one used to cast the piece.

Wax settings are generally used only in places where soldering would either be impossible or so time-consuming a task that the operation would be economically unfeasible. However, many casters stock a complete line of wax settings in all standard sizes and shapes. The waxes, almost invariably, are made from a very precise metal model and are usually preferable to any wax model you can fabricate by hand; it is one of the very few areas of specialization where the metal model-maker has the advantage. To carve a setting for a one-carat round stone would not only take longer in the wax but the fragility of the material would preclude any real precision. Indeed, in making wax settings, only a modicum of precision may be expected, and it is only for those jobs in which a truly fine hand is *not* required that you can acceptibly utilize the following special technique for creating prong settings.

The prong setting is created with the dipping procedure described in the previous section. Instead of blue wax, purple or even green might be preferable, since it will be necessary to file sharp detail into the model. Instead of a finished piece of jewelry to dip into the wax melt, you have a number of metal rods called dip sticks, each of a different shape and size.

The metal rods will, in most cases, have to be fashioned by hand. Ordinary brass rods, available in hardware stores in various thicknesses, are fairly simple to shape with files. The rods, in general, are round, and easily adapted to marquis, oval, square, baguette, and round settings. First taper the rod slightly, starting about ¾ inch (19 mm) from the end; this will provide the correct angle for all the settings. Then form the basic shapes, leaving the bottom flat (Fig. 9.7a). Polish the rods so that there will be no burr to which the wax may cling, making removal of the setting difficult.

Dip the lubricated rod into the melt, twirling it upon removal, to insure a uniform coating. Wait until the wax has cooled and slice the wax

214

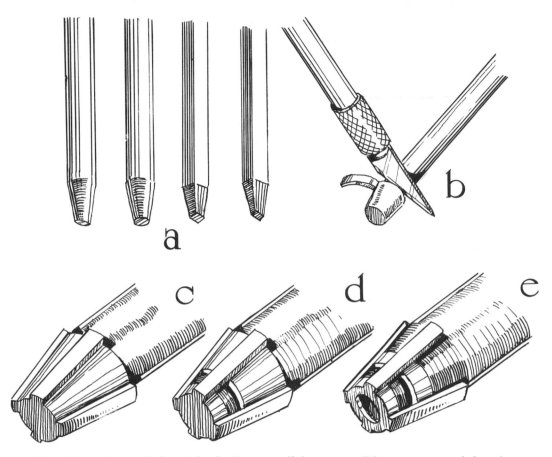

Fig. 9.7 a. Assorted dip sticks. b. Evening off the wax. c. Filing grooves to define the prongs. d. Cutting the open-work gallery. e. The completed setting.

level at the point where the tips of the prongs are to end (Fig. 9.7b). File the bottom flat. File off any irregularities in the setting. Then, using a warding file, cut down four evenly spaced grooves while the wax is still in place on the rod (Fig. 9.7c). The four high ridges will become the prongs when you begin to work the rest of the setting with your knife.

Using the very point of a number-11 X-Acto knife, or else fashioning an implement with a thin sharp chisel point, cut out the small squares which will form the open-work gallery (Fig. 9.7d). Then cut out the squares which will isolate the prongs (Fig. 9.7e). Remove the setting from the rod and touch up any imperfections with a small escapement file.

A second method of producing a wax setting is more applicable for smaller settings, such as clusters, where precision is not as much a concern as speed and overall effect. Here, as in the first method, dip the rod into the wax melt, twirl it as it is being removed so that a uniform coating is created, and let it cool. While it is still on the rod, level the top and

215

the base. Then, using a tri-corner file, cut in three or four narrow grooves, depending upon the size of the setting (Fig. 9.8a). Slice out the central third of the setting, leaving two thin separated circles on the rod (Fig. 9.8b). Then, using thin gauge wax rods laid into the grooves across both discs, touch the hot point of your finest spatula to the points of contact, connecting all the units while leaving sufficient tail on the rods to permit easy handling later, when creating the cluster (Fig. 9.8c). For even less precise but still usable cluster settings, a simplified version of the preceding approach may be employed; instead of making two circles separated by a gallery, one circle will suffice, a circle with grooves for only three wax rods. Remember, also, that when making cluster settings, quite often one prong will serve double duty, holding two stones in place; the best procedure is to make an assortment of settings—some with three prongs, some with two, and some with only one—and use them as necessary within the structure and design of your piece.

INLAYS

An inlay, very simply, is a metal unit which fits into another metal unit. Inlays are used when polishing one solid piece would be impossible and several sections are demanded. They are also used when different metals are combined in a single design; this—especially as the price of gold continues to rise—is the primary function of the inlay in the jewelry industry. One can reduce expenses by combining gold with silver while not sacrificing anything by way of design. In fact, quite often, very spectacular pieces can be produced.

The creation of a piece which contains an inlay requires at least two waxes, two metal models, two molds, and two castings. One might ordinarily imagine that these steps should be effected in order, that the two wax models would be made simultaneously, each being painstakingly and deliberately crafted to tenon perfectly—an all but impossible job right there, if the design is at all intricate. However, this is not the case. Inlays and other tight fittings require absolute precision in their creation. Wax, no matter how rigid it might be, still has considerable flexibility—especially at the thin gauges demanded of jewelry. Imagine, then, fitting one piece of wax into another piece of wax. First one would distort in order to accept the other while the second would, in turn, be distorted to fit. The two pieces would fit together perfectly *in the wax*. However, once the two are separated again, they will return to their original forms, which, when frozen in metal, will in all likelihood not fit together at all.

In order to make a well-fitting inlay, it is necessary to get one unit into its cast-metal form *before* fitting the second wax into it. The usual procedure is to make the framing piece first, in wax, taking care to leave a seat designed to accomodate the inlay (Fig. 9.9a). This unit must be cast and cleaned perfectly before anything further may be done to it.

216

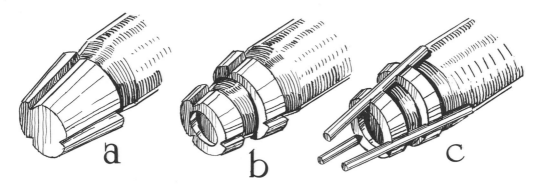

Fig. 9.8   a. Cutting the grooves. b. Separating the units. c. Attaching the wax rods.

Any cleaning later on in the process would destroy the exactness of the fit, for your precision is predicated upon the fact that the wax will be formed to the exact specifications of the metal frame; any subsequent cleaning of the seat will remove material, make the opening wider, and alter the fit.

There are two methods for applying the molten wax to the metal frame, depending upon the size of the opening to be inlayed. If the opening is small, simply dip the frame—holding it by the casting sprue—into a green wax melt, catching enough wax in the opening to fill it. If the opening is too large to be filled in this way, use a large spatula to pour the molten green wax into the inlay cavity. Fill the bottom and edges first, to insure that the wax retains the form of the seat exactly (Fig. 9.9b). Then fill in the center.

Notice that you use green wax for this project rather than the more viscous blue; this has been done to minimize contraction of the wax when it sets. Contraction will cause the inlay to pull away from the frame, leaving an imperfect fit. In order to combat this all but inevitable effect, wait until the wax sets—so that the extent of the contraction may be accurately gauged—and then insert a hot, loaded spatula into the gap left by the shrinkage, augmenting the edge with enough wax to insure a proper fit (Fig. 9.9c). You can also slit the wax, one side at a time, press the form back against the metal frame and rejoin the unit with the addition of extra wax in the center (Fig. 9.9d). Whichever method you apply to the problem, there is one certain way of determining whether the fit will be adequate after the wax inlay has been reduced by the unavoidable shrinkage which will occur in casting and cleaning. If you encounter any difficulty in popping the wax out of its metal frame, being forced to exert pressure from behind in order to extricate it, then, in all likelihood, you have sufficient material to compensate for the shrinkage. Make certain that the edge of the inlay is as clean as the edge of the frame; any drastic cleaning—even a very cursory one—will remove enough material to ruin the fit.

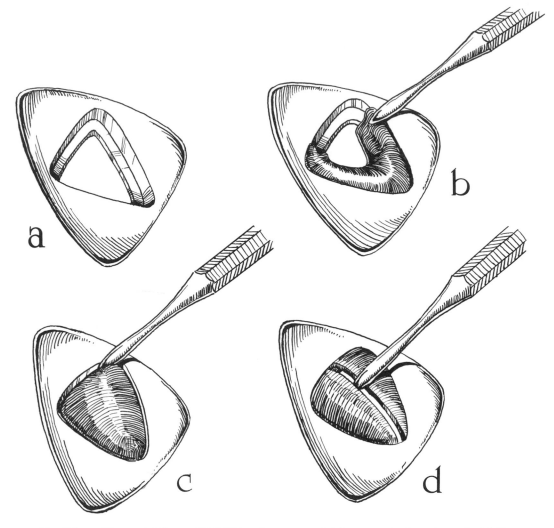

Fig. 9.9   a. The metal frame. b. Adding the wax. c. Adding wax to the edges. d. Adding wax to the center.

Inlays are most commonly created in this way; however, there is nothing to stop you—especially if the inlayed piece is significant enough—from casting the inlay first and using the dipping process to build a frame around it. This method will remove the worry over the wax pulling away from the fitted edges as it sets. In this case, as the wax contracts, it will form a tighter fit around the metal piece, so tight that it may even split. If this occurs, just squeeze the sides together on either side of the fissure and add a little wax to weld the break.

Casting shrinkage will also work in your favor. In this case, there is no need for as tight a fit between the wax model and metal model as you had been forced to achieve when the inlay was wax. There is no need for pressure to be exerted when the inlay is removed from its wax frame. Considering contraction and casting shrinkage, an over-tight fit would make the finished frame much too small to accept the inlay and you would have a difficult routing job in the metal. Instead, if the metal inlay is able to be *placed* tightly into the frame, exactly as you would want the finished pieces to fit, then the shrinkage caused by the casting and the routine cleaning and polishing of the metal should offset each other.

MODIFYING CASTING-WAX RING

This problem is fairly typical of the sort of thing encountered by a professional model-maker. You are given a wax that has been taken from a rubber mold; the original model is a diagonal dome ring, only it was designed when gold was priced much much lower than it is now. It is about 25 millimeters wide and the wall is uniformly 2 millimeters thick. Your job is to produce a ring which is less than 1 millimeter thick, and whose crown measures only 19 millimeters across the top.

First make sure that the proper casting wax has been used. The very hardest casting wax is simply too friable to be worked with any sort of ease. The touch of a saw onto the material will cause it to shatter. The very softest casting wax will not work either; it is so soft that it will deform and take on the texture of your fingerprints in a matter of minutes. For this job—and for almost every other job in which you use casting wax this way—the all-purpose medium grade wax is best. It is flexible enough to sustain the pressure of your tools, and it is hard enough to hold whatever new detail you work into its surface.

Ordinarily, when one is beginning such a project from scratch, any alteration of the basic silhouette is accomplished on the outside of the piece; wax is either added to or removed from the borders of the model. Here, however, since you are dealing with a finished ring, already hollowed out, any work to alter the external dimensions will destroy the piece altogether. All modifications must be done from the inside.

You should have at least two casting wax models of the piece on hand, as well as a small block of casting wax and two saucers of water—one warm and one cold—by means of which you can control the flexibility of the material. Dipping the wax model into warm water first, so that it will not shatter in your fingers as you work it, saw horizontally across the middle of the crown (Fig. 9.10a). Use your number-2 saw blade and cut completely through the crown until you reach the shank. During this operation, the most difficult job will be to hold the ring firmly without breaking it. A good—if rather daring—approach is to put the ring on your finger while sawing it slowly. A safer way is to wrap a wooden ring mandrel in felt and set the ring on that while sawing it. Not only will the risk of breakage be minimized, but the circlet will not become distorted while you work the model. You may, indeed, keep the ring placed on

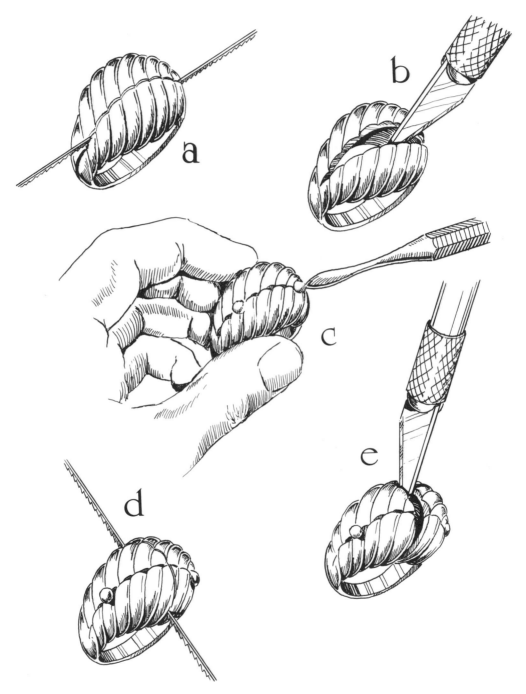

Fig. 9.10 a. Sawing the crown horizontally. b. Removing a strip from center. c. Tacking the seam. d. Sawing the crown vertically. e. Removing a strip from the center.

220

the mandrel throughout the entire procedure until you have to remove it in order to hollow out the inside.

Once the saw has cut through, remove a ⅛ or ³⁄₁₆ inch (4- to 6-millimeter) strip of wax from the center of the crown (Fig. 9.10b). The best tool for this is the number-11 X-Acto knife. Using a new blade dipped in wax lubricant and dried slightly, scrape out the wax from either side of the sawcut. Work from the center toward the sides, using a light uniform stroke until a lozenge or marquis-shaped opening has been created; such a shape will allow you to reclose the gap in the crown fairly gracefully without altering the thickness of the ring at the shank. Dip the ring into warm water to soften it and insure flexibility; then, very slowly and gently, squeeze the opening shut. Make sure that the two sides of the cut touch at all points. Make whatever corrections are necessary, and then, taking some wax on a heated spatula, tack the opening shut. Deposit the wax in two beads, each a third of the way in from the sides (Fig. 9.10c). This will leave the center free for work and will also permit you to reopen the cut if necessary.

You have now reduced the model to the appropriate width; the specifications of the job have been met. However, your aesthetic sense should at once dictate further revisions. The ring, as it is now, is disproportionately squat and, to recreate the basic proportions of the original, you must reduce the horizontal dimension as well. Therefore, using the saw, slice once again through the center of the crown; only now, the cut should be vertical. Do not slice all the way through the ring, but, rather, leave the edges joined (Fig. 9.10d). Remove a strip of wax as before.

Dip the wax into warm water to resoften it, squeeze the sides together and survey the results. If the pattern of the ring is reasonably reproduced, even with all the revisions, tack the slit together in preparation for the final bonding. If, however, the pattern is so askew that minor corrections would have no appreciable effect, open up the two blobs of wax which hold the original cut closed and shift the four sections around until a reasonably clear version of the original design appears (Fig. 9.11a). Then tack all the openings shut.

Bonding Casting Wax

Now you must add wax in order to rework the design and leave no trace of the surgery you just performed. Keep in mind, while adding the wax, that this is not carving wax; excessive heat will open up big holes in the model, destroying all the work you have done. If you can, use an electric spatula. If not, you must take special care; add only enough wax to restore the original pattern. Dip the piece frequently into cold water to prevent distortion. The new wax will be significantly darker in color than the wax of the original model. It will lighten somewhat as it sets. Remember, casting wax takes longer to set than carving wax. Take ample

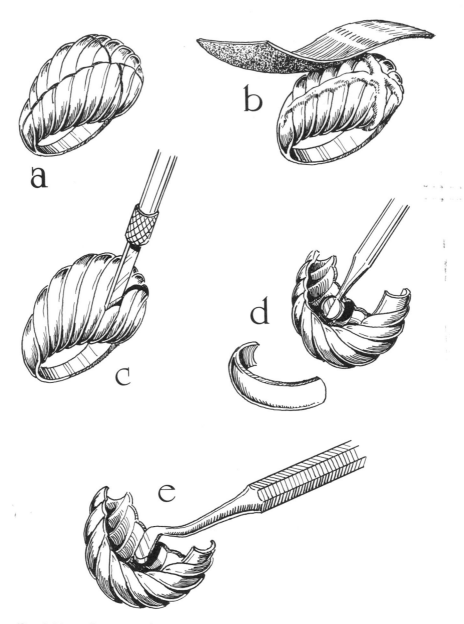

Fig. 9.11 a. Restoring the pattern. b. Reshaping the crown. c. Defining the pattern. d. Hollowing model with wax burr. e. Scraping out the hollow.

time to let the whole piece cool; you may well ruin the entire model through impatience.

Finishing Touches

When you have added enough wax to the crown, set the hot tool aside for finishing touches. Using a piece of number-2 emery paper, lightly reshape the basic contours of the ring, restoring shape and proportion to the crown (Fig. 9.11b). Do not work on the pattern until you are satisfied with the exterior shape. Then, reform the design by cutting sharp V-shaped channels into the wax you have added (Fig. 9.11c). I have found that, when working on casting wax models, a pushing action of the knife, using it as if it were a chisel, is preferable to the usual slicing one; there is less drag on the blade and the cut can be more readily controlled. Finish with a scraping motion to round out all the corners and angles, then burnish to smooth out any irregularities in the surface. There is no need to press hard on the model; the wax is soft and takes a shine readily. However, if you find that, even after burnishing, the surface is still irregular, you can use heat to create a perfect finish.

Do not attempt to use an open flame on this wax. That procedure is risky enough on carving wax; on casting wax, which melts at some 75°F lower, it would be downright foolish. Instead, turn the thermostat on your electric spatula up to its highest setting and, taking extreme care never actually to touch the surface of the wax, move the red-hot tip close to the wax to put a shine on the model. This technique is especially useful when working in concavities where heat from an open flame would not reach until the higher points had been melted down and ruined. Work carefully and the entire surface of the piece should quickly display a fine gleaming finish.

Now, you must turn your attention to the second problem; lightening the weight of the ring by reducing the thickness of the wall. Make certain that the wax has cooled completely from its exposure to the heated spatula; any contact with it while it is even slightly warm will mar the perfect finish. There are two methods which you can employ to hollow out the model. You can use specially shaped burrs designed for use on wax, or you can create your own rounded chisel and scrape away the excess material. However, before you begin, carefully examine the inside of the model.

You have split the crown twice and have rejoined the gaps from the front, taking care not to melt any more of the material than was absolutely necessary to create a bond. The front is flawless, but it is more than likely that the inside of the ring is badly marred. You may have an occasional dribble solidified on the reverse side of your bond; more important, the bond itself may not have gone all the way through to the inside of the model, leaving a distinct criss-cross channel in plain view. Not only is this scar evidence of the modification of the original ring, but it also leaves parts of the model perilously thin for casting and, later, filing. Before you can attempt any hollowing from the inside—an operation which itself might endanger the model at this stage—this channel must be filled. But the model is fragile; any excessive heat might ruin it. Were you to attempt to run casting wax into the groove, the results could range anywhere between complete destruction of the ring to an easily discernible sagging of the details on the front side of the repair. Instead, for this job—as well as for many other such superficial repairs, both on casting and on carving wax—the ideal material is inlay wax.

Inlay Wax

Inlay wax comes in stick form, usually eighteen pieces to a box. It is a very low-melting material, beginning to flow almost immediately after being introduced to the flame. All you have to do is to deposit a bit onto the surface of the wax model; it will run, like water over a stone, into the deepest recesses of the groove, filling it, while leaving the surface of the piece unaffected. This wax should never be used for structural bonding; its function is purely cosmetic, filling in imperfections and surface flaws. Any high spots left on the surface of the piece after the wax has set may be scraped off easily without undue danger to the rest of the model.

Hollowing Ring

Since the casting wax is so brittle, the usual method of hollowing out carved wax rings becomes potentially dangerous. Any slip with the tool while it is being angled into the cavity might result in a split wax model. Here, it is recommended that the shank be sawed carefully away so that work on the interior is unobstructed.

Special wax burrs that have only three blades (Fig. 9.11d) are stocked by most jewelry supply stores. These are generally available only in the round shape and only in a limited range of sizes; however, even if you cannot accomplish the complete job with them, you can at least make a good start. Because of the unique arrangement of the cutting blades, wax cannot become embedded in the grooves. However, you must be aware that it will cut very quickly—and roughly. Therefore you must approach the hollowing operation with the lightest touch you can muster. Work carefully, from the center out until you have almost the desired thickness; then switch to a more manageable manual tool.

Hand tools designed especially for the purpose of scraping out the hollows of wax models do not exist, as far as I know; but they are easily made. Select the shape of dental tool or wax carver which will best lend itself to this job. Any small chisel-shaped tool with a slight bend to it is ideally suited (Fig. 9.11e). Simply round the corners of the chisel so that a semicircular blade is created, and sharpen the entire sweep of the cutting surface. Draw it lightly across the interior surface of the model—a very fine shaving will result—repeating the operation as many times as necessary to reach a uniform thickness. Rejoin the shank to the crown, bonding the joint with casting wax from the outside; touch it up with inlay wax on the inside; polish the entire piece lightly with a buffing cloth.

MIX-AND-MATCH-CASTINGS

This section does not explain a technique really but rather an entire approach to model-making, an approach which demands its own specialized techniques, even its own specialized approach to design. I call it Mix-and-Match-Castings. In this approach, the model-maker/designer uses waxes pulled from existing molds to create something brand-new.

Mix-and-Match-Castings are most often used as a way of conserving money and making new pieces by modifying old ones slightly. Yet it need not be as strictly production-oriented as it sounds. If the model-maker is thoroughly familiar with his resources—the molds at his disposal—and if he is able to integrate different elements into a new piece, a very nice product can be the result.

You must have a complete knowledge of the castings available. If the molds have been made from your own pieces, there is no problem of course; not only will you know all the pieces of which you have castings but, since the style of all the pieces will have been created by the same artist, individual elements gleaned from different pieces will, more often than not, fit together harmoniously without too much effort. The difficulty comes when you have inherited a batch of molds and are told to create from them. Quite possibly these molds represent the work of dozens of different model-makers, each with a different style and technical capabilities. Your best procedure, in this case, is to secure a wax of every piece, appraise it and memorize it; in this way, you will know your resources when the time comes to use them.

An extraordinarily large number of "new" jewelry creations are produced by mixing and matching castings. Most of these are fairly unimaginative and graceless; however, the process by no means precludes originality and beauty. Simply exercise good taste and appreciate the integrity of each individual piece of jewelry, looking at each model as something quite unique.

The first type of model construction deals with pieces that do not fit together physically and must be modified in order to form a unit. In this situation, the pieces must be shaped individually, as you would form pieces of ordinary carving wax. These are then bonded by the casting wax itself or, in sections where a deal of work must be done to render the design harmonious, by molten carving wax. Extreme care must be exercised when introducing the carving wax to the casting wax model; the heat required to melt the carving wax is more than sufficient to burn right through the model. Add a very small deposit of green carving wax to the surface of the model; then build up a thicker deposit upon the first. The two waxes will bond nicely and, of course, the carving wax will be a pleasure to work. It is not an extraordinary occurrence to carve an entire new section from carving wax and fit it onto a casting wax model, bonding the two together with casting wax and touching up the seam with inlay wax.

225

The second type of Mix-and-Match-Casting model requires very little in the way of basic alteration. It is merely a bonding of two surfaces which fit flush, a job which—had the units been cast into metal—would have fallen to the production solderer. In this category are the various seal rings and identification bracelets to which ornaments are affixed, earrings which have been applied onto standard ring shanks, or cufflink frames deliberately designed to accommodate a motif or a setting in their centers. These items usually demand more of the model-maker in terms of speed and productivity than in aesthetic sensibility. When producing them, the model-maker must be aware not only of the time he will spend on them, but of the time it will take the production jeweler to clean and polish them as well. Obviously, the method used for bonding cannot be the same as the one employed for pieces which require some alteration; you cannot run a hot tool along the seam, flow in the inlay wax, and then smooth out the joint. Nor can you employ the method used to bond flush joints of carving wax; a hot needle thrust through the back plate would melt away too much wax to form a proper bond. There are, however, two methods which will do the job satisfactorily.

Crazy Glue

The first is the simpler method—but it should be reserved only for extremely delicate bonding, which requires but one or two tiny points of contact and where *any* application of heat would destroy the details of the piece: Crazy Glue. A needle dipped into the opening of the container will deposit enough of this extremely fast-drying cement to bond small sections of wax together. The joint, of course, will not be a permanent one—only molten wax will form a permanent bond—but it will be strong enough to hold the pieces in place throughout the investing process. Nor will a small amount of glue foul the investment in the burnout process, or even leave a residue in the cavities. But exercise discretion when using it; too heavy a reliance on this handy expedient could ruin the surface of your model and endanger the casting process as well.

Sticky Wax

The second method of joining casting wax sections together is much more versatile, can be used on much larger areas, and is perfectly safe for all types of casting. This method utilizes an extremely useful substance: sticky wax.

Sticky wax usually comes in stick form, either colorless or red, and is available in boxes which contain a dozen pieces. It is a very soft substance, somewhat resembling Mold-A-Wax but much more gummy, and melts at a fairly low temperature. As its name implies, its salient characteristic is its stickiness; with very little heat—well before it begins to flow—it is able to bond to any other type of wax: casting wax, carving wax, even sheet wax.

A very little bit of this material is all you should need; too thick a slice will leave a gap between the two sections you intend to join. Once you have the wax on the point of a knife, hold both the sticky wax and one of the two surfaces to be bonded *near* the flame, keeping both in constant motion (Fig. 9.12a). Your objective is simply to warm the wax—not to melt it. A moment or two should be sufficient; then apply the sticky wax to the casting wax piece. If the pieces have been warmed properly, it should adhere with no difficulty (Fig. 9.12b). In order to bond your two casting wax pieces together, hold each piece—the one with the sticky wax, the other without it—near enough to the flame to heat them

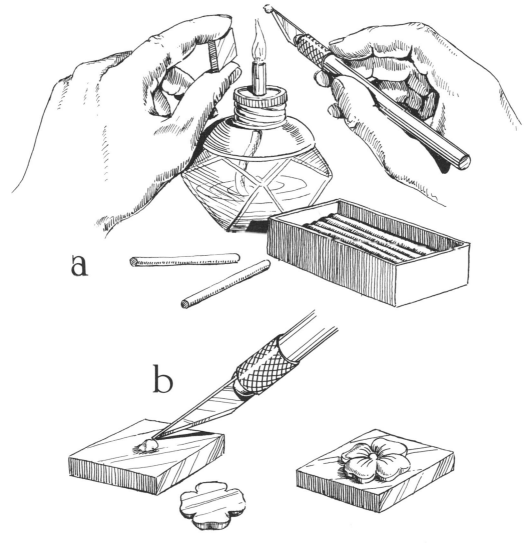

Fig. 9.12 a. Preparing the surface. b. Applying sticky wax.

both; then just press them together. The bond will be strong enough to survive the investing operation and, since the adhesive is, after all, wax, no difficulty should ever arise in the casting.

The uses of this material are, obviously, many. It can be used to bond joints where a minimum of heat is demanded; it can be used to tack pieces in place so that they may be appraised, shifted if necessary, and finally bonded permanently, or it can be used to fill in tiny irregularities in a joint which is not completely flush. Like so many of the expedients we have reviewed in this chapter, the uses of sticky wax are only as limited as one's imagination. Each of the methods described here is really only a beginning, a direction for you to follow; once you have learned these few simple techniques, your own common sense and curiosity should enable you to advance well beyond them.

Chapter 10

Finishing the Metal Model

GRINDING, cleaning, and polishing castings is the domain of the production jeweler: a man whose worth to the industry lies primarily in speed, rather than in precision. No member of the shop is as dissimilar to the model-maker; and yet, it is essential that model-makers learn the production jeweler's trade: not for speed, not on every casting, but to manicure the casting of the original model to absolute perfection. The rubber mold—from which every other casting is to be created—is made directly from this metal model. It must be perfection itself; the slightest mote will be reproduced tens or hundreds or even thousands of times.

The importance of casting the original wax cannot be overestimated. If you have a choice among casters, select the best one. Even if his price is many times more expensive than that of the standard production casting house, it is simply not worth the risk to the original model. But even if you have located the best and most dependable casting house in the country, your instructions to the caster should be very explicit. *Always* cast models in sterling silver. Fourteen-karat gold, the standard metal for castings in the jewelry industry, is too hard a material for the model-maker to work comfortably. Bronze is also too hard, and brass cannot really capture the finer detail work of the original wax. Silver flows best into the investment mold; it is hard enough to hold every detail of the original and soft enough to be worked with comparative ease. Not only should the casting be in silver but the silver should, if at all possible, be "bombed."

BOMBING THE SILVER

Bombing is a chemical process whereby the oxidation, which has formed on the model due to the intense heat of the casting process itself,

229

is removed and the surface once again attains the gleam of precious metal. Bombing *can* be done at home, in some well-ventilated spot, but it entails the use of a heated cyanide solution which actually explodes when the catalyst is thrown into the pot. It is much better, much safer to pay an extra dollar and give this unpleasant job to the caster. Be careful, though, that your caster will actually bomb the piece and not put it into a tumbler to restore the shine. A tumbler is a simple apparatus resembling a small motorized drum which contains several handfuls of small steel pellets; when the machine turns, these pellets pound the casting so that it is burnished to a high luster. Tumbling is a cheap form of polishing, fine for cheap castings: not for your precious original, which can lose much of its hard-won detail in the process.

REMOVAL OF SPRUES

Be careful, also, that you instruct your caster to leave your entire sprue network intact. Casters, when they remove sprues, use a very large snips. If your model is delicate, less than a millimeter in thickness as most models are, the pressure of these snips can distort it; it can even pull the sprue off altogether, leaving a hole or a crack in the model. Even more important, if you allow the caster—who relegates such minor jobs to apprentices—to cut off the sprues, there is always the chance, especially if the model displays intricate contours, of parts of the casting being clipped too close or even being clipped away altogether.

The removal of the sprues is the proper job of the model-maker, and the proper tool to use is the saw; it takes longer than the snips, but there is virtually no risk involved. Insert a number-2 saw blade into your frame and deliberately saw off each sprue, allowing at least 1.5 millimeters of sprue to remain; otherwise, you stand the chance of skinning the model with your sawcut (Fig. 10.1b). But a saw is capable of removing the sprue only on flat and convex areas; in those places where the sprue has been set into a concavity, it is necessary to employ a wheel-shaped burr in order to cut laterally (Fig. 10.1a). Be careful with this tool, though; unless you maintain absolute control, it can whirl around the sprue and cut into your model or your finger. If you find it too difficult to control, use a large round high-speed carbide burr to accomplish the same thing. Here, too, do not attempt to cut the sprue down to the surface of the model; the chances of abrading the model are too great.

Before completely removing the sprue, you should see clearly where the imperfections in the model are located. Remove any incrustations of oxidized material, called fire-scale, which might have accumulated in the crevices. You can do this with your old standby: the fiberglass brush. Just scratch it across the surface of the silver; it will pick out loose fire-scale and put a superficial shine on the metal—enough of a shine for any filemarks, porosity, nodules, or poorly formed details to show up with absolute clarity. Another way of accomplishing the same end, more

230

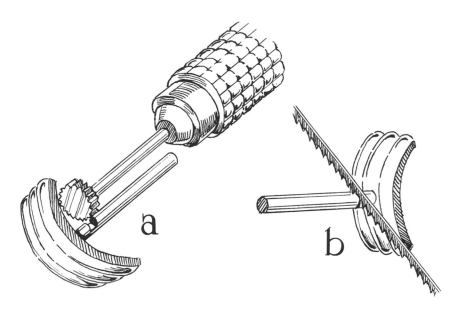

Fig. 10.1 a. Removing sprue with burr. b. Sawing off sprue from surface.

quickly but with somewhat less precision is to use metal brushes attached to your flexible shaft handpiece. When working with this kind of brush, you must wear safety goggles; the wires are apt to snap off and fly into your face.

These metal brushes come in two styles: steel and brass. In general, unless there is a great deal of scale on the piece, the steel brush is too rough for working on silver; the brass brush is recommended (Fig. 10.2a). With it, you can put a nice shine on the piece without endangering the surface.

Your first job is to grind the sprues down to the level of the surface. On flat, convex, and even on fairly shallow concavities, the most efficient tool is a separating disc mounted on a threaded screw mandrel. There are three varieties of such mandrels: the plain screw; the reinforced head mandrel, to be used with separating and sanding discs, grinding wheels and polishing buffs and brushes; and the tapered screw mandrel which is used with felt buffs (Fig. 10.2b). Just screw the separating disc, a disc of stiff Carborundum paper with a reinforced hole at the center, onto the reinforced head mandrel, snap it into the flexible shaft handpiece, and gingerly grind down what remains of the sprue (Fig. 10.3a). Try, if you can, to leave the slightest bit of a knob remaining; you will have better control if you take this last bit of sprue down later, with a file.

In the deeper concavities, however, the separating disc is incapable of reaching base level; here, you must work entirely with the various burrs at your disposal. You can screw a Carborundum wheel onto the reinforced head mandrel and grind away the sprue—but only if the concavity is wide enough to accommodate the size of the wheel (Fig. 10.3b).

231

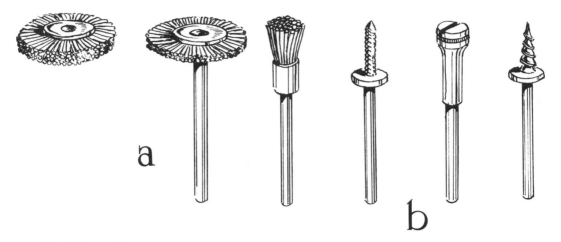

Fig. 10.2   a. Wire brushes. b. Mandrels.

Other grinding implements are more versatile: the standard steel burrs used on the wax; diamond-point burrs that are impregnated over the cutting surface with real diamond grit; red stone points in which the cutting stone is mounted on a $\frac{3}{32}$-inch shaft (Fig. 10.3c). Of these, the red-stone points are preferred. The metal burrs leave too coarse a track; the diamond-points are too expensive and require too much care while being used. Simply select the red-stone point whose size and shape seems most useful for the particular concavity in which you must work. Then, very slowly and deliberately, cut down the sprue a little at a time until you reach the surface. The burr will leave a lightly scratched surface which will be no problem to smooth later, with finer abrasives.

Texturing

It is at this point in cleaning up the model that you can texture the back if desired. The texture should be a distinct one. Professional jewelers use a pneumatic hammer which leaves a stipled texture in the metal. Perhaps not wishing to invest several hundred dollars in such a specialized instrument, you can do very nicely with steel burrs, particularly the round burr and the hart burr. By working slowly and carefully, you can incise either a pock-marked pattern or a series of ridges into the model. However, there is a two-fold danger involved in texturing the back of the piece. You can make your model perilously thin, even piercing it inadvertently, or you can lose control of the burr and watch as it scours the entire front surface. With regular measuring, however, you should be able to texture the piece with no difficulty.

Final Cleaning

This operation, actually, has already begun. The red-stone burrs have worked well in the hollows, but now you must turn your attention

232

to the major areas of the piece, which, in most cases, are either flat or convex. For this job, the best tool is the smallest barette escapement file, cut-3 or even cut-4. With the round and half-round escapement files, you should be able to define all the details and rid the model of all major imperfections (Fig. 10.4a). The surface should all gleam at this point. Any areas inaccessible to the file, and requiring more control than the red-stone points can provide, can be worked fairly nicely with a scotch stone: a long bar of abrasive material which can be shaped with coarse emery paper into whatever type of point is necessary for the job (Fig. 10.4b). The scotch stone leaves a mark that is similar to the mark left by the red-stone points: a fairly light system of scratches.

To remove these purely superficial imperfections, turn to the milder abrasives: emery papers, rubber wheels, brushes and buffs with various polishing agents. At this stage of the job—the cleaning stage—you must try to attend to all the little motes and dull spots which have been left over from the grinding operation. In order to accomplish this, you must often use mechanical equipment that cannot be wielded with pin-point accuracy; therefore, in striving to achieve a gleaming surface, you run the risk of blurring much hard-won detail. Always do as much as possible by hand; the principal tool here should be emery paper.

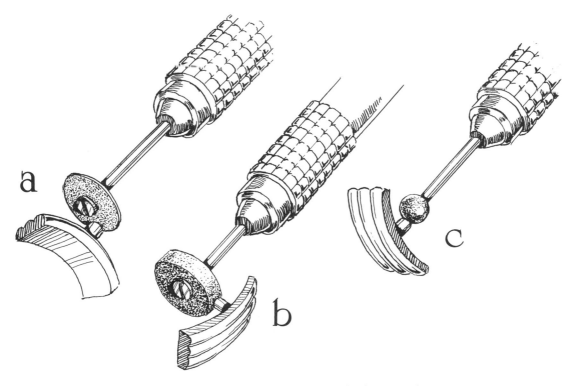

Fig. 10.3   a. A separating disc. b. A Carborundum wheel. c. A red-stone point.

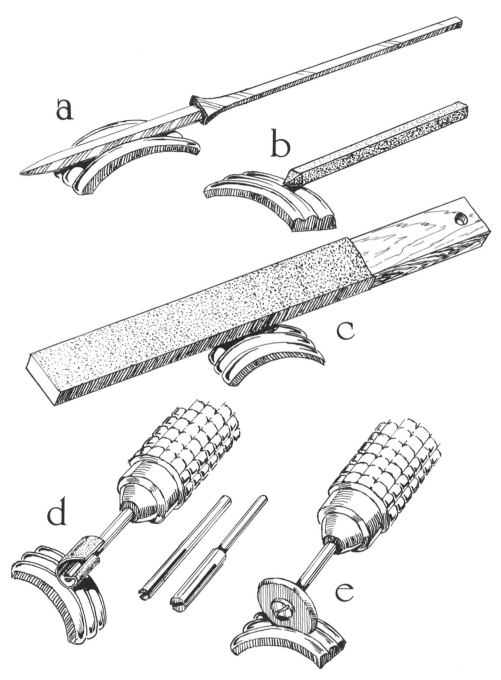

Fig. 10.4   a. Barette file for cleaning. b. Specially shaped scotch stone. c. Using emery paper. d. Slotted mandrel with emery paper. e. The rubber wheel.

There is a wide range of grits available in emery paper: 4, 3, 2, 1, 0, 2/0, and 4/0, the finest. With this range of abrasives, either by clipping the emery paper onto a special holder, or by wrapping it around a stick or file or drill bit, or even by simply folding it into whatever shape is most useful to you at the time, you may manicure the surface of your model almost to perfection (Fig. 10.4c). Do not become impatient with the slowness of this particular operation; take your time, working from the roughest surface to the finest. Take care to overlook no imperfection but scour the entire surface until it is as perfect as you are able to make it. Do not begin work with the rest of the mechanical cleaning and polishing implements until you are absolutely certain that you have accomplished as much as possible with the emery paper. Only then should you go to the flexible shaft machine to clean the model.

There are many types of abrasives that you may use on the machine. Foremost among these is a homemade tool that you might find very useful, not only for work on the metal but for work on the wax as well. Take a broken or worn-out burr and saw it off so that you are left with a uniform shaft; then, with a very fine sawblade, slit it halfway up the length. Fit a piece of emery paper securely into the slot and you have a remarkably useful tool (Fig. 10.4d), which you can use for the coarsest grinding to the finest polishing, depending upon what grade of emery paper you fit into the slot.

In addition to this split mandrel (it may be purchased also), you have at your disposal an assortment of rubber wheels of various hardnesses and sizes which can be fixed onto the reinforced head mandrel. These wheels, however, should be used sparingly; they should never be considered as a replacement for the emery paper despite the fact that they can remove imperfections in a few seconds. They can also remove detail in a few seconds. Or flatten off the top of a curve. Or incise a subtle rut in the silver. The rubber wheels should be used only when the shape or contour of the area to be cleaned prohibits use of the emery paper, which would apply to the concavity in the back of the piece.

If you have textured this area with your metal burrs, the entire surface will be rough to the touch. A light touch first with the red-stone points will remove any metal which might have been raised above the surface level. Then a rubber wheel, impregnated with pumice grit, should be played over the entire hollow to remove the scratch marks left by the stone (Fig. 10.4e). Here too you must take your time, using a very light pressure on the wheel. An overly strong pressure will actually force the rubber—which gives—down into all the tiny hollows of the texture, softening the effect and often totally eradicating it. After the pumice wheel has served its function, you have a choice between either a hard or a soft rubber wheel in order to brighten the details of your texture.

If you are forced to use the rubber wheel on the front of the model, you must do several things in order to make the wheel itself useful for

235

the job. In most cases, the diameter of the wheel will simply be too big to allow it to be worked in whatever small concavities might require refinement. To reduce the size of the wheel, just take an old knife that has outlived its usefulness, and hold the edge against the rubber wheel as you run the motor. The result will be a rut in the metal and a much smaller wheel as the rubber is ground away. The edge of this wheel will be flat and may be used in just that way, if the situation demands it. If, however, the situation demands a finer cutting edge, the rubber wheel can be further modified by holding the knife at an angle to the wheel and grinding down a razor edge on the rubber—very useful for cleaning out grooves or for removing those last occasional imperfections.

Engraving

If you examine your piece and discover that a distinct softening of the detail work has occurred, now is the time to freshen it. This requires reengraving of details directly in the metal.

For those who have been accustomed to working only in wax, the very hardness of the silver might be intimidating. But you are not called upon to carve the material, simply to redefine shapes that are already there. Here, the traditional tool of the metal model-maker—the engraving tool with a palm handle—should stand you in good stead. Engraving tools, like most of the other equipment, come in a variety of cutting surfaces (Fig. 10.5a), each blade having its own specific function. In most cases, the fine knife blade is the logical choice; after all, you simply wish to sharpen details, not to create them.

But, in using the engraving tool you must be careful; unlike the wax techniques, in which a light touch is almost mandatory, here you must exert physical pressure in order to achieve results. You must hold the handle against the heel of your hand and push the tool into the metal. The point *must* be ground as sharp as possible; otherwise it can slip across the surface of your model, putting an irreparable gash in the metal—or in your hand. In order to take precautions against such a thing happening, not only must the point be sharpened, but the piece itself must be held securely while it is being worked. Professional engravers use a so-called engraving ball to hold their piece fast. Depending upon the extent of the work you intend to do on the model, you can put a piece of rubber on the bench pin, to secure the model against slippage, hold it in a ring clamp (Fig. 10.5b), or else borrow a technique from the stone-setter and melt your model onto a shellac stick.

A shellac stick is a thick wooden stick—a length of broom handle will do—which has been heated over an open flame and rolled in flakes of shellac resin. The shellac needs very little heat to adhere to the stick and gradual reheating will build up a fairly thick wad of shellac. When you have built up the shellac to approximately the size of a golfball, press the softened resin against any flat metal surface so that one end of the

236

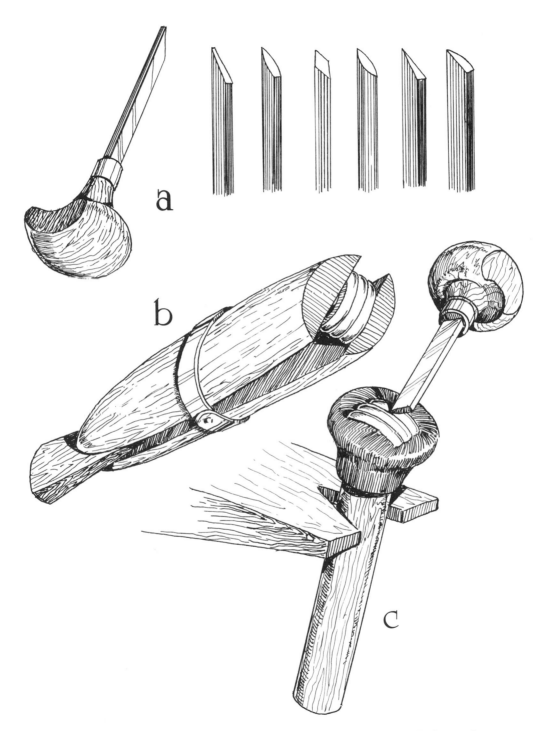

Fig. 10.5 a. Engraving tools. b. A ring clamp. c. Holding model on shellac stick.

237

wad is flattened. Heat your model and press it into the shellac; when the shellac cools, you will have a very secure grip on the piece and should be quite comfortable engraving it. To make your job even easier, cut a V out of the bench pin and rest the stick against that while working; you should have maximum control over the tool (Fig. 10.5c). To remove the piece, simply heat the shellac, pry the model loose and soak it for a while in alcohol to dissolve any resin which might have remained attached to it.

If you find engraving too much of a challange, use the flexible shaft machine equipped with small brand-new burrs. Or you can use either a carbide or diamond scribe to freshen the details a little. Even though silver seems terribly hard, when compared to wax, it is actually a very soft metal and rather easy to work by hand.

Burnishing

Burnishing is an essential part of the cleaning process. Again, you must apply pressure in order to achieve results. Only this time, instead of cutting into the metal, you actually push the metal around, closing over tiny imperfections. Burnishing is the final recourse when a spot is just too inaccessible for any other cleaning instrument to be effective. There is a small assortment of burnishing tools available, each of specially hardened and polished steel, each having a different shaped point (Fig. 10.6a). To use the burnishing tool, hold it firmly in the hand with the thumb set in the concavity behind the polishing surface; place the point onto the surface which is to be worked and with as much physical strength as you can muster, press down and push the tool until all the tiny imperfections and scratches have been covered over and disappear from the surface of the model (Fig. 10.6b).

POLISHING

Polishing, very simply, is the application of different abrasive pastes to the surface of the metal model by means of an assortment of brushes and buffs. There is a wide assortment of such pastes, all of which are usually used on a large production polishing machine (Fig. 10.7), but which may be used to good effect with your miniature polishing apparatus as well. These abrasives generally come in bar form, either in quarter-pound or one-pound sizes, and may be purchased from any jewelry supply house. Basically they contain abrasives of different cutting efficiency suspended in a paste which permits them to adhere to the surface of the metal. Those which are most useful for our purposes are Bobbing (a coarse abrasive used for extremely rapid polishing and cutting); White Diamond (a slightly less severe abrasive which is used for rapid polishing); Tripoli (the standard polishing agent, used in every production shop as its standby); and Grey Star (a lighter abrasive used for spot polishing).

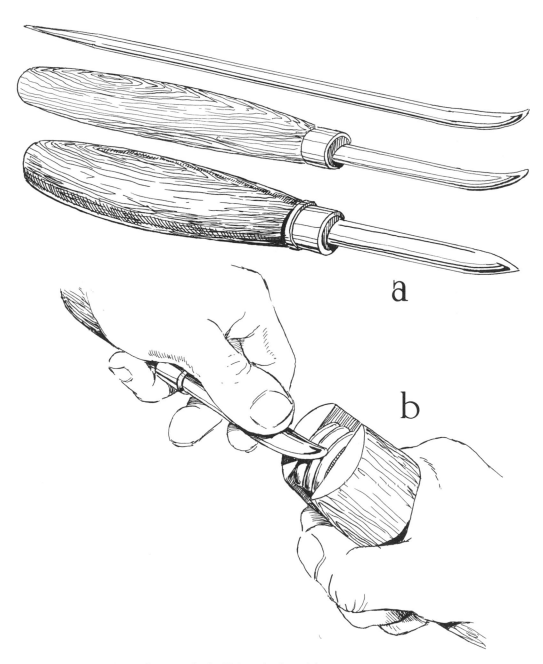

Fig. 10.6   a. Burnishing tools. b. Using the burnisher.

These polishing pastes are generally applied to the model first by means of stiff bristle brushes and then by various types of buffs and bobs. The bristle brushes come in two general shapes: the wheel, which is fixed onto the reinforced head mandrel, and the porte—or bristle-end—brush, which comes mounted on its own shaft (Fig. 10.8a). Snap

239

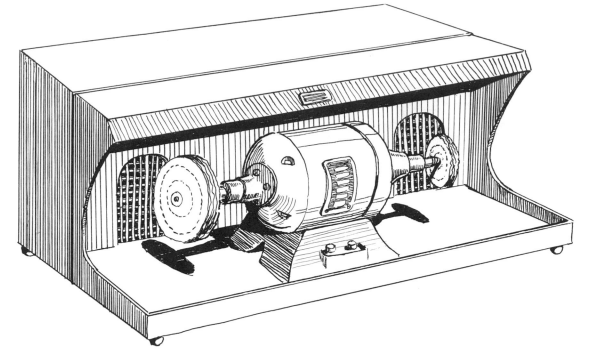

Fig. 10.7   Polishing machine.

the appropriately shaped bristle brush into the handpiece, step on the rheostat and touch the bristles to the bar of Tripoli (the preferred polishing agent); enough Tripoli will stick to the brush to polish a small section of the model. Just repeat the procedure every time you wish to work a new section. You will soon notice that, despite the dull gray-brown film of Tripoli which now coats the model, there is a soft uniform glow to the metal which it never attained during the cleaning operations. Here too, you must be careful and not exert too much pressure on the tool or overwork any one particular area; even this relatively mild abrasive can—if used with a heavy hand—ruin all your work. If you want to check any part of the piece, to see if you have a nice uniform shine, just immerse the model in a boiling solution of water and a little dishwashing detergent; the film will soon disappear and you will be able to view your work critically with no obstruction.

Buffing

When you have been satisfied that absolutely no mark remains, no dull or unpolished section is left, neither front nor back, you may begin the final polishing operation: the buffing. Here, the same abrasives are employed with the buffs—and there is quite a large assortment of such implements on the market. Begin by using the hard-packed felt buffs which come in a wide variety of shapes and sizes (Fig. 10.8b). Select the

240

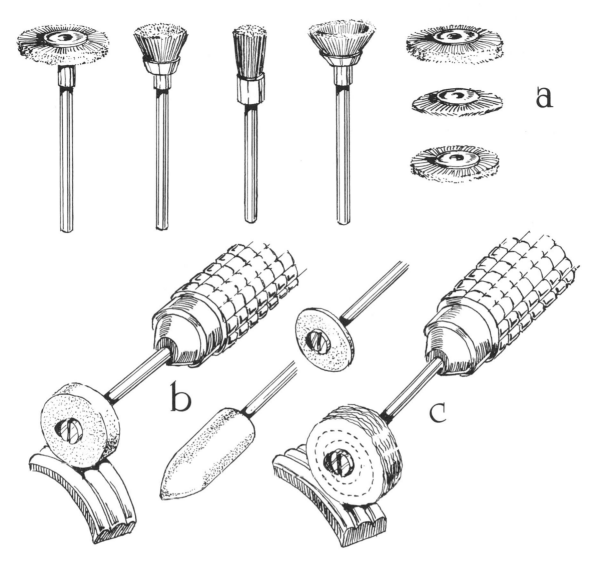

Fig. 10.8   a. Finishing bristle brushes. b. Felt buffs. c. Cloth buff.

buff which is most useful for whatever section you have chosen to work; fasten it onto the tapered screw mandrel; coat it with Tripoli and with even a lighter touch than you had employed with the brushes—both with your foot pressure on the rheostat and with your hand—buff the surface to a high gloss. In order to check the results of your labor, take a piece of flannel or other soft cloth and wipe the paste from the surface of the metal. If you find that the *entire* surface, from the highest points to the most remotely recessed grooves, is glowing, you may now shift to the final polishing implements: the cloth buffs.

Cloth buffs are actually many individual circular sheets of different types of cloth joined into a ¼-inch thick wheel by a metal hub (Fig. 10.8c).

There are three types of such buffs, each differing from the others by the types of cloth used: muslin, cotton flannel, or chamois. After fastening the buff to the reinforced head mandrel, and snapping it into the hand-piece, run the machine while dragging the edge over some rough surface—an ordinary file cleaner is ideal—so that the individual cloth discs become separated.

Run the muslin buff into the Tripoli and then, again lightly touch the edge to the metal surface of your piece. Try, when you are buffing your model, to arrange it so that the buff turns in the same direction as whatever detail you might be polishing. By separating the discs, you allow each one to press down into inaccessible spots, completely polishing the surface of the model. It is not necessary to dab the buff into the Tripoli each time you move to a different surface area; all the cutting and heavy polishing should have been accomplished by now. The cleaner the buff the better. Just let the Tripoli which still adheres to the model serve as the polishing agent. A very bright shine will begin to work its way through the paste. If you wish a still higher shine, change to a cotton flannel buff, and repeat the procedure.

MODEL WASH-OUT

Before you can apply the final finish to your piece, you must wash the Tripoli paste completely off the surface of the model; otherwise it will continue to cut—even after you no longer desire it to do so.

The professional production shop has an entire wash-out set-up. Most shops have an ultrasonic cleaner which utilizes sound waves to pry the dirt loose from the model. A less sophisticated method is to immerse the piece in a special boiling solution for several minutes until the dirt has been boiled away. In either case, the piece is subjected, as a final wash-out operation, to a hard blast of steam which is generated by a special engine designed to remove whatever final specks of dirt or grease might still remain on the model.

The ordinary model-maker, however, not wishing to invest thousands of dollars in this specialized equipment, can do an admirable job with the most mundane of implements. A pot of boiling water with a few spoonsful of any ordinary household cleanser poured into it, either a dishwashing detergent or an all-purpose cleanser, will serve nicely as a cleaning solution. The job can be facilitated by fitting an ordinary sieve over the rim of the pot so that the piece lies suspended, completely immersed on all sides in the boiling solution. This procedure will loosen, but not remove, the dirt from the surface of the model. In order to get rid of the Tripoli still clinging to the metal, take a *soft* toothbrush and gently scrub away the loosened deposits. Repeat this operation, boiling and brushing, until the piece is absolutely clean. If any dirt remains in

242

the recesses, turn on the bathtub tap full force to blast it out. Pat the piece dry with a soft cloth; it must be completely dry and free of grease before the final process—the rouging—can be begun.

Rouge Finish

Rouge is a finishing, not a polishing agent; its action is not an abrasive one but a burnishing one. It comes in various grades: dry red, used for finishing gold; medium-dry red, used for gold or silver; and medium green or black, used for silver. Fit a *fresh* cotton flannel or chamois buff onto the reinforced head mandrel. Rake it across the file cleaner, and then take up some rouge on the edge of the cloth wheel. Again working the wheel in the direction of the details, buff the surface of the model. The gleam which results will be a brilliant one. Wash the surface clean of any rouge build-up and the model is completed.

You have created a piece of jewelry. You have worked it up from an original pencil or water-color rendering, have anticipated and overcome all possible difficulties, and have made a wax model. You have watched that wax being cast into silver and, now, you have cleaned and polished the metal model to perfection. It is ready to be put into production. Your job is done.

Appendix

Avoirdupois Weight

27.33 grains	=	1 dram
16 drams	=	1 ounce
16 ounces	=	1 pound

Troy Weight

24 grains	=	1 penny-weight (dwt.)
20 dwt.	=	1 ounce
12 ounces	=	1 pound troy

Metric Weight

1.56 grains	=	1 gram
10 grams	=	1 decagram
100 decagrams	=	1 kilogram

Douzieme Gauge

.0074 inch	=	1 douzieme
12 douzieme	=	1 ligne

Comparison of Troy Weight and Metric Weight

Dwt	Grains	Grams
0.10	2.40	0.16
0.20	4.80	0.31
0.30	7.20	0.47
0.40	9.20	0.62
0.50	12.00	0.78
0.60	14.40	0.93
0.70	16.80	1.09
0.80	19.20	1.24
0.90	21.60	1.40
1.00	24.00	1.56

Metric Conversion

Millimeter	Inch
0.1	.004
0.5	.020
1.0	.039
1.5	.059
2.0	.079
2.5	.098

Saw Blade Sizes

Number	Inch
5/0	.0080
3/0	.0095
1/0	.0110
1	.0120
3	.0140
5	.0158
10	.0215

Burr Sizes

Number	Millimeter
5/0	0.5
3/0	0.7
1/0	0.9
1	1.05
5	1.7
10	2.7
15	3.8
20	5.0
25	5.9
30	8.0

Wax Gauges

Gauge	Millimeter
6	4.11
8	3.28
10	2.59
12	2.06
14	1.63
16	1.30
18	1.02
20	0.81
22	0.64
24	0.51

Ring Sizes

Size	Diameter (inch)	Circumference (inch)
0	.454	1.429
1	.486	1.528
2	.520	1.632
3	.552	1.735
4	.584	1.835
5	.618	1.943
6	.650	2.045
7	.683	2.15
8	.716	2.25
9	.748	2.35
10	.781	2.46
11	.814	2.56
12	.846	2.63
13	.878	2.76

Specific Gravity of Precious Metals

24-kt. gold	19.36
18-kt. yellow gold	15.58
14-kt. yellow gold	13.07
14-kt. white gold	12.61
14-kt. red gold	13.26
14-kt. green gold	14.20
10-kt. yellow gold	11.57
platinum	21.45
10% irid. plat.	21.54
palladium	12.00
silver	10.53
sterling	10.40
copper	8.94

Index

Page numbers in *italic type* indicate information found in illustrations.

246